Germany and the Middle East, 1871–1945

Germany and the Middle East
1871–1945

Edited by
Wolfgang G. Schwanitz

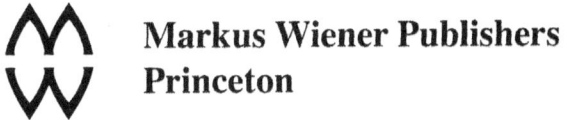
Markus Wiener Publishers
Princeton

Second printing, 2020

Copyright © 2004 by the Department of Near Eastern Studies, Princeton University

Reprinted from *Princeton Papers: Interdisciplinary Joutrnal of Middle Eastern Studies*, volumes X–XI.

All rights reserved. No part of this book may be reproduced or transmitted in any form or by any means, whether electronic or mechanical—including photocopying or recording—or through any information storage or retrieval system, without permission of the copyright owners.

For information write to:
Markus Wiener Publishers,
231 Nassau Street, Princeton, NJ 08542
www.markuswiener.com

Library of Congress Cataloging-in-Publication Data

Germany and the Middle East, 1919-1945 / Wolfgang G. Schwanitz, editor.
  p. cm.
  Includes bibliographical references.
  ISBN 978-1-55876-298-5 (pbk. : alk. paper)
  1. Germany—Relations—Middle East. 2. Middle East—Relations—Germany. 3. Germany—Civilization—Middle Eastern influences. I. Schwanitz, Wolfgang.
  DD258.85.M53 S39 2002
  327.43017'4927'09041—dc21
  2002151810

Contents

Maps, Illustrations, and Documents	vii
Preface and Acknowledgments	ix
The German Middle Eastern Policy, 1871–1945 *Wolfgang G. Schwanitz*	1
The German Mission to Afghanistan, 1915–1916 *Thomas L. Hughes*	25
"When Continents Awake, Island Empires Fall!" Germany and the Destabilization of the East, 1919–1922 *Hans-Ulrich Seidt*	65
"The Jinnee and the Magic Bottle": Fritz Grobba and German Middle East Policy, 1900–1945 *Wolfgang G. Schwanitz*	87
German-Saudi Relations and Their Actors on the Arabian Peninsula, 1924–1939 *Uwe Pfullmann*	119
German Research on the Ancient Near East and Its Relation to Political and Economic Interests from Kaiserreich to World War II *Stefan R. Hauser*	155
Berlin – Ankara – Baghdad: Franz von Papen and German Near East Policy during the Second World War *Karl Heinz Roth*	181
In the Shadow of the Moon: Arab Inmates in Nazi Concentration Camps *Gerhard Höpp*	217
About the Authors	241

Maps, Figures, and Documents

Map 1	The most critical time for the Allies in the Middle East between mid-1940 and 1942	13
Map 2	Iraq: For a brief period a German foothold in the Middle Eastern door in May 1941	14
Figure 1	The German Kaiser Wilhelm II visits the Ottoman Empire and Jerusalem in 1898	x
Figure 2	Afghanistan's ruler Emir Habībullah and his sons 'Ināyatullah (left) and Amānullah	24
Figure 3	Soldier and Scholar: Major General Oskar Ritter von Niedermayer, Ph.D. (1885–1948)	64
Figure 4	An Intellectual and Revolutionary: Karl Radek alias Karl Sobelsohn (1885–1939)	69
Figure 5	Comrades in Arms: Enver Pasha (1881–1922) and Friedrich Sarre (1865–1945)	74
Figure 6	The foremost German Middle Eastern envoy for 25 years, Dr. Fritz Grobba (1886–1973)	86
Figure 7	Knowledge Transfer to the U.S.: Cover sheet of manuscript MS # P-207, 1955–1957	90
Figure 8	The Ibn Saʿūd: King ʿAbd al-ʿAzīz (1880–1953), who built the kingdom of Saudi Arabia	118
Figure 9	Reza Shah and the crown prince before the Apadana relief excavated by Eric Schmidt	154
Figure 10	Prophecy: "Hitler is great, and Papen is his prophet," after Papen's Vienna mission 1938	180
Figure 11	Record: Papen's appointment by Hitler that was only recently discovered in Moscow	184

Figure 12	Papen and Sarachoğlu shaking hands after the German-Turkish Friendship Treaty in June 1941	186
Figure 13	Adolf Hitler (1889–1945) and Franz von Papen (1879–1969) at Obersalzberg, July 1940	188
Figure 14	The Moroccan Mohamed Bouazad was killed in the gas chamber of Mauthausen in 1945	216
Document 1	An American evaluation of the Axis propaganda in the Muslim world in 1941	16
Document 2	Foreword by former General Franz Halder to Dr. Grobba's supplement to MS # P-207	107
Document 3	Fritz Grobba's final remarks to MS # P-207 on the Middle East written for the U.S. Army	109
Document 4	Al-Kailānī's and al-Husainī's assistants visited a Berlin concentration camp in July 1942	218
Document 5	About 1,130 prisoners of Islamic faith within German concentration camps, June 1944	222
Document 6	Anti-Semitism or anti-Judaism? An Arab question and the official German answer in 1942	231

Preface and Acknowledgments

This contribution owes a great deal to the good advice and cooperation offered by its authors. Most of the papers are the result of a joint effort at the panel "Germany and the Middle East, 1919–1943" at the Twenty-Fifth Anniversary Conference of the German Studies Association. Held at the beginning of October 2001, it was considered as the first international conference in Washington D.C. after the catastrophic day in September rocked our world.

We present with this work new research results of the historical mosaic of links between North America, the Middle East, and Europe. The articles cover different topics and different parts of the 1871–1945 time period, and thus contribute toward a new interpretation of the whole picture. A follow-up study will address the United States, the Middle East, and the divided Germany. In this work, the term "Middle East" includes in its widest definition the Near East. All together it is the area in Asia and Africa between and including Arab North Africa in the west, Iran, Afghanistan, and Pakistan in the east, the Fertile Crescent, Turkey, and Cyprus in the north, and the Arabian Peninsula in the south. Of course this is a practical matter; and the authors each indicate their respective historical and geographical approach to that term. Regarding the transliteration of Middle Eastern languages, we have applied a modified style.

Among those who have generously supported this outcome with their time and counsel are Professor Bernard Lewis and Professor Şükrü Hanioğlu of Princeton University, to whom I would like to express my gratitude. Finally, special thanks are due to editor Brigitte M. Goldstein for translations that included most of the attached historical documents, to Susie Lorand, and William Blair. Last but not least, I am very grateful to our publisher, Markus Wiener.

Wolfgang G. Schwanitz
Browns Mills, N.J.

Figure 1. Emperor Wilhelm II visits Jerusalem in 1898

The German Middle Eastern Policy, 1871–1945

WOLFGANG G. SCHWANITZ

When the German Reich was established in 1871, the neighboring countries of Great Britain, France, and Russia were already expanding their overseas colonies into empires. During the next four decades, while those empires continued to grow, Berlin was forced to develop a policy toward North Africa and West Asia that was quite different from those of the other European powers.[1]

First, there was nothing much left in that region to be claimed. The territories of what became known as the Middle East were already distributed among neighbors of Germany. Thus, keeping the status quo in the region was most likely to serve the national interests.[2] Trade, commerce, and a peaceful penetration especially in open-door areas were cornerstones of Berlin's Middle Eastern policy. This was also true during the *Deutsche Orient-Gründerjahre*. These "German Orient founding years" started in 1884 and lasted three decades.[3] It was a time in which Germany explored new regions in Africa and Asia. Berlin established colonies in West and East Africa, becoming a small colonial power.[4] But it was also an era in which the Germans intensified their economical, cultural, and military relations to the Middle East with its wide lands from Turkey via Palestine and Mesopotamia to Egypt and Mauritania. The first striking feature of Berlin's Middle Eastern policy in peacetime appeared: respecting the status quo and refusing any colonies in the region.[5]

Second, the Eastern Question—who would get which part of the declining Ottoman Empire—had caused many conflicts. It was Chancellor Otto von Bismarck, until 1890 the main foreign politician with a distaste of colonial acquisitions, who regarded the Eastern Question as a means for his policy toward the neighbors in Europe. The Middle Eastern policy constituted politics re-directed to neighboring colonial powers. He opined that the European and American policy came first and the Middle Eastern policy had to serve the primary policy. Thus, and this is the second feature, Berlin's Middle Eastern policy was always subordinated to a primary policy toward Europe and America.[6]

Third, the Middle East was not promising enough for a great design of German policy. Otto von Bismarck used to put it this way: the Eastern Question is not worth the bones of a single Pomeranian musketeer. For example, the German policy toward Egypt was then considered a question not between Berlin and Cairo, but between Berlin and London. In the chancellor's eyes there was not much to expect from direct relations with Egypt, but Egypt made an effective "stick"[7] to be used against London to disturb some alliances between neighbors of Germany. He used this *bâton égyptien* diplomatically. Since Berlin had no colonies in the region, it slipped into the role of a key mediator in European conflicts over the Orient. Thus, the third striking feature of Berlin's Middle Eastern policy was a diplomacy of mediation, namely during a series of conferences on African frontiers and Asian topics since the 1880s.[8]

1. Policy background and the "German Orient founding years," 1884–1914

The three features of Berlin's Middle Eastern policy in peacetime were respecting the status quo and renouncing territorial claims in the region, the subordination of this secondary policy to the always primary policy toward Europe and America, and the diplomacy of mediation in Oriental conflicts. Unlike the other great powers, Germany did not rule over any Muslims in the Middle East.[9] Therefore, the Germans gained a critical perspective on the Middle Eastern empires of their neighbors and all the troubles they caused. It is no wonder that the mainstream of German politicians and academics had a sympathetic view of anti-imperial tendencies and their nationalistic or Islamic expressions. How was the background of Berlin's Middle Eastern policy shaped?

Mainstream politicians were interested in keeping the Ottoman Empire together. Only in this way they would secure their historical, economical, cultural, and military relations with Istanbul (Constantinople) as the foremost regional power. Historically, the German states had established their own contacts before the German Reich was created. Andreas Mordtmann was consul general of the Hanseatic League in Istanbul in 1847 and developed the ties to the Ottoman Empire. Prussia had had Protestant missionaries in Ottoman provinces such as Palestine since 1841. A year later Ernst Gustav Schultz became Prussian consul in Jerusalem. Johann G. Wetzstein was his colleague in Damascus starting in 1848. In 1846 Saxony's parliamentarian Robert Georgi supported the idea of a new Suez Canal in Egypt and promoted the related study mission.[10]

In the economic field, the Deutsche Bank in 1888 won a concession to build a railroad from Izmir to Ankara. It was built as far as Ankara four years later, then extended several times: in 1896 to Konya, in 1914 to Samara, and in 1940 to Baghdad.[11] As Egypt celebrated the opening of the Suez Canal in 1869,[12] Prussia's crown prince, Friedrich Wilhelm (the father of the Emperor Wilhelm II), witnessed the event. From Morocco to Iran, from Greater Syria to Arabia, German capital invested heavily in railroads, raw material processing, financing, engineering, aviation, and automobiles. In 1906 three German banks founded Al-Bank Ash-Sharqī Al-Almānī, the German Orient Bank, under the auspices of Dresdner Bank. It grew among eight similar banks to become the largest overseas bank and played a central role in foreign trade.[13] Until World War I, Germany ranked third—after Great Britain and France—in trade volume with the Ottoman Empire and its provinces. This rank and the exchange pattern of industrial products versus raw materials prevailed until World War I.

The core of Germany's cultural ties to the Middle East—see Stefan Hauser's contribution to this volume—evolved in science and research. Although the Germans did not possess possibilities like the French after Napoleon's conquest of Egypt in 1798, German study of the Orient, or *Orientalistik*, profited from the work of other Europeans. The French *Description de l'Egypte, publiée par les ordres de Napoléon Bonaparte* influenced Egyptology, archeology, and the study of Islam, or *Islamwissenschaft*, but the latter field had its own traditions already.[14]

Heidelberg established a professorship in Arabic in 1609. Johann Jacob Reiske founded the discipline of Arab history, literature, and culture, or *Arabistik*, at Leipzig in 1748. Heinrich Leberecht Fleischer of Leipzig was a co-founder of the Deutsche Morgenländische Gesellschaft (German Oriental Society) in 1845. In Berlin Eduard Sachau taught Oriental languages in 1876, succeeded by Eugen Mittwoch. At the start of the "German Orient founding years" the politician August Bebel edited *Die Mohammedanisch-Arabische Kulturperiode* (The Muhammadan-Arab Period of Culture), popularizing findings of Islam scholars such as Alfred von Kremer, Gustav Weil, and Aloys Sprenger. From 1887, dragomans[15] attended the Seminar für orientalische Sprachen (Seminary of Oriental Languages) in Berlin in preparation for the foreign service. Carl Heinrich Becker began teaching Oriental culture in Hamburg in 1908. In Berlin the Deutsche Gesellschaft für Islamkunde (German Society for the Study of Islam) began its periodical *Die Welt des Islams* (The World of Islam) in 1912. In the same year, the Orientalische Kommission (Oriental Commission) was set up at the German Academy of Sciences in Berlin. It served as a nucleus for several academic institutes.[16]

Cultural exchanges with the Middle East included a broad variety in art, medicine, and literature. The travelers and explorers to Arabia were often gifted artists who painted what had impressed them. Johann Ludwig Burckhardt delivered early sketches about Mecca and Medina. A race between the so-called Orient photographers like Rudolf F. Lehnert and Ernst H. Landrock and Orient painters such as Wilhelm Gentz inspired the fantasy of the German public. A kind of Oriental fever led Germans to "orientalize" their architecture. Businessmen discovered markets in the Middle East for pre-fabricated palaces in an Oriental style. Carl Wilhelm Valentin von Diebitsch delivered to the viceroy of Egypt a completely pre-fabricated guesthouse made of cast iron for the ceremony opening the Suez Canal. This *al-qaṣr al-būrūsī*, or Prussian Palace, is still the best hotel address on the island Al-Gazīra in Cairo. Maximilian Koch, Theodor Bilharz, Robert Koch, Franz Pruner, and Sebastian Fischer laid the foundations of tropical medicine.[17]

A similar tradition developed in literature. Johann Wolfgang von Goethe studied intensively the life of Muhammad and the Qurʾān.

The German Middle Eastern Policy

Friedrich Schiller raised the question of how a Turk would discover and describe Europe. Johann Gottfried Herder collected Oriental literature. The European Enlightenment brought attempts to reconcile three world religions, as Gotthold E. Lessing suggested in his theater show *Nathan, der Weise* (Nathan, the Wise Man). The poet Friedrich Rückert also taught Oriental poetry. Gustav Weil translated the *Thousand and One Nights*. Wilhelm Spitta directed the National Library in Cairo. Thinkers like Karl Marx and Friedrich Engels discussed Oriental history, policy, and literature.[18]

Germans developed military relations with the Middle East in two main ways. They sent missions to the Ottoman Empire and the Arab provinces, and they received Ottomans for training. German physicians formed the medical vanguard in the Ottoman army, as was also the case under Muhammad ʿAlī. The Ottomans hired advisers like Colmar von der Goltz in the 1880s. They sent officers like Mukhtar Pasha and Ahmad ʿIzzat Pasha for training to Berlin, Potsdam, or Vienna. After Emperor Wilhelm II visited Istanbul in 1898, the exchange of personnel increased. Shevket Pasha organized systematic training of Ottoman troops by Germans in 1909. Most notably, Enver Pasha served as military attaché in Berlin for three years until 1911.[19]

German relations with the Middle East advanced under the wary eyes of London, Paris, and St. Petersburg. The primary policy toward these immediate neighbors framed the secondary German Middle Eastern policy. Politicians in Berlin did cultivate their wish for an alliance with London. Whereas the French were historically too close to the Germans and the Russians economically too far away, they regarded the British as very similar. Apart from the former's Magna Carta, democratic tradition, and colonial empire, the maritime power and the continental power had much in common. Could the British and the Germans really complement each other in world policy? This idea became popular again after Otto von Bismarck left office and Wilhelm II took over the foreign policy. But the old dream of an axis between Berlin and London was not meant to be.

There was still another consideration for Berlin that jeopardized Germany's ability to keep a distance from Oriental affairs. Aligned powers like Austria or Italy could trigger, with their policy in the Ottoman Balkans or in the province of Tripoli, a chain reaction that could force Germany into hostilities against Great Britain and

France. Otto von Bismarck was very much aware of that risk. He avoided such a domino effect that could hit the edges of Europe and ignite an all-out war in the center. But the chancellor's cautious diplomacy was much less rooted in the mind of Wilhelm II, who tried a world policy of his own. He attempted to expand the recently established German Reich from a medium-sized power into a great power.[20]

2. Berlin's Middle Eastern policy in wartime and the "Jihad made in Germany"

Berlin's Middle Eastern policy in peacetime and during the course of the three decades of "German Orient founding years" until 1914 emphasized maintaining the status quo, pursuing a secondary policy with peaceful penetration of the region, and mediating in Oriental conflicts. Then, for reasons that cannot be discussed here, the always-feared "Sarajevo effect" dragged Europe and the world into a war starting in the peripheral Balkans.

If one considers Berlin's switch from a secondary peacetime to a primary wartime Middle Eastern policy against Great Britain, France, and Russia (and their colonial Middle Eastern hinterland) there is one unique feature: The jihad "made in Germany."[21] It was already a topic in the first year of the war. A dispute erupted between two founding fathers of the study of Islam in Europe. Their discussion indicated the general attitude toward the war that was first frenetically welcomed and expected to be very short.

Did the Germans push the Young Turks to proclaim a jihad after entering World War I against the British, the Russians, and the French? Indeed, they did, maintained the leading Dutch Arabist C. Snouck Hurgronje, who blamed his German colleagues—among them Carl Heinrich Becker—for having supported this "jihad fever." The Dutchman insisted this jihad was an intellectual weapon "made in Germany." Supposing this were true, replied the German scholar of Islam: had not Berlin and Istanbul every right to do so? But this, wrote Hurgronje, hurts humanism and religious peace. "There is no taboo for religion," Becker answered.[22]

The jihad developed as a concerted German-Ottoman campaign. It consisted of five stages: Max von Oppenheim's design to revolutionize the enemy's colonial hinterland; agitating for jihad by the Berlin-based Oriental News Department; the Ottoman fatwa; Shaykh Sālih's commentary on the fatwa; and the realization of the jihad. It was used as a weapon to globalize the war. However, it was a slap in the face to the Enlightenment. Although Hurgonje's criticism hit the mark, Becker held to a chauvinistic approach. To understand the German Middle Eastern policy, it is worthwhile to look into these five elements of the jihad according to the German design.

Max von Oppenheim served as an archaeologist and diplomat in the Middle East for twenty years, and Wilhelm II read his reports recommending the jihad.[23] After the war began, the German General Chief of Staff, Hellmuth von Moltke, wanted Enver Pasha to proclaim the jihad to weaken the enemies from within. The kaiser asked him to enter the war too: he wanted the sultan to call for a jihad in Asia, India, Egypt, and Africa to get Muslims fighting for the Caliphate. Berlin and Istanbul cooperated closely in planning and realizing the jihad. Even some academics in Berlin expected to see "Islamic fanatics fighting for Germany."[24]

The jihad was the idea of Max von Oppenheim, the German "Abu Jihad." Before the Ottomans entered the war on the side of the Central Powers, he designed a master plan at the end of October 1914: "fomenting rebellion in the Islamic territories of our enemies."[25] The emperor confirmed Oppenheim's suggestion to incite Muslims to jihad under the leadership of the Ottoman sultan-caliph. This was the plan: The sultan proclaims the jihad against the British, the French, and the Russians. Berlin delivers money, experts, and material. The targets are Muslims in British India, French North Africa, and Russian Asia. The call to fight goes out in several languages according to psychological factors. Berlin creates an Oriental News Department in the Foreign Office. The rebelling of Muslims in India is the key to victory. Expeditions are to be sent to Afghanistan to trigger an uprising from there (see the contribution by Thomas L. Hughes). The Germans provide intelligence to the Muslims, while the Turks incite them to rise up against their foreign masters. Islam, concluded Max von Oppenheim, will be one of our sharpest weapons against the British. Let's mount a joint effort to make it a deadly strike.[26]

Max von Oppenheim (later succeeded by Karl E. Schabinger and Eugen Mittwoch) became the head of the Oriental News Department.

Oppenheim employed a dozen academics and native Muslims. Some called his strategy of jihad a "war by revolution."[27] But it was an asymmetrical war, waged by incitement to jihad and by anti-imperial uprisings. The aim was a double strategy between front and colonial hinterland to support the fight at the fronts by keeping troops busy in the wide lands of Islam. Of course, it raised some questions. Was the Ottoman sultan accepted as caliph by all Muslims? Was it permitted to them to fight with infidels against infidels and "their" Muslims?

As Max von Oppenheim had suggested, a fatwa answered this. The shaykh of Islam affirmed five points on November 11, 1914.[28] To summarize: After the enemy of Islam attacked the Islamic world, His Majesty the Padishah of Islam orders a jihad as a general mobilization and individual duty for all Muslims in all parts of the world according to the Qur'ān. Since Russia, England, and France are now hostile to the Islamic Caliphate, it is also incumbent upon all Muslims who are being ruled by these governments to proclaim jihad against them and to actually attack them. The protection of the Ottoman Empire depends on the fact that all Muslims hasten to participate in the jihad; if some refrain from doing so, it is a horrible sin and they deserve divine wrath. For Muslims of the named enemy countries it is absolutely forbidden to fight against the troops of Islamic lands even if the enemies force them to do so; otherwise they deserve hellfire for murder. It is a great sin for Muslims under the rule of England, France, Russia, Serbia, Montenegro, and their allies to fight against Germany and Austria, which are the allies of the Supreme Islamic Government.

According to this fatwa the sultan-caliph was the sovereign over all Muslims. It was permitted to them to fight with infidels against infidels and "their" Muslims. The latter not only had no right to fight back, but had to turn against their foreign overlords. Shaykh Sālih ash-Sharīf at-Tūnisî confirmed this new doctrine of jihad on the side of the Austro-German Central Powers. Enver Pasha had asked Shaykh Sālih to travel to Berlin to popularize the jihad among the Germans. For this purpose Shaykh Sālih wrote a commentary. His *Haqīqat al-jihād* (The Truth of Jihad) was published at the beginning of 1915 by the German Society for the Study of Islam. Martin Hartmann of the Seminary of Oriental Languages in Berlin wrote a friendly foreword and the dragoman Karl

E. Schabinger added an afterword. Both recommended that text as a "development of jihad." What did it mean? A "partial jihad" was possible: on the side of allied infidels and just against certain enemy infidels. This jihad was an individual duty for all Muslims. A peace between the world of Islam and Europe would be possible if there were no longer any foreign occupation of Islamic lands.[29]

In the end, the execution of the jihad was disappointing for Max von Oppenheim and his Oriental News Department in the Foreign Office. It turned out that the majority of Muslims ignored the jihad, although Germans spent a lot of money for expeditions—such as the one headed by Werner Otto von Hentig and Oskar von Niedermayer to Kabul—and for pan-Islamic propaganda printed in Berlin like the weekly *Al-Jihād*. Nevertheless, Schabinger concluded that the seeds of an uprising had been planted. One day there would be an accumulation of colonial people ready to turn against their rulers.[30] The German General Staff drew a much less favorable conclusion: it was an illusion that the jihad would decide the war.[31] And on the other sides? As early as the middle of 1916 a French source concluded about the declarations of jihad that it had moved many people to action in the name of Islam; "they failed, indeed, but they caused no end of trouble to the Entente Powers."[32]

Indeed, this jihad was a concerted German-Ottoman action. Planned as an export of an Islamic uprising or revolution into the enemy's colonial hinterland, its idea was truly made in Germany. It was unfortunate that renowned German Oriental experts like Carl Heinrich Becker, Martin Hartmann, Ernst Jäckh, and Max von Oppenheim unleashed the old genie of pure religious hatred. Others like C. Snouck Hurgronje remained steadfast against this use of jihad and defended basic values of humanism and enlightenment. The most distinctive features of Berlin's Middle Eastern policy during World War I were not the 30,000 German troops fighting as part of the Ottoman army, the two attempts to capture the Suez Canal, or General Hans von Seeckt's role as the last Ottoman chief of staff. Of course, from a Middle Eastern viewpoint, the foremost element was that the Ottomans sided with the Germans.[33]

What was unique was, after the switch from a secondary peace to a primary war policy, the "jihad made in Germany." Thus, the German discipline of Islamic study lost its innocence not long after its birth.

3. The Republic of Weimar returns to a secondary Middle Eastern policy

After the Germans lost the war and overthrew their Emperor along with his "world policy," the German Reich was no longer a monarchy but became the Republic of Weimar. As such, a one-third smaller Germany was bound to comply with the victors' demands. Reconstruction and reform was the order of the day. Berlin returned to its secondary Middle Eastern peace policy. As the Treaty of Versailles ruled, Germany lost its Central African colonies. The new republic was even freer to concentrate on trade, commerce, and culture, reestablishing two of the prewar pillars of German Middle Eastern policy: respecting the status quo and disclaiming any territories. The third pillar, mediating in Oriental disputes, was excluded since Germany was given no role in international relations at all, and that promoted thoughts about vengeance in Berlin (see the contribution by Hans-Ulrich Seidt).

The Foreign Office broke with some older traditions by making reforms at the beginning of the 1920s. Both the classical diplomat of noble descent, trained in jurisprudence, and the dragoman, who knew Oriental languages as well as judicial matters, were replaced by a wider range of experts from all disciplines. Thus, it was possible for Berlin to regain most of its lost positions.

Germany again became the third-ranking country in foreign trade with the Middle East. One question that was discussed often in Berlin was whether or not to support industrialization in the region. Finally, the argument that if Germany did not do so, the competition would take this business over, prevailed. The Germans were attractive partners especially for Middle Eastern nationalists who looked for alternative suppliers to new emerging countries like Saudi Arabia (see the contribution by Uwe Pfullman) and Iraq. Students who had studied in Germany since 1920 returned to their homelands. They advanced there professionally and favored Germany in a climate that became hostile to the new British and French Mandatory powers.[34]

The Republic of Weimar applied a secondary Middle Eastern peace policy, cautiously avoiding trouble with London and Paris. Nevertheless, the Germans remained very critical of declining empires in the region[35] and supported Arab nationalists in their desire to rid themselves of foreign masters. In this light there was a natural basis for cooperation between the Germans on the one hand and the Arabs, Turks, and Persians on the other. It was not difficult for the old guard of diplomats like Dr. Fritz Grobba to exploit all the feelings that were nurtured by the experience of having fought and lost on the same side in the war. After the Treaty of Versailles, Berlin possessed no navy or other military tools. Thus, it had a diminished interest in the Middle East. Apart from economical and cultural relations, the region lacked importance for Berlin and returned to playing a marginal role.

London had decided to support a Jewish homeland in Palestine. As the waves of new Jewish immigrants, *olim chadashim*, arrived there, Palestine became a focal point. Berlin tried not to get involved in this project and kept its distance. Nevertheless, anti-Semitism was on the rise in Germany and did influence the fate of the region, indirectly at first. Moreover, some politicians in Berlin saw the emigration of Jews to Palestine as a solution to problems in Central Europe. But the most dangerous development was that the advanced Jewish assimilation in Germany was in jeopardy and with it some of the most important results of the European Enlightenment. Throughout the 1920s the inhumane nature of German racism became obvious. What appeared in the following decade was in no way a surprise. Even founding fathers of Islamic studies like Carl Heinrich Becker tended to divide humankind into "higher" and "lower" races.

4. The secondary and the primary Middle Eastern policy of Nazi Germany

From his election in 1933 until World War II, Adolf Hitler pursued a secondary peace policy toward the Middle East. He was much more interested in a division of labor with London: he accepted the British Empire while believing that Eastern Europe ought to be a completely German domain for *Lebensraum*. He readily left political "responsibilities" for the Middle East to Great Britain and Italy,[36] maintaining the tradition established by the first chancellor Otto von Bismarck, who regarded colonial outposts in Africa and Asia as nothing but trouble. Hitler's racial views, known to the public since 1920, must have influenced his lack of interest in creating German colonies or territories in the lands of "colored people."

An examination of German Middle Eastern policy under Hitler confirms that the region was of no concern to him. He built a Berlin-Rome axis with clear functions for Italy in the Middle East, and hoped for an understanding with London. Arab nationalists like Grand Mufti Amīn al-Husainī of Jerusalem were more interested in him than vice versa. An additional factor on the German side was the shortage of convertible money because most of it was being spent on re-armament. All this was to be changed by three factors.

First, if a disagreement or war arose with London, Paris, or Moscow, the Middle East could become one of the major battlegrounds. For this reason, even in peacetime, German planners were interested in French- and British-influenced territories and immediate neighbors of Russia such as Afghanistan and Turkey. That Franz von Papen became Hitler's ambassador to Ankara showed the major importance of this country for him (see the contribution by Karl Heinz Roth).

Second, the Middle East could become a primary matter if positions of Axis partners like Italy and Japan were in danger. Then Berlin could be dragged into conflicts. A common German policy was to avoid such risks in a region of secondary importance. The Middle East was not even important to Germany as a source of raw materials. Instead, Germans relied on Europe for raw materials like oil from the Balkans, and rare materials like tungsten from Portugal or chrome ore from Turkey. There was no need for deliveries from the Middle East or for military bases there.

The third possibility for increasing Berlin's interest in the Middle East was in case the plan of *Blitzkriege* ("lightning wars") in Europe failed. In that event, the region would become more important as a battlefield to entangle as many enemy troops as possible, as a source of fighting support, and as a base for reaching war targets in Russia or blocking British access to the Suez Canal. Just for this eventuality, the concept of a "jihad made in Germany" became important again. But Hitler, of course, did not expect it to be needed. Thus, the region was supposed to be mainly reserved for Italians. The Germans and Japanese had only economic interests. Accordingly, the Tripartite Treaty of Berlin codified the areas of influence a year after World War II began.

After Germany started World War II in September 1939, all three of the above scenarios played roles. Hitler did not achieve an agreement with London. Instead, a war against Great Britain followed. Most Brit-

THE GERMAN MIDDLE EASTERN POLICY

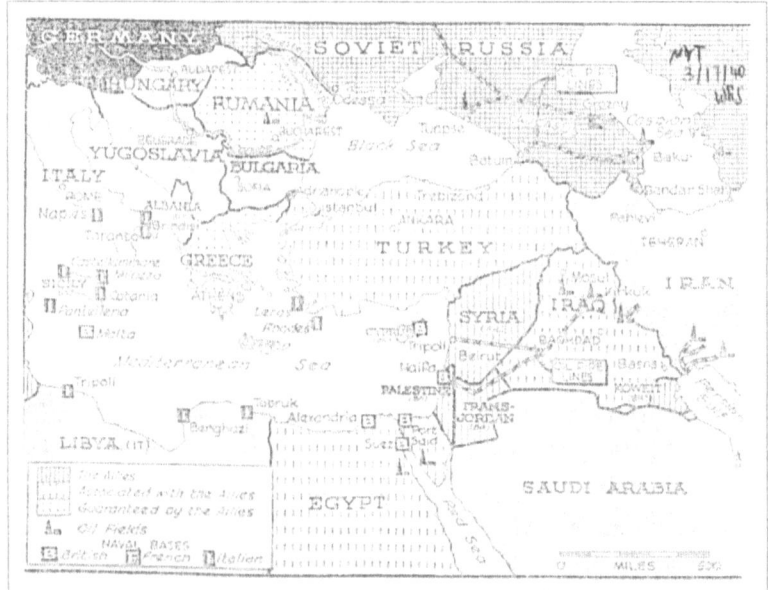

Map 1. The most critical time for the Allies in the Middle East between mid-1940 and 1942. (Source: *The New York Times*, March 17, 1940. Copyright © 1940 by the New York Times. Reprinted by permission.)

ish-influenced countries like Egypt broke off their relations with Berlin at the beginning of World War II. Going a step further, they declared war on Germany shortly before the end of the war. Berlin then switched from a secondary Middle Eastern peace policy to a primary Middle Eastern war policy. Although this policy was directed against London, Berlin played no major role in the Middle East, since it had to take the Italian policy in the region into account. After the fall of France in mid-1940 the Middle East became more accessible for the Germans. But Hitler showed no interest in French colonies.[38] Again, he concentrated on continental Europe.

In the most critical period of World War II, from June 1940 until November 1942 (see map 1), Hitler regarded the Middle East as a potential battleground, but never as a field of a greater engagement — a position that only a victory against Russia could have changed. To be prepared, his Order Number 32 called for German Middle Eastern plans to pave the way for later battles against the British. There, too, he would inflict an "uncompromising war against the Jews." Furthermore, he explained to the Grand Mufti of Jerusalem at the end of November 1941 that this relentless war naturally would include an active opposition to the Jewish national home in Palestine. Germany would be "willing to solve the Jewish problem step by step and it would appeal at the proper time to non-European nations as well." The current battle against the "Judeo-Communist Empire in Europe" would decide the fate of the Arab world too. He hoped that the coming year would it make possible for Germany to thrust open the Caucasian gate to the Middle East, but his *Blitzkrieg* failed at the Stalingrad front in November 1942. In the same month, General Erwin Rommel lost the battle of Al-ʾAlamain in an attempt to reach the Suez Canal, and the Allied forces landed in Morocco and Algeria. Hitler's plan had failed.

Besides, the Germans at first had had no foot in the Middle Eastern door, except briefly after an anti-British development in Iraq (see map 2). Rashīd ʿAlī al-Kailānī began a military coup in April 1941 in Bagh-

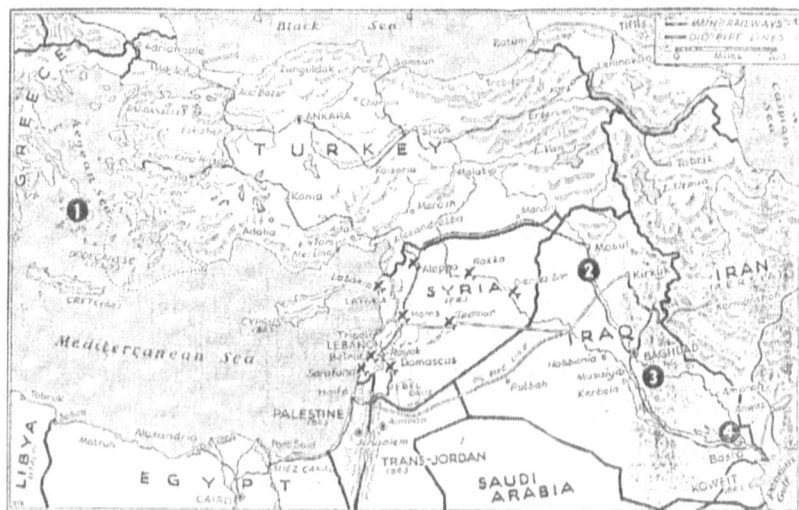

German planes, flying presumably from the Nazis' newly acquired island bases in the Aegean Sea (1), are said to be arriving in Syria for action in Iraq. Many of Syria's military airdromes, the chief ones of which are shown on the map by airplane devices, are reported to be already under German control and thus subject to British attack. Nazi planes are declared to have landed around Mosul (2), where there are extensive oil fields, and north of Baghdad (3), the Iraqi capital. British bombers raided the railway near Baghdad, a small arms factory at Musaiyib in the same area and barracks at Amarah in the neighborhood of the port of Basra (4).

Map 2. Iraq: For a brief period a German foothold in the Middle Eastern door in May 1941. (Source: *The New York Times*, May 16, 1941. Copyright © 1941 by the New York Times. Reprinted by permission.)

The German Middle Eastern Policy

dad. The Germans intervened there by airplanes at the beginning of May. But at the end of that month the British forces prevailed, forcing the Iraqi premier and his followers to flee, though Hitler had ordered limited support for them. Rashīd ʿAlī al-Kailānī—like Grand Mufti Amīn al-Husainī—ended up in exile in Berlin, and both spent the wartime there as guests of the German government. Both conspired from there against the Allies (see the American evaluation in document 1, "Axis Propaganda in the Moslem World," 1941).

The Grand Mufti helped the Germans by declaring a jihad against the Allies in broadcasts to the Middle East, and the Palestinian leader found German supporters. At the critical juncture after the fall of Paris, Max von Oppenheim forwarded an adapted version of his old jihad plan. The time had come, he wrote, to oppose England in the Middle East. There were two tasks: getting reliable news from the region and inciting rebellion in Syria and its neighbors. General aims were keeping British troops there, cutting off the oil supply for the British navy, and blocking Suez Canal traffic. Dr. Grobba would be best suited, in cooperation with influential natives like Shakīb Arslān of Greater Syria, to organize the uprisings that would weaken British positions in Egypt and India. A government under the leadership of Amīn al-Husainī should be established in Palestine, and only the Jews who had lived there before the First World War should be allowed to stay.[39]

A most challenging, but more or less unwanted, Middle Eastern involvement started for Berlin after the Italian dictator asked his German counterpart to support his troops against the British in Libya. Thirty days after Benito Mussolini requested help, German troops landed there. A month later General Rommel arrived, leading the newly founded German Africa Corps into the battles that would direct them close to Alexandria. Since the Germans also occupied Crete, it looked as if the Middle East would be the next big battleground. But Hitler had already ordered the attack against the USSR for late June 1941. Its outcome spared the Jews in the Middle East from the Holocaust and the region from a terrible experience.

Many Middle Easterners, like many Germans, did not recognize the nature of Nazi Germany. But some leading thinkers, among them the Egyptian poet Taufīq al-Hakīm, grasped it better. On the other hand, young Egyptian officers like ʿAbd an-Nāsir and Anwar as-Sādāt placed their hopes of ridding their country of the British on the Germans. It

AXIS PROPAGANDA IN THE MOSLEM WORLD

The Arab is a born dissenter and a lover of intrigue. In a country as small as Palestine, there have at times been as many as six different political parties functioning at once. Under such circumstances, there will always be found groups who will lend themselves to Axis propaganda, if only to spite their enemies.[1]

The Arabs are, however, united in one general purpose: To free their world from the domination of French and British masters. Arabs in Syria, Palestine, Egypt, and Iraq are apparently blinded[2] to Italian imperialism in Libya and Ethiopia and to German domination of Europe by their anxiety to get rid of British control. This arises not only from a desire to play all European powers off against each other but from a naiveté which assumes that anyone who is against Britain is automatically a friend of the Moslems. They fail to realize that, in case of a British defeat, there would be a substitution of Axis for British imperialism.

[1] An example seems to be the pro-Axis minority among the predominantly pro-British Druses.

Arab animosity toward foreigners and non-Moslems may be discriminated as follows:

A. *Anti-British sentiment.*

Despite the wishful thinking that continues to exist in Britain,[2] dislike and mistrust of Britain are strong throughout the Arab world, as well as in Iran and India. There are two reasons for this: One is British support of the Jews in Palestine and of other minorities for the apparent purpose of dividing and ruling the Arab states; the other is the reluctance of Britain to grant independence to mandated territories. The Arabs place little trust in British promises, which have been often broken in the past. Their distrust of British methods leads them to look for ulterior motives in every move made by Britain. If anything adverse happens, they automatically blame the British, without bothering to look into the facts of the case. This makes it easy for Axis propaganda to stir up Arab feeling; how easy is shown by the killing of the British Consul Mason at Mosul after German propaganda had accused the British of being responsible for the death of King Ghazi. The acquisition by Iraq and Egypt of their independence only after years of rebellion have convinced the Arabs that force is the only means by which they can extract what they regard as their rights from the British.[3]

[2] But see the realistic article, *Arab Nationalism and the War*, in Round Table (London), September 1941, pp. 698–708.
[3] An illustration of the strength of this attitude is the unpopularity of the Nashashibi faction in Palestine and the support by the Arab population, both in and out of Palestine, of the Mufti Hājj Amīn, who is the apostle of force against the British. What success the Axis powers have had is playing up to this state of mind can be judged from the fact that the Mufti is now in Berlin.

The Zeesen radio has lately been giving unusual attention to the exile and persecution of Arab leaders by Britain, and this cannot help but have considerable effect upon the Arabs.

The Assyrians who were at one time entirely pro-British now contain a considerable element which denounces Britain for having let the Assyrians down in Iraq.

The Arabs are very sensitive and bitterly resent the attitude of superiority of many Britons whom they meet.

B. *Anti-American sentiment.*

This is of recent growth. It is a result of two things: (1) The expression by American public officials of sympathy with political Zionism (which they usually misjudge as being purely religious and cultural) in Palestine. This has resulted in a tendency in all parts of the Arab world (strongest in Palestine and Syria) to suspect the United States of siding with the Jews against the Arabs in Palestine. (2) America's increasingly close alliance with Britain has led the Arabs to believe that we support Britain's policies in the Arab world. The attitude of India toward the United States has taken a very definite turn for the worse as a result of the promulgation of the Atlantic Charter, from which India was specifically excluded. All these factors are being fully exploited by the Zeesen radio in broadcasts to the Near East and India as evidence of the hypocritical attitude of the United States in preaching independence and self-determination for minorities on the one hand, while supporting British imperialism on the other.

C. *Anti-Jewish feeling.*

While Palestine is the focus of the problem, anti-Semitism has had an important effect on the Arabs of Syria and even of Saūdi Arabia, within whose boundaries there is hardly a single Jew. There can be no doubt that the situation created by the Zionist program in Palestine has caused the position of the Jews to deteriorate throughout the Arab world. Despite what Zionists say abroad for outside consumption, there are too many Jews in Palestine (and abroad) who adhere to the attitude expressed by William B. Ziff in *The Rape of Palestine:* The Jews are entering Palestine by divine right and intend to "make the Arabs go back to the desert where they came from." In North Africa there are grounds for anti-Jewish feeling which are separate from the Palestinian problem. Ever since the Arab invasion, the Jews there have been a despised element of the population, and this antipathy has been increased since the nineteenth century by the undoubted part which the Jews have played in facilitating foreign control of both French and Spanish Morocco.

Zeesen has recently been reading anti-Jewish passages from the Koran, emphasizing that the Jews are the "enemies of Islam."

D. *Anti-French feeling.*

This flourishes in all areas where the French are in control and existed even before the end of World War I: Witness the testimony of the King-Crane report which expressly states that under no circumstances did either the Syrians or Iraqis want a French mandate, a mandate which Syria subsequently was

Document 1. An American evaluation of the Axis propaganda in the Muslim world in 1941.

The German Middle Eastern Policy

> forced to accept. Anti-French feeling is relatively useless as an Axis propaganda implement as long as German-controlled Vichy retains holdings in the Arab East, except under the aspect of anti-de Gaullism in regions which might come under Free French control. Moreover, the setting up by the Free French of an "independent" Syrian state has stolen some of the Axis thunder. Zeesen propaganda blasts concentrate on denouncing Taj-al-Din, its head, as merely a de Gaullist-British tool.
>
> E. *Anti-Bolshevik feeling.*
>
> The educated and propertied classes among the Arabs, who largely control public opinion, are extremely apprehensive of socialism and more particularly of a Bolshevik socialist revolution. Through broadcasts and other means of propaganda, the Axis powers have succeeded in impressing on the Arab world the belief that they are engaged in saving capitalist civilization from the menace of Bolshevism. Propertied Arabs feel that a Nazi regime would not seriously damage their position, whereas a Bolshevik regime would exterminate them and the system under which they are accustomed to live. Ambitious Arab leaders tend to conceive of themselves as future heads of states, freed from British or French domination, each a miniature Reich with its Fuehrer or Duce, subservient perhaps to the Axis, but each with a considerable measure of "absolute" power
>
> F. *Moslem conservatism and prejudice.*
>
> This makes an appeal to conservative Moslems throughout the entire East, from Morocco to India.
>
> Many approaches can be used to exploit this: Anti-Christian bias, xenophobia, concern for Moslem minorities, etc. Recently Zeesen has been playing up the alleged suppression of the Moslem minorities in Russia; another curious anti-British blast from Zeesen accuses the British of being Pagans like the pre-Islamic Arabs and thus the natural enemies of Islam. It is doubtful whether such ridiculous appeals to presumed Moslem ignorance are going to help the Axis cause.
>
> G. *Food shortage and economic ruin.*
>
> The German radio at Zeesen has repeatedly stated that the food shortage in Morocco (especially in the Spanish Zone and Tangier) is being caused by the British blockade. In German broadcasts to the rest of the Moslem world, including Palestine, Egypt, Syria, Iraq, and Iran, it is made out that the British army is systematically stripping these countries, leaving the population to starve. At present the food situation does not appear to be bad except in Spanish Morocco and Tangier, but if it should become serious in other Moslem countries, this propaganda might have serious results. The announcement that Britain is stripping India of food is often repeated by Zeesen which adds that Britain means to sacrifice millions of Indian lives in a vain attempt to resist the Axis.

was not German racism or anti-Semitism that attracted them, but the thorough and fast modernization of Germany under the Nazi dictatorship. Arab nationalists originally admired the fascism of Mussolini, and consequently also Hitler, as an alternative to Anglo-Saxon democracy and as a modernistic movement. Berlin used this tendency in a selfish and ultimately antihuman manner to create trouble for the Allied Powers. Thus, the German Middle Eastern policy found a wider echo within radical Arab nationalism. The Middle East became again just a means for German "out-of-area" aims toward Europe and America. As Middle Easterners became aware of this nationalistic approach, their disappointment accumulated, along with their potential for anti-Westernism.

5. Germany's Middle Eastern policy: Patterns and prospects

Otto von Bismarck based Berlin's secondary Middle Eastern peace policy on three pillars: respecting the status quo, renouncing territorial claims, and mediating conflicts. The most striking paradigm was the subordination of this policy to the always-primary policy toward Europe and America. Although the German Middle Eastern policy was direct and active, especially in trade, commerce, and cultural exchange, there was the same ranking of regional priorities as in the primary policy. First came the Turkish heartland, then the countries under British or French influence, most notably Greater Syria (*bilād ash-shām*, including Palestine and Lebanon), then the other French-influenced territories, especially Algeria and Morocco, and finally the Russian Muslim lands in Central Asia.

This order of priorities did not change during either world war. What changed was Berlin's switch to a primary Middle Eastern war policy directed against Great Britain, France, and Russia. Even then the warfare was asymmetrical, weakening the enemies' colonial hinterlands from within by incitement to jihad. During World War I the Ottoman sultancaliph, the shaykh of Islam, and a Tunisian mufti promoted the concept, whereas during the Second World War it was the exiled Iraqi prime minister and the Grand Mufti of Jerusalem who promoted it. In both cases, the result was a new mixture of critical approaches to European Middle Eastern empires and of nationalistic aspirations in the declining or former Ottoman Empire.

During both wars, Berlin had no explicit design for the Middle East, and no direct goals other than two unsuccessful attempts to conquer the Suez Canal: once with the Ottomans from the East, the other time with the Italians from the West. But this direct military involvement resulted from claims of its coalition partners. Berlin's original aim in World War I was to fight the European great powers and to keep the Ottoman Empire as it was. After it broke apart, Berlin was willing to respect the national independence of former provinces of the Ottoman Empire. During World War II, Germans favored the idea of a Greater Arabian Empire or a federation associated with free countries of the region such as Saudi Arabia and Egypt. Of course they were to be allied with the Axis powers. Clearly, Berlin would not follow the lead of Rome for long. On the contrary, it would end up dictating the Middle Eastern policy of its junior partner.

Some politicians and academics claimed after World War II that Berlin lost its biggest chance for victory after the fall of Paris: had Hitler chosen the Middle East rather than Soviet Russia as the next big battleground, he might well have succeeded in the fight against London. Although Winston Churchill supported this speculation in his memoirs, the nature of Hitler and the racism of the Nazi system made such a choice unlikely. The dictator was completely oriented toward Eastern Europe. He excluded the Middle East from the beginning as an area for a greater engagement in the sense of a special German expansion.

On the other hand, some officers in the Foreign Office worked against Hitler. According to the foremost German envoy to Arab countries, Fritz Grobba, they prevented Hitler from discovering the "Middle Eastern chance"—if it existed—in the short period of the anti-British revolt in Iraq. It is no wonder that Hitler talked in the final days in his bunker about the failed agreement with London. If the senseless war against the British could have been avoided even until early 1941, he said, America would not have entered the war. The "false great powers," France and Italy, he claimed, could have dropped their untimely "policy of greatness." That would have allowed the Germans a "bold policy of friendship with Islam." Thus, without the war against the British, Adolf Hitler reasoned further, London could have turned to the Empire whereas Germany could have concentrated on her real mission: the eradication of Bolshevism.[42]

This reasoning leads to another conclusion about Berlin's Middle Eastern policy. In wartime it became as ideologically oriented as it had been secondary and commercially oriented during peacetime. Its central goal became supporting the war through the export of certain ideologies. During World War I this meant the export of an Islamic revolution. Germans incited jihad in a subtler fashion during World War II. The Nazis added the deadly racism leading to the Holocaust in Europe and the instigation of anti-Jewish sentiments in the Middle East. This was oil on the fire of the Arab-Jewish dispute about Palestine. The project of Jewish assimilation failed in Europe because of the mass extermination of Jews by Germans. Thus, the question of Palestine arose in a new light in the region. There were also Arabs among prisoners in the Nazis' concentration camps. On the other hand, the Grand Mufti of Jerusalem and the Iraqi premier sent their envoys to visit a concentration camp near Berlin, as a recently discovered report by Dr. Fritz Grobba indicates (see document 4). Thus, both leaders and their entourage knew about such camps and were able to anticipate their use in the coming genocide (see the contribution by Gerhard Höpp).

After World War II, Middle Eastern policy was not a high priority for the governments of the divided Germany. East Germany essentially went along with the Soviet Union and the Warsaw pact, while West Germany followed the United States and NATO, subordinating German interests to those of their allies. For example, when Bonn recognized the state of Israel in the mid-1960s, ten Arab states broke off diplomatic relations with West Germany and most of them recognized East Germany at the end of that decade. Germany also had and still has to deal with the burden of the Third Reich; often its policies regarding Israel have been based on moral rather than political criteria.[43]

Now, after reunification, Germany finally has the opportunity to pursue a genuine primary Middle Eastern peace policy of its own. The new hierarchy in Berlin's policy-making toward the Middle East seems to be:

- Firstly, the focus on truly bilateral or multilateral questions that are framed regionally between Central Europe and the Middle East.

- Secondly, the influence of bilateral or multilateral security matters on relations with the U.S. and other third parties.

- Thirdly, the influence of this bilateral and regional policy toward growing problems of multiple identities in Europe and the Middle East.

Berlin's new primary Middle Eastern policy indicates a paradigmatic change from the traditional threefold secondary style (respecting status quo, renouncing territorial claims, mediating conflicts) to a primary style. This is an opportunity that also implies risk.

Regionally, Berlin's Middle Eastern peace policy will be influenced by the cultural patchwork that Europe is becoming. In the past, the East-West divide determined Germany's alignment. Now regional and even local factors related to North-South conflicts play a larger role. Berlin takes into account its growing minorities of Jews and Muslims in shaping its Middle Eastern policy, and there is a sensitive mixture of foreign and domestic policy factors in the new period of globalization.[44] Until recently, Berlin had made the trans-Atlantic relationship a fundamental pillar of its foreign policy. This pillar was shaken during the Iraq crisis of 2003, when some German politicians opposed the attack by a U.S.

and British coalition. Whether Germany in the future will follow NATO or the EU, and what role a common European defense and possible European military intervention force will play, remain to be seen.

Notes

1. Gregor Schöllgen, *Das Zeitalter des Imperialismus* (Munich, 2002); idem, *Imperialismus und Gleichgewicht. Deutschland, England und die orientalische Frage* (Munich, 2000).
2. For the Prussian tradition of keeping the status quo overseas, see Ulrich van der Heyden, *Rote Adler an Afrikas Küste, Die brandenburguisch-preußische Kolonie Großfriedrichsburg in Westafrika* (Berlin, 2001), 14–15.
3. My overview of the German Orient founding years 1884–1914 is in August Bebel, *Die Muhammedanisch-Arabische Kulturperiode* (Berlin, 1999), 173–83.
4. Horst Gründer, *Geschichte der deutschen Kolonien* (Paderborn, 1995).
5. For German colonial pressure groups, see Axel Fichtner, *Die völker- und staatsrechtliche Stellung der deutschen Kolonialgesellschaften des 19. Jahrhunderts* (Frankfurt, 2002).
6. Diktat Bismarcks, Bad Kissingen, 15.06.1877. In Heinz Wolter, *Otto von Bismarck, Dokumente seines Lebens* (Leipzig, 1986), 320–21.
7. Martin Kröger, *"Le bâton égyptien" – Der ägyptische Knüppel, Die Rolle der "ägyptischen Frage" in der deutschen Außenpolitik von 1875/76 bis zur "Entente Cordiale"* (Frankfurt, 1991).
8. Imre Josef Demhardt, *Deutsche Kolonialgrenzen in Afrika* (Hildesheim, 1997).
9. For German Muslim subjects in Central Africa, see Carl Heinrich Becker, "Ist der Islam eine Gefahr für unsere Kolonien?" in Carl-Heinrich Becker, *Islamstudien, Vom Werden und Wesen der islamischen Welt* (Hildesheim, 1967), 156–86.
10. Otto Robert Georgi and Albert Dufour-Feronce, *Urkunden zur Geschichte des Suezkanals* (Leipzig, 1913).
11. Manfred Pohl, *Von Stambul nach Bagdad* (Munich, 1999); and Jürgen Franzke, *Bagdad- und Hedjazbahn* (Nürnberg, 2003).
12. Wolfgang G. Schwanitz, ed., *125 Jahre Sueskanal* (Hildesheim, 1998).
13. Wolfgang G. Schwanitz, *Gold, Bankiers und Diplomaten: Zur Geschichte der Deutschen Orientbank 1906–1946* (Berlin, 2002).
14. Gereon Sievernich and Hendrik Budde, eds., *Europa und der Orient 800–1900* (Berlin, 1989).
15. For the history of dragomans, see Maria Keipert and Peter Grupp, eds., *Biographisches Handbuch des deutschen Auswärtigen Dienstes 1871–1945* (Paderborn, 2000), xxxv–xxxvi; Bernard Lewis, "From Babel to Dragomans," in *Proceedings of the British Academy* 101 (1999): 37–54.
16. Johann Fück, *Die arabischen Studien in Europa* (Leipzig, 1955); Holger Preissler, "Die Anfänge der Deutschen Morgenländischen Gesellschaft," in *Zeitschrift der Deutschen Morgenländischen Gesellschaft* 145, no. 2 (1995): 1–92; Wolfgang G.

Schwanitz, "Deutsche Orientalistik wohin?" in *Asien, Afrika, Lateinamerika* 23, no. 1 (1995): 51–82.

17. Elke Pflugradt-Abdel Aziz, *Islamisierte Architektur in Kairo, Carl von Diebitsch und der Hofarchtitekt Julius Franz – Preußisches Unternehmertum im Ägypten des 19. Jahrhunderts* (Bonn, 2003); Uwe Pfullmann, *Durch Wüste und Steppe, Entdeckerlexikon arabische Halbinsel* (Berlin, 2001); Eugen Wirth, *Die orientalische Stadt im islamischen Vorderasien und Nordafrika*, 2 vols. (Mainz, 2000); Bolko Stegemann, *Auf den Spuren des Orientmalers Wilhelm Gentz* (Krefeld, 1996); Stefan Koppelkamm, *Der imaginäre Orient, Exotische Bauten 18. und 19. Jahrhunderts in Europa* (Berlin, 1987).
18. See my overview in Bebel, op. cit.
19. Wolfgang Petter, "Die deutsche Militärmission im Osmanischen Reich," in Klaus Jaschinski and Julius Waldschmidt, eds., *Des Kaisers Reise in den Orient* (Berlin, 2002), 87–99.
20. Ernst Berner, "Kaiser Wilhelm II.," in Paul Seidel, ed., *Hohenzollern Jahrbuch* (Berlin, 1898), 1–17.
21. Wolfgang G. Schwanitz, "Djihad 'made in Germany': Der Streit um den Heiligen Krieg (1914–1915)," in *Sozial.Geschichte* 18, no. 2 (2003): 7–34.
22. C. Snouck Hurgronje, "The holy war 'made in Germany', 1915," in his *Verspreide Geschriften* (Bonn, Leipzig, 1923), vol. 3, 257–58; Carl Heinrich Becker, "Die Kriegsdiskussion über den Heiligen Krieg," in his *Islamstudien*, op. cit., 281–304.
23. Martin Kröger, "Max von Oppenheim—mit Eifer ein Fremder im Auswärtigen Dienst," in Gabriele Teichmann and Gisela Völger, eds., *Faszination Orient. Max von Oppenheim, Forscher, Sammler, Diplomat* (Köln, 2001), 106–39.
24. Ernst Jäckh, *Der aufsteigende Halbmond* (Stuttgart, 1915).
25. Archiv Sal. Oppenheim Jr. & Co., Oppenheim 25/10, *Max Freiherr von Oppenheim, Denkschrift betreffend die Revolutionierung der islamischen Gebiete unserer Feinde* (Berlin, 1914).
26. Ibid., 136.
27. Donald McKale, *War by Revolution, Germany and Great Britain in the Middle East in the Era of World War I* (Kent, 1998).
28. "The Ottoman Jihad Fatwa of November 11th, 1914," in Rudolph Peters, *Jihad in Classical and Modern Islam* (Princeton, N.J., 1996), 55–57.
29. Shaikh Sālih ash-Sharīf Al-Tūnisī, *Haqᵒqat al-Jihěd*, translated from Arabic by Karl E. Schabinger, foreword by Martin Hartmann (Berlin, 1915).
30. Karl Emil Schabinger Freiherr von Schowingen, *Weltgeschichtliche Mosaiksplitter, Erlebnisse und Erinnerungen eines kaiserlichen Dragomans*, ed. Karl Friedrich Schabinger Freiherr von Schowingen (Baden-Baden, 1967).
31. Reichsarchiv, ed., "Jildirim," *Deutsche Streiter auf heiligem Boden* (Berlin, 1925), 65.
32. "Secret French Report, 01.06.1916," in Jacob M. Landau, *The Politics of Pan-Islam. Ideology and Organization* (Oxford, 1994), 102.
33. Efraim Karsh and Inari Karsh, *Empires of the Sand: The Struggle for the Mastery in the Middle East 1789–1923* (Cambridge, 1999).
34. Wolfgang G. Schwanitz, ed., *Araber, Juden, Deutsche* (Berlin, 1994).

35. L. Carl Brown, ed., *Imperial Legacy: The Ottoman Imprint on the Balkans and the Middle East* (New York, 1996).
36. Heinz Tillmann, *Deutschlands Araberpolitik im Zweiten Weltkrieg* (Berlin, 1965); Lukasz Hirscowicz, *The Third Reich and the Arab East* (London, 1966).
37. Nazi minister Hans Frank claimed to have coined the phrase "axis Berlin-Rome" in September 1936. He talked with the Italian foreign minister Ciano about "a European car that would be driven ahead on the axis between the (Italian) Fascism and the (German) National Socialism." Mussolini used that term, an "axis on which all European states rotate," in his speech of 1 November 1936. A year later he joined the Anti-Comintern Pact. It was common in Anglo-Saxon countries to use "Axis powers" to include Japan after the Tripartite Pact of 27 September 1940 created the "axis Berlin-Rome-Tokyo."
38. Chantal Metzger, *L'Empire colonial français dans la stratégie du Trosième Reich (1936–1945)* (Brussels, 2002), tomes 1, 2.
39. Political Archive of the Foreign Office, Nachlass Werner Otto von Hentig, vol. 84, Memorandum Max von Oppenheims, 25.07.1940, 7 pp.
40. Israel Gershoni, "Egyptian Liberalism in an age of 'Crisis of Orientation': Al-Risēla's Reaction to Fascism and Nazism, 1933–1939," in *International Journal of Middle East Studies* 31 (1999): 551–76; Israel Gershoni, "Confronting Nazism in Egypt—Tawfiq al-Hakim's Anti-Totalitarianism 1938–1945," in *Tel Aviver Jahrbuch für deutsche Geschichte* 26 (1997): 121–50.
41. Anwar el-Sadat, "Rommel at El-Alamain: An Egyptian view (1942)," in Bernard Lewis, ed., *A Middle East Mosaic* (New York, 2000), 314–16.
42. Joachim C. Fest, *Hitler, Eine Biographie* (Berlin, 1997), 1011.
43. At the request of the U.S., Bonn had participated in a secret deal to deliver weapons to Israel; West Germany recognized the state of Israel in an attempt to resolve the crisis.
44. Wolfgang G. Schwanitz, "'Gharbî, Sharqî, Ittihâdî': Zur Geschichte der deutsch-ägyptischen Beziehungen 1945–1995," in Ghazi Shanneik and Konrad Schliephake, eds., *Die Beziehungen zwischen der Bundesrepublik Deutschland und der Arabischen Republik Ägypten* (Würzburg, 2002), 43–54. Wolfgang G. Schwanitz, *Deutsche in Nahost 1945–1965* (Frankfurt, 1998), vols. 1, 2; Wolfgang G. Schwanitz, "'Salami tactics': Akten über doppelte deutsche Nahost-Gesandte 1950–1966, Das Nationalarchiv II im College Park und die Quellenkritik," in *Orient* 40, no. 4 (1999): 597–630.

Figure 2. Emir Habibullah and his sons Enayatullah (left) and Amanullah

The German Mission to Afghanistan 1915–1916

THOMAS L. HUGHES

It was no accident that the Afghan factions in November 2001 chose Bonn as the site for the conference that would form the first post-Taliban government for Afghanistan. Two months later, hundreds of German troops arrived in Afghanistan for peacekeeping and police-training work, with Germany also providing the largest European contribution toward economic reconstruction. Nor was it accidental that in June 2002 the *loya jirga* in Kabul, convened to legitimize an interim government, met under a gigantic German-provided tent, complete with air-conditioning, lighting, sound facilities, cushions, tea services, and six thousand meals a day. Mindful of Germany's long history of friendly involvement in Afghan constitutional discussions, the United Nations, in coordinating the event, again turned to Germany.

Shortly before World War I, one of his ambassadors told Kaiser Wilhelm that hostilities with Russia were not inevitable and that future developments in foreign affairs were hard to predict. "Oh," the lighthearted kaiser is said to have replied, "the gift sometimes occurs—to sovereigns frequently, to generals occasionally, but to ambassadors almost never." The 1915 German mission to Afghanistan was an attempt to make one of the kaiser's predictions come true. This mission was aimed at influencing the ruler of a landlocked kingdom thousands of miles away, a fellow sovereign who, like the kaiser himself, was not quite sovereign, but who proved to be very canny in his own predictions and adept at hedging his bets about them.

For two years, in the midst of World War I, Afghanistan was the goal of a German mission operating at the vortex of four clashing empires — the German, Ottoman, Russian, and British. In addition to their ten-month stay inside Afghanistan, the Germans' arrivals and departures involved more months of high adventure, heroic personal drama, narrow escapes, and legendary feats of survival. In Kabul itself, the mission's life with the Emir Habībullah had much of the aura of an *opera buffa*. But as a British adversary, General Sir Percy Sykes, later wrote: "The German Mission to the Emir created a crisis of the first magnitude in Afghanistan and was a source of the gravest anxiety in India."[1]

I backed into a fascination with this story in 1978 when I discovered that Werner Otto von Hentig, the diplomatic leader of the wartime venture, was alive in Germany. His father and my grandfather were cousins, and I had heard rumors about his extraordinary career. An initial meeting led to frequent visits and letters, which continued until von Hentig died in 1984 in his ninety-ninth year. Despite his great age, he remained fit, trim, and quick of step. His brain was clear and sharp. He spoke fluent English, among many other languages. Following our long walks in the woods or other venues for historical chitchat, I took meticulous notes.

All this led me to read the published accounts in English of his famous journey, including the reputable standard works by Americans like Ludwig Adamec, Louis Dupree, and Milan Hauner. I am familiar with most of the British authors from Percy Sykes to Peter Hopkirk, whose accounts are vivid but sometimes shaky. Raja Mahendra Pratap, the Indian prince who was the titular head of the German mission, has left us an exotic genre with titles like: "My German Mission to High Asia: How I joined the Kaiser to enlist Afghanistan against Great Britain" (*Asia Magazine*, May 1925).

Von Hentig himself published several accounts in German of his mission. His *Ins Verschlossene Land* (Into the Closed Land) was rushed into print by Ullstein in Berlin in 1918, the last year of the war. It sold three hundred thousand copies, and appeared later in translation in more than a half dozen European and Near Eastern languages, including Turkish, Arabic, Armenian, and Hebrew, but never in English. Another German edition of one hundred thousand copies appeared in 1928 on the occasion of King Amanullah's state visit to Berlin, when Hentig was again among the participants.

Hentig gave me an unpublished English translation, which he himself revised in the 1930s as details of his secret activities in Kabul emerged. Some of these appeared in his 1962 memoirs, *Mein Leben: Eine Dienstreise*. His papers are in the Swiss Bibliotheca Afghanica.

The 1915 Hentig mission wound its way from Berlin to Vienna to Constantinople to Baghdad to Isfahan where, supplemented by Oskar Niedermayer's contingent, it went on to Herat and Kabul. But it is essential to remember that this Afghanistan saga is just one part of a much larger story. German efforts by the end of 1914, especially after the stalemate on the Western front, were also directed toward contesting British activities in Mesopotamia and the Gulf, destabilizing the Russian and British presence in Persia, and persuading the Persians themselves to support the Central Powers—always with an eye on Turkish support toward making inroads in the Caucasus. Much was in motion elsewhere in the Muslim world. Indeed the German Afghan mission's chances for success depended upon simultaneous successes by the Central Powers in these neighboring campaigns.

Before turning to the dramatis personae of the mission per se, let me offer some vignettes from a century ago that evoke the flavor of the times, especially as they bear on the postures of the major contestants.

The Southern *Drang nach Osten*

Pre-war German influence was strong and growing in the Ottoman Empire and Persia. The German General Colmar Freiherr von der Goltz Pasha had begun organizing the Ottoman army in the 1880s. Prussian civil servants were helping Turkey to modernize. German archaeologists and secret agents were at work. Baron Max von Oppenheim, the leading German Orientalist, was active mapping the region. Pan-Germanists in the nineteenth century had already stated the case for creating Germany's India out of the ruins of the Ottoman Empire. The

Konya to Baghdad Railway, not quite completed at the time of the 1915 mission, symbolized this geopolitical drive.

The Persian shah, like the Ottoman sultan, saw Anglo-Russian imperial rivalries as carving up his domains. Tehran also thought of the new and powerful German Empire as a possible counterweight. German investment, banking, and commercial interests, teachers, and even settlers were invited in. The German legation had close relations with Persian "democrats." Persian liberal nationalists were overwhelmingly pro-German and pro-Turkish. Swedish officers in the Persian Gendarmerie were pro-German. Several of the German officers in the 1915 Afghan mission had lived and worked in Persia before the outbreak of the war, and at least three of them—Hentig, Niedermayer, and Walter Röhr—were already on good personal terms with the German minister, Prince Henry XXXI of Reuss. Also by 1915, the escape of hundreds of German and Austrian POWs from Tashkent had turned their Tehran legations into armed camps.

Years earlier, in 1898, the kaiser's own triumphal visit to Constantinople, Jerusalem, and Damascus (planned by Thomas Cook & Son) gave him a platform to proclaim publicly: "Three hundred million Muslims around the world have a friend in the German Emperor." He failed to mention that most of them were subjects of his English grandmother, Queen Victoria. In turn, the British noticed, of course, that the kaiser conveniently had almost no Muslim subjects of his own and no Islamic unrest stirring in his domains.

The cultivation of the Ottoman Empire, and through it the Islamic world, was an important element in the "New Course" of the German Empire after Bismarck's fall in 1890. It met with little resistance in German official circles. Some residual Bismarckians fretted that the Iron Chancellor's policy of avoiding antagonizing Russia and Great Britain would be undermined by an active Near Eastern push, but they were overridden.

Incidentally, the kaiser even had a little trouble in his own household over the Eastern Question. His wife, the Empress Augusta Victoria, personified the pious Prussian womanly virtues of the "three K's—Kinder, Kirche, Küche" (children, church, kitchen). Already on their visit to Damascus in 1898, she had questioned the propriety of the kaiser's personally paying for a new marble tomb for Saladin, especially since the kaiser was the Protector of the Johanniterorden, the Order of St. John of

Jerusalem, which dated from the Crusades. On that same trip, she had heard in Constantinople disquieting stories about the sultan's harem. Staunchly proud of her own seven bouncing children, she later learned to her dismay that the emir of Afghanistan boasted over one hundred offspring. Armed with such information, she reminded Wilhelm that, after all, he was the head of the German Protestant Church and that Muslim practices were something else again.[2]

Her husband heard her but did not heed. One hopes that in 1914 the kaiserin was spared the news that German propaganda in the East was referring to her restless husband as "Haji Wilhelm Mohammed" and that Asian bazaars were buzzing with rumors that he had secretly converted to Islam following a pilgrimage, incognito, to Mecca. Passages in the Qurʾān were found that showed the kaiser had been ordained by God to free Muslims from infidel rule.

Embittered by Great Britain's entry into the war, German officialdom, military and civilian alike, wasted no time in assessing this opponent's vulnerabilities in Central Asia. There are memoranda to the Foreign Office from Helmuth von Moltke and the General Staff as early as August 2 and 5, 1914, advocating awakening Islam toward revolution in India. The point was strongly reinforced by the famous Swedish explorer Sven Hedin (1865–1952), who arrived in Berlin two weeks later. By far the most expert Western visitor to Central Asia, he claimed that the East was ripe for revolt and that the Afghans were "burning with desire" to free India from the British. His view was reflected in another memorandum from the General Staff on August 24, which predicted that the Indian revolution would begin with an "invasion by the Emir of Afghanistan." These themes were repeated in Chancellor Theobald von Bethmann-Hollweg's famous September Memorandum on German war aims in which he refers to "our machinations in Afghanistan and India."[3]

The Ottoman Empire, its decline arrested somewhat by German influence and involvement, still retained considerable prestige in the Muslim world. Along with Afghanistan, it was almost the only Muslim land to escape foreign control. The sultan purported to speak for Islam and continued to claim the cherished title of caliph, a claim supported in Afghanistan and India. In January 1913 there was a coup d'état of notably German flavor in Constantinople, led by the German-trained minister of war, Major Enver Pasha. The figurehead Sultan Mehmed V was allowed to remain on the throne.

When, after a two-month delay, the Ottoman Empire did join the war on the German side, Enver quickly arranged for the sultan-caliph to proclaim a jihad, or holy war, against Britain. The German Foreign Office or Wilhelmstraße (named for the street on which the German Foreign Office was located) immediately ordered copies of the proclamation forwarded to Berlin for translation and use in propaganda leaflets among Muslim troops in enemy armies. The summons, which called upon Muslims everywhere to rise and slay their Christian oppressors, was transmitted through a network of mullahs, assisted by Turkish, German, and Indian agents. The German Foreign Office predicted that the sultan's actions would awaken the fanaticism of Islam and might lead to a large-scale revolution in India.

In August 1914, at the outbreak of the European war, Emir Habībullah of Afghanistan had declared neutrality, but he was seriously concerned when Turkey joined it in October. For the next three years, he repeatedly told the British agent in Kabul that he was "anxious about Turkey's great religious attraction for Afghans in particular. The influence of Turkey on his subjects was a matter of supreme importance to him."[4]

Adamec says that after Turkey entered the war, Enver Pasha reported he had received a message from the Afghan emir asking whether the Afghans should attack Russia or Britain. This seems very inconsistent with the emir's grip on reality. Probably Enver used some more ambiguous verbal report, along with other evidence that the Indian frontier tribes were stirring, to encourage the Germans to join in an Afghan mission. Originally Enver's own concept was for a Turkish-dominated Pan-Islamic mission containing a few Europeans. This was the basis for the initial involvement of Wilhelm Wassmuss and Oskar Niedermayer in a 1914 mission that collapsed.

In short, as Vartan Gregorian has written: "The entry of the Ottoman Empire into the conflict ... aroused widespread Pan-Islamic and nationalist sentiment in [Afghanistan] ... The overwhelming majority of the Afghan nationalists and modernists were sympathetic to the Turkish cause ... In general, public opinion in Afghanistan was on [the Turkish-German] side, as it was in India and Persia, where even the peasants and tribesmen seem to have been anti-British and anti-Russian."[5]

Despite this fortunate combination of interests in the Muslim world, there were German-Turkish tensions as well throughout the war. Command and control disagreements aborted the Wassmuss-Niedermayer mission when they refused to work under Turkish command. There were growing tensions between the German diplomats and the German military in Turkey, with the military in the ascendancy in the last months of the war.

In Constantinople during the war, there also were political disputes between the Germans, both civilian and military, and the Ottoman regime. For example, both Protestant and Catholic churches in Germany were greatly disturbed by the massacres of the Armenians, and successive German diplomats in Turkey who protested the massacres too vigorously in 1915–1916 were in effect declared personae non gratae and removed.

Although not well known outside Germany, there was, in fact, an anti-Turkish uproar among German Christians over the Armenian Question. Thus the elderly Grand Duchess Louise of Baden, daughter of Kaiser Wilhelm I, sister of Kaiser Friedrich III, and aunt of Kaiser Wilhelm II, promptly wrote to Theobald von Bethmann-Hollweg demanding to know what he was doing about the Armenian horrors. The chancellor sent the Prussian representative at the Baden court to pacify her and explain that despite his continuous and emphatic protests, horrible things had happened. Discussion of the issue, however, only seemed to incite new persecutions as well as growing anti-German sentiment in Turkey. The situation was extremely delicate, and all this at a time when the alliance had special value. [6]

Indian Revolutionaries and British Apprehensions

Resistance to British colonial rule in India had been growing in the Indian diaspora during the pre-war decade, not only among strident young Indians in Britain and South Africa who were under constant surveillance, but also among more strident Indians in Japan and in anti-colonial circles in the United States. Following the Boer War in 1899, anti-British collaboration was especially close between the discontented Indians and Irish in New York. They looked forward to the day when Irish and Indian troubles would combine to destroy British imperialism. Ethnic societies were organized.

India House was a prestigious pioneer model for Indian students. A staff member of the *Gaelic American* helped publish the newspaper *Free Hindustan* until the British persuaded American authorities to close both papers down. In 1908 joint Irish-Indian meetings were held twice a week, for example, at the New York home of Muhammad Barakatullah. Seven years later he joined the German mission to Afghanistan. He probably coined the widely used phrase: "England's difficulty is India's opportunity." In case of war, with an Irish rebellion tying up the British on the home isles, and with British and Indian forces away from India in Europe, the opportunity for the use of force inside India and on its borders would beckon. In case of a revolt against Britain, many Indians assumed that German help would be on the way.

For some years, India had touched and enlivened the German imagination, risking war with England, and prominent Germans like Friedrich von Bernhardi certainly took account of the Indian situation.[7] Indian revolutionary literature in 1913–14 regularly referred to an approaching Anglo-German war and possible German help in the revolutionary struggle. In the early months of 1914, German newspapers repeatedly featured articles on Indian distress, social unrest, and British colonial high-handedness. Secret societies which would provide arms and explosives were said to flourish inside India and abroad, especially in California. Later it was learned that the German Embassy in Washington, the famous Franz von Papen in particular, was paymaster for many of the arms destined for India.

By September 3, 1914, the Foreign Office in Berlin had agreed that Germany would assist the Indian nationalists, and for the next few weeks there were almost daily Indian-German meetings to discuss next steps. On September 9, two months before the jihad was proclaimed, the kaiser declared that Muslims in the Entente armies would not be treated as belligerents but would be sent to the caliph in Turkey when taken prisoner. Indian revolutionaries continued to arrive in Germany and in early 1915, the Indian Independence Committee was formally set up in Charlottenburg and subsidized on a regular monthly basis by the Foreign Office.

Inside British India, Muslims and Hindus alike showed new signs of restiveness under imperial rule. Several prominent Hindu leaders left India in 1914 to campaign abroad for Indian freedom. One was Mahendra Pratap, who would formally head the German mission of 1915. The world war and Pan-Islamic feeling also tended to bring traditionalists and modernizers together in India, as it did in Afghanistan. Thus, before long, the All-India Muslim League, founded in 1906 to protect Muslim rights and promote loyalty to the British government, joined the Indian Congress Party in the Lucknow Pact of 1916 and demanded Indian self-rule.

The English knew full well that the only hands that could set India afire were those of the emir of Afghanistan. Parliamentary debates in 1914 made clear how alarmed they were about potentially adverse developments in that part of the world. For generations they had fought—and Kipling had popularized—the Great Game between the British and Russian empires for control over the high mountain ranges in and adjoining Afghanistan, from which invaders might pour down into the plains of British India. Under these circumstances, British imperialism had little tolerance for Afghan sensitivities. Even that eminent Victorian Alfred Lord Tennyson was once described, in inverted Victorian word order, as being "all for putting up with no nonsense from the Afghans."[8]

And as far as India itself was concerned, by the end of the Victorian era, it was regarded not only as the jewel in the Empire's crown, but also, by someone like Jowett, the Master of Balliol College Oxford, as a vast laboratory for high-minded British social experimentation. Indeed Balliol alumni were fated to be prominent in the growing Indian entanglement. Often it was a story of Balliol chasing Balliol—as Balliol viceroys, like the arch-imperialist Lord Curzon, used the services of Balliol's Indian Secret Service spy chief, Sir Charles Cleveland, to track down some of Balliol's most promising Indian revolutionary alumni like Shyamaji Khrishnavarma, the founder of India House in Highgate, London, and later proponent of German-Indian wartime collaboration. The latter was instrumental in urging Raja Mahendra Pratap to leave Geneva for Berlin in early 1915 to join the German mission to Afghanistan.[9]

Russia's defeat in the Russo-Japanese War in 1905 had enabled Britain to emerge as the apparent winner of the Great Game. In a treaty with Britain in 1907, negotiated over the heads of the Afghans who had no say in the matter, Russia gave up her interest in Afghanistan and left control of the emir's foreign policy in British hands. The Government of India asserted its responsibility for relations with Afghanistan, Persia, and the Persian Gulf sheikhdoms through a network of resident agents and governors. At the same time Persia was divided into three zones—a Russian north, a neutral center, and a British south. The Persians, of course, were not consulted.

British intelligence went to work full-time to uncover and obstruct Indian revolutionary cells inside and outside the Subcontinent. The Japanese, supposedly Britain's allies, gave sanctuary to many Indians over British protests. Delhi tried its best to drain the swamp of revolutionary remittances that found their way to India via Batavia, Burma, Siam, and Persia. British wartime accounts describe dozens of revolutionary plots, missions, schemes, and attempts at landings, most of which were foiled.

Countering German intelligence operations and planning anti-German ones received, of course, the highest priority, and before long the German-Islamic connection became a major focus. The British wartime director of information, John Buchan, dramatized his countrymen's fears in his famous 1916 novel "Greenmantle." These excerpts provide its flavor:

> The secret may be in Constantinople. But it is moving eastwards. The secret is known in Germany. It is life and death...I can put it no higher and no lower. If the East blazes up, our effort will be distracted from Europe. Germany's like a scorpion: her sting's in her tail that stretches way down into Asia...The stakes are no less than victory and defeat. We have laughed at the Holy War, the Jehad that old von der Goltz prophesied. But I believe that old man with the spectacles was right. There is a Jehad preparing. There is a dry wind blowing through the East, and the parched grasses wait the spark. The wind is blowing towards the Indian border. The Germans know, and that is the card with which they are going to astonish the world.[10]

Buchan goes further and one of the characters in his novel introduces another element into the British threat analysis. He refers to Enver Pasha and asks how this "adventurer and a collection of Jews and gypsies have got control of a proud race." Another character tells us: "If you look into the matter, you will find that the Jew is at the back of most German enterprises."

The British director of information had already introduced this subject in an earlier (1915) novel, *The Thirty-Nine Steps* where we learn about "a subterranean movement, engineered by very dangerous people.

This is the return match for the pogroms. The Jew is everywhere...with an eye like a rattlesnake. He is the man who is ruling the world just now, and he has his knife in the empire of the Tsar."

Ironically this British assumption about Jewish-led German imperialism is not just a novelist's poetic license, but reflects official British certainty that they were in fact up against a German-Jewish conspiracy. This assumption pervades both diplomatic dispatches and commonplace political views.

The British knew that Kaiser Wilhelm had had friendly conversations with Theodor Herzl years before, and that Wilhelm had recommended to the sultan that he consider establishing a Jewish homeland in his Palestinian territories. They knew that Wilhelm had persisted over the years in urging the sultan to improve and modernize his regime by increasing the number of his Jewish advisers. The British also suspected the Young Turks of being under the influence of Jewish intellectuals. Lord Kitchener, the British minister of war, worried that the caliph had fallen into the hands of Jews and Germans who might use him to undermine Britain's position in India.

The British knew that Sven Hedin was supplying the German General Staff with his maps, the best in the world, of Central Asia—and that Hedin had a great-grandfather who was a rabbi. They knew that in 1915 the celebrated German researcher, Baron Max von Oppenheim, was in charge of anti-British activity in Turkey where he was personally urging Muslim leaders to support Germany and the jihad. A British official reported, with satisfaction, that "his propaganda was not well received among Constantinople religious communities owing to his Jewish origin."[11] So there were many plays within the play in the mindsets of the great powers as they set about creating and reacting to the German Afghan mission.

The Mission's German-Indian Leadership

The mission is largely the story of three young men—two Germans, Werner Otto von Hentig and Oskar Niedermayer, and an Indian, Mahendra Pratap. All three were twenty-nine years old when the mission began. The three were thrown together by circumstances in an enterprise that was not carefully organized. At one time or another, there were several dozen participants. They were recruited gradually, some of them preceding others in the field. Still others were added and several were separated en route.

The first of the three on the ground in Turkey and Persia was First Lieutenant Oskar Niedermayer. He had been chosen in 1914 to participate in the military component of the aborted mission headed by Wilhelm Wassmuss. Both Germans opted out of the earlier project, since the Turks refused German control and they, in turn, did not want to participate in a Turkish-dominated enterprise. Wassmuss then embarked on his own exotic adventures with the tribes of southern Persia, and was at the center of the most dramatic British intelligence coup of the entire war. In evading British capture, Wassmuss abandoned his codebook. This famous accident eventually enabled the British to read German official cable traffic to and from the Washington Embassy, including the legendary Zimmermann telegram that arguably was instrumental in bringing America into the war in 1917.

With Wassmuss out of the Afghan mission, Niedermayer "worked himself into a leading position" with the remaining group, as Adamec puts it, and he returned to Persia to await developments. Niedermayer was a Bavarian artillery officer who had studied geography, geology, and philology at the University of Erlangen. Between 1912 and 1914, he undertook a privately funded research journey across Persia to India that had a lifelong effect on his professional career.

By all accounts, Niedermayer was a resourceful, ambitious activist of exceptional physical and mental abilities, with a keen eye for the main chance. He is invariably referred to as resilient and "iron-willed." All these attributes fully applied to his colleague von Hentig as well. They were essential to both men in enabling the mission to reach Afghanistan, and equally essential later when both escaped from it. But conceptual differences were there at the outset. Niedermayer unsuccessfully sought the integration of the larger Hentig group (Germans, Austrians, Indians, and Afridis) into the smaller Niedermayer group under his orders and subject to martial law. As Niedermayer saw it, the Hentig diplomatic mission was to be grafted onto a Niedermayer military mission.

As far as Hentig was concerned, the reverse was the case—the Niedermayer mission was grafted onto the Hentig mission. Hence the seeds of their future antagonism were planted in a confusion of command and control. At different times during the mission Hentig certainly exerted full control over the group that accompanied him from Berlin to Isfahan (April to July), and he continued to do so in Persia in the weeks before July 22 when his and Niedermayer's groups were deliberately kept apart. Once they arrived in Afghanistan, the diplomatic-political aspects of the mission were clearly predominant with Hentig in charge. He alone had official credentials—named as *Kaiserlicher Vertreter* (imperial representative) in the chancellor's letter to the emir—and he alone was responsible for the mission's finances. The ambitious military insurrectionist goal of the mission—and with it Niedermayer's hopes and expectations—never materialized, despite the latter's best efforts to maximize his own role.

At times, Niedermayer and Hentig seem to have made reports independent of each other. In any case, orderly reporting channels were disrupted from the outset. In theory, the German ambassador in Turkey, von Freiherr Hans von Wangenheim, had overall supervision, but he was in Germany taking a cure most of the summer of 1915. His substitute in Constantinople, Prince zu Hohenlohe-Langenburg, seems to have had little or no contact with the Afghan mission. Shortly after returning to Turkey, Wangenheim died, on October 25, the day before the mission's first meeting with the Emir. His successor, Count Wolff-Metternich, largely preoccupied with, and undone by, the Armenian Question, also seems to have played no consequential role in the Afghan story. Moreover, what reporting there was from the mission in Kabul had to go via Prince Reuss in Tehran, and his role, in turn, was jeopardized with the deterioration of the Persian situation itself in 1916.

In March 1915, Lieutenant Werner Otto von Hentig was serving on active duty with his regiment, the famous Prussian Third Cuirassiers, on the Russian front, when he was ordered to report to the General Staff in Berlin for what turned out to be the Afghanistan assignment. Before the war he had studied at a variety of universities—Grenoble, Königsberg, Berlin, and Paris—before earning a degree in international law from Bonn. He practiced law briefly in Vienna and then joined the Diplomatic Service. His pre-war assignments were: attaché in Peking 1910–12, in Constantinople 1913, and then secretary of legation in Tehran 1913–14.

Thus Hentig also spoke Persian and had traveled widely in the Asian world. Moreover he had the advantage of growing up in a prominent Prussian family where Chancellor Bernhard von Bülow, Field Marshal von der Goltz, and other luminaries were household names. An excellent horseman and cavalry officer, Hentig spent several weeks every summer in the early years of the century with his parents and siblings at Schloss Friedrichstein, Graf Dönhoff's splendid East Prussian castle. Dönhoff, who also had served on diplomatic assignments in Asia, encouraged the young Hentig to join the Foreign Service. That service now asked the army to grant Hentig leave so he could assume the diplomatic leadership of the Afghan venture.

The German and Indian planners in Berlin needed a prominent Indian figure as titular head of the mission to Kabul. They found this person in Raja (Kumar) Mahendra Pratap, a Rajput feudal lord with a commanding presence. Excited about the war and the prospects for Indian freedom, he left India at the end of 1914 for Europe determined to boster these prospects.

Pratap was a man of good family. He says he was "called Kunwar Sahib of Mursan by some and Raja Sahib of Hathras by others." He was the younger son of Raja Ghanshiam Singh and an adopted son of Raja Harnarain Singh, whose ancestors were independent princes in India until the British conquest of their land in the early nineteenth century. Pratap had donated his ancestral palace, five villages, and half his fortune toward the founding of a technical and literary school for boys and girls. He lived in northern India at Dehra Dun.

Pratap attended Indian National Congress meetings as early as 1906. He and his wife went around the world in 1907, visiting Berlin, Paris, London, New York, Washington, Tokyo, and Shanghai. He received praise from Gandhi, Tagore, and Nehru. On returning from another European tour in 1911, Pratap offered to go to South Africa with Gandhi in 1912, but the latter settled for a financial contribution instead.

In August 1914, Pratap wrote: "I began to feel decisive sympathy for the Germans who were fighting this dirty British Empire."[12] At the end of the year he set sail for Europe to see how he could help. Upon his arrival in Geneva, the charismatic Indian prince was promptly sounded out about an active role with the Germans. As a condition, Pratap insisted on talking things over with the kaiser personally, and a private audience was promptly promised.

Pratap arrived in Berlin on February 10, 1915, and left with the Hentig mission two months later. As the so-called "Prince of India," he was taken up in an airplane to view the Russian front. He sat to the right of Field Marshal Mackensen at a grand banquet. In Berlin, Pratap stayed at the Hotel Continental where one of his fellow guests was the Irish emissary, Sir Roger Casement, who was later hanged by the English.

After several conversations with Foreign Office personnel, the ubiquitous Undersecretary Arthur Zimmermann accompanied Pratap to the Bellevue Palace for his interview with Kaiser Wilhelm. Pratap has left a report of this encounter that begins: "After entering the palace, while lackeys in livery were removing our wraps, I was amused to see my honorable companion (Zimmermann) stop for a minute before a mirror to give his mustachios an extra upper twist" to emulate those of the famous man Pratap was about to meet.

Pratap reports an animated twenty-minute conversation during which the emperor displayed "in perfect English his extraordinary knowledge of Indian affairs." Inquiring particularly about the Punjab states bordering Afghanistan, Wilhelm spoke of Jind, Patiala, and Nabha, and of their strategic position in case of a military move from the Afghan side. "I told him that if Afghanistan should enter the war, this would greatly enhance the chances of an Indian uprising against England. I said that I would gladly go to Afghanistan and do all that I could to help. The Emperor appeared highly satisfied. He conferred upon me the Order of the Red Eagle (second class). When I left he called in a loud, cheery voice, 'When you go to Afghanistan, please give my personal greetings to His Majesty the Emir!' It was a very friendly, informal, and touching call."[13]

The necessary documents were prepared. Special letters from the emperor and the chancellor to the emir were written in German and Afghan. Letters from the Chancellor to twenty-six princes of India were printed in German, Hindi, and Urdu, and bound in handsome red leather covers. Pratap goes on to say: "Dr. von Hentig, who has been summoned from the front to accompany me, will also carry a letter from the Chancellor to the Emir saying 'Dr. von Hentig will introduce the high-born Raja Mahendra Pratap who is working for India's freedom. Any help extended by the Afghan government will be highly appreciated by Germany.'"[14]

Pratap chose a half dozen Afridi and Pathan volunteers from among the Indian POWs at Zossen prisoner-of-war camp to join the group. They were Hindus. But the most important addition to the Indian side was the well-known Muslim mentioned earlier, (Maulvi) Muhammad Barakatullah, the second-ranking member of the Indian Revolutionary Committee in Berlin.

Pratap and Barakatullah had met on several previous occasions. The latter, then age fifty, was the very clever son of a Bhopal State servant. In England, in 1895, he first met Nasrullah Khan of Kabul. He was about to meet him again, in the Afghan mission, together with Nasrullah's brother, the emir.

Barakatullah had spent six eventful years in New York, from 1903 to 1909, promoting anti-British and pro-Indian propaganda. Subsequently, from 1909 to 1914, he taught at the University of Tokyo as professor of Hindustani, taking time out in 1911 to visit Constantinople, Cairo, and St. Petersburg. In Japan he continued his agitation, including publishing pamphlets in Urdu and English for distribution in Asia, until the British intervened with the Japanese to put a stop to his activities. He returned to the United States briefly in May 1914, but within a few months he was helping organize the Indian Independence Committee in Berlin, his trip to Germany being paid for by the German Consulate in San Francisco.

These newspaper statements from Barakatullah in 1912 indicate the direction of his thinking:

> There is really one man who holds the peace of the world in the hollow of his hand, and that man is Emperor William of Germany... In case of a European war, it is the duty of the Muslims to be united, to stand by the Khalif, and to side with Germany... All that is required is a leader, and that leader will arise in Central Asia, probably in Afghanistan. The firing of an Afghan gun will give the signal for the rising of all Islam as soon as she is ready and willing to open her gates for believers to fight under the green banner of the prophet, or under her own.[15]

Before the mission got underway, Hentig added two more Germans. One was a major, Dr. Karl Becker, another crack horseman who spoke

Persian. He was acquainted with the tropical diseases of the area from two years of work at the German hospital in Tehran. The trip eventually led him into Russian captivity. The other was Walter Röhr, a young merchant who had lived in Persia for many years and spoke Turkish and Persian dialects like a native. He was Hentig's future brother-in-law, and at the end of the mission in Kabul, he accompanied Hentig all the way to the east coast of China.

When they left Berlin, the group carried, in addition to a supply of gold, a cumbersome collection of specially selected gifts for the emir and his closest associates. They represented, says Hopkirk, "the best in up-to-date German technology"—elaborate watches, gold fountain pens, gold-topped canes, hand-ornamented rifles and pistols, binoculars, cameras, compasses, a cinema projector, and the very latest German invention—a dozen radio alarm clocks. The amount of one hundred thousand pounds sterling was deposited in Hentig's name with the Deutsche Bank in Constantinople.

Before leaving, the Hentig group attended a ceremony in Berlin celebrating Bismarck's one hundredth birthday on April 1, 1915, where the Afridis were photographed presenting arms to Prince Wilhelm, the eldest son of the crown prince. Pictures of the event later showed up in an English periodical in Afghanistan. On April 10, 1915, this unusual collection of motivated people was ready to move.

Through Turkey and Persia

As early as the spring of 1915, the British viceroy in Delhi, Lord Hardinge, was worried about "alarming reports" from the Northwest Frontier that the German embrace of Islam was attracting widespread credibility among the generally pro-Turkish tribes. He warned London that the presence of German agents with armed parties in Afghanistan would make it doubtful that the emir could maintain his neutrality.

So the itinerary and character of the Hentig mission, as it moved south through Europe to Turkey, was already the subject of keen interest for British intelligence. Assuming this much, Hentig split up his group into smaller parties, starting out on different days, and planning to rendezvous in Constantinople. Hentig and Pratap, with a German orderly and an Indian cook, traveled by way of Vienna. There, at the Hotel Imperial, they spent six hours with ʿAbbas Hilmi, the deposed khedive of Egypt, who had been expelled after a twenty-three-year reign in Cairo. His story reinforced everyone's anti-British enthusiasm.

From Vienna they proceeded by rail via Budapest, Bucharest, Sofia, and Adrianople to Constantinople.[16] Once there, they settled in for three weeks at the Pera Palace Hotel, while Hentig completed travel arrangements. Official Ottoman letters were indited by skilled Persian scribes at the Sublime Porte. They too were addressed to the emir and the princes of India, supplementing the official German letters previously prepared in Berlin.

Hentig and Pratap were received by the war minister, Enver Pasha, whom Hentig recalled meeting when Enver had visited East Prussia before the war. Now they met again on a day when the English were making a furious assault on the Turks in Gallipoli; but "Enver appeared quite unruffled," Hentig recalled. Enver ordered Lieutenant Kasim Bey, a Turkish officer who had previously served in Persia and whom he personally trusted, to join Hentig as the Ottoman representative on the mission.

The war minister also arranged a visit with the sultan for Hentig and Pratap. They were taken by private carriage to the beautiful Dolmabahche Palace on the Bosphorus, through the Garden of Paradise, into the ceremonial reception hall where the chief Court Chamberlain served them with coffee and cigarettes. After elaborate preliminaries, including a "salaam" and "special unction," they were ushered into the presence of the aged sultan. Clad in a black frock coat, with a red fez on his head and a huge diamond on his ring finger, he sat on a divan and invited his guests to sit on richly upholstered chairs opposite him. The chamberlain translated into French the sultan's Turkish words of welcome, and Hentig then retranslated them into English for Pratap. The sultan was cordial, solicitous about the health of his guests, and apprehensive over the dangers of their prospective trip. As a benediction, he invoked Allah's blessing on the whole enterprise.

In early May 1915, Hentig's party of some twenty people, now including two Afghans from the United States who had joined the expedition, left Constantinople and were ferried with their luggage across the Bosphorus to the Asiatic side. They set out for Baghdad on the new but unfinished railway. The group crossed the Taurus Mountains on horseback, a hundred pack animals carrying their accompanying luggage. This was the route previously taken, Hentig noted, by Alexander the

Great, the Apostle Paul, and the German emperor Friedrich Barbarossa. The Euphrates was in flood, and Hentig had to have houseboats put together for the final stages of the journey to Baghdad itself, the key point for all land routes to Central Asia.

Baghdad was assumed to be full of British spies, and Hentig once again dispersed his group for security. He later wrote: "We departed from Baghdad on June 1, 1915. Eight days later we were on Persian soil. At that time the Russians controlled the north, the British the south. We Germans ruled Middle Persia to a certain extent. We had a substantial position and the strong sympathies of that part of the population who were free to declare themselves and become politically active. We even had the confidence of the rapidly growing democratic party, of circles of the nationalistic clergy, and of self-confident tribesmen loyal to the Shah."

Near the Persian frontier at Krynd, they were welcomed by the Ottoman military commander Rauf Bey, who was later briefly prime minister (Rauf Hüseyin Orbay) under Atatürk. "The Turkish officers were splendidly mounted," Pratap wrote, "and their prancing steeds and glittering arms made a brilliant spectacle." On June 14, the Hentig party reached Kermanshah, the capital of western Persia. Many in the group were already sick with malaria and remained there, attended by Dr. Becker. Hentig left for Tehran to organize the mission's next moves with Prince Reuss and Niedermayer.[17]

On July 3, 1915, a few days after the Hentig and Niedermayer groups had separately left Isfahan heading east, the viceroy in Delhi informed London of the steps he had taken to obstruct the Germans in Persia and to prevent their entrance into Afghanistan.[18] Money was no object. The Secret Service was told to be liberal in paying the locals for information on the Germans' movements. Russian troops and local pro-British militia were ordered to capture and annihilate the German expedition. British-Indian cavalry was sent into Persia along the Afghan border to intercept the Germans. British allowances paid to the tribes on the Indian-Afghan border were raised. The subsidies to the Afridis were more than doubled. Strenuous attempts would be made to bribe influential mullahs to oppose the message of the jihad.

Three days later, on July 6, the viceroy warned Afghan Emir Habībullah himself that armed parties of Germans, Austrians, Turks, and Indians were en route to Afghanistan. If by any miracle they should actually cross the Afghan frontier, the viceroy asked the emir to arrest, disarm, and intern them until the end of the war. In reply, the emir reasserted his neutrality and promised to treat the Germans in the way the viceroy requested.

Now began a new German-British version of the Great Game, fought on a secret battlefield of covert operations, intelligence intercepts, false messages, misleading signals, feints and diversions, and a mutual hankering for luck. It is a four-sided story of the competing secret services of king, kaiser, sultan, and czar. All foreign troops, whether Russian, British, or German, were illegally in Persia in the first place, and were therefore somewhat wary of the Persians as well as very wary of one another. Most of their moves were wartime secrets, and secrecy has not always been the friend of accuracy. Accounts written later by the protagonists are often difficult to square with one another in this high-stakes mid-summer struggle in the formidable Persian salt desert.

Amusingly enough, Hentig, at age ninety-five, was in touch with some of the British officers who were assigned to track him down in the Persian sands. He once showed me a letter written on the starched stationery of the London Athenaeum Club from one of his nonagenarian British opponents of yesteryear. It read something like this: "My dear Hentig: Well do I recall that fateful July afternoon in 1915 at Wadi X in that hellish desert, when you and your fellows were vainly looking for a waterhole, and we damn near captured you. Must have been dreadful for you, simply dreadful. I hope you haven't experienced anything like that since. Yours faithfully, Brigadier so-and-so hyphen-so-and-so, OBE VC CMG etc."

Isfahan in the summer of 1915 was the center of German power in Persia. The German consulate there was all-important. The ruling clergy were pro-German. "We felt at home there," said Hentig, "before going into the formidable desert, which normally was considered impassable that time of year." It was in Isfahan where the Niedermayer and Hentig groups reconnoitered at the end of June. It was decided that the groups would proceed separately, travel several days apart, and combine forces again at Tebbes, halfway between Isfahan and the Afghan border. The sick companions, who were earlier left behind in Kermanshah, now rejoined Hentig. Camels and water bags were purchased in Isfahan for the desert.

The Hentig group traveled with twelve packhorses, twenty-four mules, and a camel caravan. Hentig hired Persian messengers to go ahead to pick up advance impressions about village attitudes and enemy whereabouts. The local drivers had to be on constant lookout for robbers along the way. Skeletons from time to time confirmed that they were headed in the right direction. Hentig did not disclose the contents of the loads to others in his party—which boxes, for instance, contained the gold and the gifts. The group traveled mostly at night to avoid the raging daytime heat, which often reached 120 degrees Fahrenheit. The sought-after watering places were usually dried up or enemy-occupied. Water when it was found was usually non-potable. Food was obtained in small places or brought by messengers for men and animals. During the forced marches, the Indian dignitaries often proved to be as much a burden as a blessing. They were hardly a match for the German leaders in vigor, discipline, or stamina.

The ensuing saga was one of wits and endurance, punishing heat, choking dust, poisonous snakes, brigands and ambushes, threatened desertions by Persian guides and opium-addicted camel drivers, betrayal by nomads to enemy spies, and spreading dysentery, delirium, and despondency among many participants who faced possible arrest should they succeed in reaching Afghanistan. Hopkirk, relying heavily on Niedermayer, has provided by far the most readable and dramatic account available in English.

During their daring forty days and forty nights crossing the Persian desert from Isfahan to the Afghan frontier, the Germans made frequent tactical feints to elude Russian and British patrols. These included sending deliberately false dispatches designed to be intercepted by the enemy to mislead them about German whereabouts, composition, numbers, and intended route of the march. This disinformation worked. It threw British and Russian border patrols off the track and extended their deployments, just as the Germans intended.

After twenty days in the desert, Hentig's men dragged themselves into Tebbes on July 23, 1915. Except for Sven Hedin, no known European had ever trod the ground of this city before. There were palm trees, food, and water. The governor and the grandees of the city welcomed the group. Here, according to Pratap, "the Niedermayer rearguard finally caught up. With them was an ex-African explorer, Wilhelm Paschen, and six Austrian and Hungarian soldiers who had escaped from Russian prison camps. They and their firearms were very welcome."

It was now a race for time, as the mission knew it had been spotted. There were British and Russian troops with machine guns ahead of them, and two hundred miles to go to the Afghan border. The German wireless sets had been left behind, and Niedermayer, now in military command, ordered the kaiser's bulkier and heavier gifts for the emir, as well as bales of propaganda, buried in the desert for retrieval later. Urgent messages of alarm flashed from London to Delhi to St. Petersburg.

In London the fabled British intelligence chief, Commander Hall, had not yet deciphered Wassmuss's captured codebook. But it was deciphered by September. This historic British intelligence triumph may have played a direct role thereafter in handicapping the German Afghan mission in Kabul.

Niedermayer now emerged as a brilliant tactician; he dispersed the overall group into three patrols—to divert the Russians in the northeast and the British in the southeast, while searching for a way through the enemy lines. The strategy succeeded in luring enemy patrols hither and yon, the Germans zigzagging from place to place in forced marches, keeping just ahead of enemy informants describing yesterday's whereabouts. Dr. Becker's camel caravan was lost, and he himself experienced escape, betrayal, and then capture and Russian imprisonment on an island in the Caspian Sea.

But Becker's German colleagues gave the British the slip. Described as dried-up skeletons, the group crossed the Afghan frontier on August 19, 1915, seven weeks after setting out from Isfahan. Ahead of them still lay days of dry water holes choked with camel dung before they reached Herat. Pratap says that there were a total of fifty horsemen now in the party.

On Afghan Terrain

Henceforth, Hentig's diplomatic and negotiating responsibilities indisputably came to the fore. Barakatullah, who already enjoyed some fame in the Muslim world, was sent ahead by Hentig to ingratiate himself with the governor general of Herat and to tell him that the group had an urgent personal message from the kaiser for the emir, as well as many gifts. The governor was impressed and quickly sent several noblemen in medieval clothing to greet the visitors, who were invited to consider themselves guests of the Afghan government. The governer provided a great caravan of kitchen utensils and servants, and an armed escort of one hundred mounted men arrived to accompany the mission to Herat.

Hentig had saved the blue cuffs to his white curassier's uniform and wore his spiked helmet. He mounted the horse he had ridden since Baghdad and led the procession into Herat. They were acclaimed by the curious villagers they encountered along the way, including the village women who were allowed to appear on the rooftops to applaud this unusual spectacle.

The group entered Herat on August 24, 1915, and was ceremoniously welcomed by the Turkish colony and troops commanded by a Turkish captain. The visitors found Herat a paradise of orchards and gardens, cool and green. They feasted on oriental delicacies and tasty melons. "A light and festive Viennese spirit pervaded the scene," Hentig wrote, "with exotic flowers and upwardly pointed shoes." The visitors were housed at the emir's provincial palace, a fortified edifice on the eastern edge of the city.

Several days later, the governor general, in full dress, paid them an official visit. Hentig explained that they had come to establish official relations, recognize Afghan sovereignty in foreign affairs, inform the emir about the course of the war, and provide the Indian prince—who in a sense was the equivalent of the emir—with the means to reach the Indian border. British agents reported to Delhi that Hentig also showed the governor the sultan's proclamation of jihad, and promised that if Afghanistan would take part in the war, Germany would send officers to help and, after victory, would arrange for the cession to Afghanistan of India as far as Bombay and of Turkestan as far as Samarkand. Perhaps greatly embellished in Delhi, this report was promptly sent on to London.[19]

Despite the emir's promise to the British, the visitors were given the freedom of the town. It soon became obvious that the governor in Herat treated the foreign emissaries with great consideration. The governor disclosed that the group could expect to leave for Kabul, four hundred miles to the east, in another two weeks' time. Meanwhile, so that they would appear more presentable, Hentig, Niedermayer, and

Röhr received freshly tailored uniforms and their horses were provided with new saddles and the services of blacksmiths, all at the governor's expense. The visitors were carefully watched but royally entertained and allowed to tour Herat's ancient buildings.

On September 7, 1915, the group left Herat for Kabul on another harsh twenty-four-day march via the Hazarajat route through the barren mountain ranges of central Afghanistan. The easier, though longer, route would have been the southern one via Kandahar, avoiding the mountains. But the Afghans obviously wanted to minimize the chances of stirring up any ferment in the Indian frontier region. En route, the Germans paid for their local services again, as in Persia, and became popular as a result.

The First Weeks in Kabul

The mission reached the Afghan capital on October 2, 1915, to a welcoming "salaam" by the Turkish community in red fezzes. An Afghan honor guard in Turkish uniforms performed a military parade. "In the streets and from the roofs, they saluted us with shouts of joy," Hentig wrote. "We could read in their faces the hope that with our coming a new day was dawning for Afghanistan." All the visitors were accommodated as guests of the state in the Bagh-I-Babur, the emir's palace in the suburb of Babershah on the outskirts of Kabul, where they were also supplied with provisions.

Despite their initial welcome, however, it soon became evident that they were, in effect, confined—given the comfortable hospitality of controlled asylum in a stately building, amid gardens and fountains. However, there were armed guards outside the compound protecting them, since, so the Afghans said, they were "in danger from British secret agents" and therefore always had to be escorted by Afghan guides.

It was obvious that the emir was in no hurry to receive his foreign guests. He was away from Kabul, reportedly in Paghman, his summer palace in the mountains. He was biding his time, probably finding out what he could about the members of the mission and keeping in touch with the British. Requests for an audience were met with polite but noncommittal replies for nearly three weeks. It took the threat of a hunger strike by Hentig, Niedermayer, and others to produce action.

Hentig meanwhile was preparing for his first encounter with the emir, and he had a good mental conception of the Afghan ruler. Habībullah was forty-five, short and heavy, with gold-rimmed glasses. He monopolized his primitive kingdom. By virtue of his divine right, he thought he owned the entire country. Every Afghan national theoretically belonged to him. He might claim one for his army or another for his harem where, in fact, he spent much of his time with his many wives and concubines. On his one official trip to India in 1907, he offered his hand in marriage to several English ladies, but this only had the negative effect of adding to the conviction among many Afghans that their ruler was overly friendly with their traditional enemy.

The emir owned the only newspaper in the country. The only drug store belonged to him, and prescriptions were filled only with his personal approval. Only the emir was allowed to photograph, acquire antiques, and collect stamps. Stamps coming into the country on letters from Peshawar, for instance, were removed by the postmaster general and presented to the emir. He did found Habibia College, the country's first public school, although his critics said that it was built merely to house his offspring. The emir owned the only automobiles in the country, naturally Rolls-Royces. When driving in his own car, he sat in the front seat next to the driver; in the back seat was his aide-de-camp with a pistol, or one of his sons with a loaded gun.

The emir's brother, Nasrullah, was prime minister or, as the Germans thought of him, chancellor of the Reich. He was a man of deep religious conviction who wanted to strengthen the religious bonds between the Afghanistan and the rest of the Islamic world. Nasrullah dealt with the borderland tribes, while Habībullah cultivated his relations with Delhi. Nasrullah spoke Pashto fluently, while the emir had only a limited command of it. Nasrullah wore tribal dress, while Habībullah fancied British-type uniforms.

It was clear from the outset that Nasrullah would be more sympathetic to the German mission than his brother, the emir. Of the latter's many sons, the eldest commanded the army, while the strongest personality among the princely brothers was Amanullah, who, like his uncle Nasrullah, already showed pronounced pro-German tendencies.

Finally, on October 26, 1915, more than two months after the mission had entered Afghanistan, three Rolls-Royces came to deliver its ranking members to the emir's retreat in Paghman. To everyone's advantage, the privacy afforded by the mountainous location kept the proceedings somewhat protected from the snooping British agent in Kabul.

Audiences with the Emir

When they were ushered into the emir's presence, the latter began the audience himself with a prolonged address. To the group's discomfort, the ruler said: "I regard you as merchants who will spread out your wares before me. Of these goods I shall choose according to my pleasure and my fancy, taking what I like and rejecting what I do not need." With Röhr translating all this to and from the Persian, the emir then asked Hentig to tell him what he and his company had to offer.

Hentig said the members of the mission did not consider themselves merchants. They had come to recognize the emir's sovereignty and autonomy, establish diplomatic relations, and inform him of the world situation. The Indian colleagues would describe their ideas of liberating India, Kasim Bey would speak for the Ottoman Empire, and Niedermayer would explain how Germany would win the war in the West.

Letters from the kaiser, the German chancellor, and Enver Pasha were presented. When Hentig handed the emir the kaiser's typewritten letter, the emir expressed some doubt about its authenticity. It did indeed contrast with the other letters written in beautiful Persian and handsomely bound in leather. Actually a similarly bound formal letter to the emir, describing the purposes of the mission, had been signed by the kaiser a year earlier, in September 1914, but it went into too much detail and carried the name of Wassmuss as the leader of the expedition. That letter had been withdrawn when the Wassmuss mission fell apart. The Foreign Office had then settled merely on a largely perfunctory letter of personal greetings to the emir from the kaiser, fearing that more might be awkward if it fell into British hands.

Hentig now had to explain to the emir that the kaiser was very busy at his field headquarters where the typewriter was the only instrument available before the group's hurried departure. The emir then asked why the German emperor had chosen such young men for the mission, and Hentig explained that older men would probably not have survived the arduous journey. Apparently without being completely convinced, the emir said he accepted these explanations. Pratap, Niedermayer,

Kazim Bey, and Barakatullah then made individual presentations and the negotiations began, with time out for prayers and lunch.

Pratap and Hentig sat at the richly laden head table on either side of their host and were personally served by the emir with morsels that had been specially prepared and pre-tasted for him. The ruler's drinking water, Hentig noted, was taken from a locked silver samovar and his glass had a special opening. Personal precautions aside, the emir was now all cordiality.

There was another eight-hour meeting between the emir and the mission leaders at Paghman in late October, and subsequent meetings at Kabul. The routine was similar each time. The emir would start with a lengthy discourse, describing his sleep, his digestion, his exercises, and his reading. In return, Hentig would lecture on political science and history. Eventually the now familiar themes would again be pressed upon the emir: breaking with Britain and declaring independence, accepting recognition by the Central Powers and joining them as an ally, allowing influential mullahs to follow the jihad, and permitting the passage of Turkish troops to India. The emir always listened attentively and asked many questions.

Habībullah was nothing if not astute. In due course he replied that Afghanistan would not shirk its duty as a Muslim power. Unfortunately it was squeezed between two giant empires, the Russians and the British. Doubly unfortunately, Germany and Turkey were far, far away. The emir's troops would defend themselves fanatically, but they had no experience fighting modern European armies with their sophisticated weapons. Also, if he were to break with Britain, how would he pay his troops? He would lose his British subsidy and his bank account in Delhi. So if he were to enter the war, as the mission desired, he would first need arms, money, and large numbers of German or Turkish soldiers. There seemed to be some major logistical difficulties.

The mission held out the hope that Persia would be entering the war, and certainly much that had recently happened there under Prince Reuss and Wassmuss was encouraging. Niedermayer stated the case for an eventual German victory, and pointed out how isolated the emir might then be if he were still to cling to his British connection. The Indians held out the prospect of favorable territorial revisions if Afghanistan actively supported the cause of Indian independence. When Kasim Bey explained the Turks' desire to prevent a fratricidal war among Muslims upon the Turkish troops reaching India, the emir replied that this matter needed further study.

These themes were pressed in more meetings held separately, at the emir's request, with the Indians one day and the Germans another. Both groups also regularly met with, and were encouraged by, Prime Minister Nasrullah at his residence. Various members of the mission also met secretly with what Pratap calls the "Amanullah party." Rumors about these peripheral conversations undoubtedly reached the emir, increasing the risks all round.

As Hentig later wrote: "It is worth remembering that in the recent history of Afghanistan, probably the only ruler to have died a natural death had been the Emir's father. All the Emir's thoughts were directed towards preserving his life and power. To enter into dealings with his brother was disapproved of. To speak with his sons, other than in his presence, aroused suspicion." Nevertheless, members of the mission continued to confer with both Nasrullah and Amanullah. Germans, Indians, and Turks alike were encouraged by the obvious friendship and support of both.

The Russians now protested to the British about the emir's permissive attitude toward the mission. The viceroy, equally worried, had earlier suggested that a personal letter from King George V was needed, and one was soon forthcoming. Addressed to the emir and handwritten by the king on Buckingham Palace stationery, it compared favorably with the kaiser's typewritten letter, and praised Habībullah for his unwavering neutrality. The emir's subsidy from Delhi was also increased.

One way or another, British intelligence also obtained several messages addressed to Prince Reuss in Tehran, to whom all of his former friends in the German delegation seemed to be reporting. Sir Percy Sykes says that a letter from Niedermayer to Reuss was intercepted in November 1915. It said: "We were, at last, received by the Emir in a friendly manner on October 26. His explanations did not give us much hope. Please send as soon as possible the Turks for my expedition."[20]

Even Walter Röhr was writing to Reuss that month, and the British intercepted a letter of his that read: "I believe it is quite possible to draw Afghanistan into the war if about one thousand Turks with machine guns and my expedition arrive here." Needless to say, copies of these letters quickly reached the emir through the British agent in Kabul.

But the most dramatic of the covert operations involved a coded report from Hentig on the situation in Kabul, which was entrusted secretly to a Persian courier with orders to ride swiftly to Tehran and deliver it personally to Prince Reuss. Unknown to the Germans, the courier had once worked for the Russians. He headed for Meshed and handed over the Hentig message to Russian officials there. They passed it along to St. Petersburg, where it was deciphered, given to the British Embassy, and sent on to London and Delhi.

Hentig, like Niedermayer and Röhr, asked for the one thousand Turks that might be enough to propel Afghanistan into the war. Then Hentig added two elliptical sentences that positively invited an unhappy upgrading by the British: "Perhaps internal revulsion of feeling is necessary here first. We are determined to go to any lengths." In Delhi the Viceroy pounced on this formulation and quickly made it more menacing. "Necessary internal revulsion" obviously meant that the Germans were planning a coup d'état in Kabul, and "going to any lengths" obviously meant that they were prepared to assassinate the emir.

The viceroy promptly warned Habībullah of the danger to his throne and his life, enclosing the text of Hentig's inflated message with Delhi's own ominous interpretation of its meaning. The viceroy explained: "I am perfectly confident that the success of such a plot is impossible, and that Your Majesty is perfectly secure. At the same time, I think it right that you should know what manner of men are your present guests in Kabul."

Of course, this British ploy was unknown to Hentig at the time. In retrospect, however, it seems that shortly after the viceroy alerted the emir to his prospective assassination, Hentig and the emir were meeting once again for another installment of their talks. "Among the latest German technological marvels which we brought with us to impress the Emir were pocket alarm clocks," Hentig later said. "One day while the Emir and I were negotiating, my alarm clock suddenly rang. He turned deathly pale, his jaw dropped as though paralyzed, and he waited for the bomb to explode. I think he would have signed anything that moment, and in spite of my showing him how the alarm clock worked, it was one of our shorter sessions."[21]

When he recovered from his close call with the alarm clock, the emir resumed his policy of procrastination. Indeed his posture for the remaining months of the German stay is best described in the words of a former British viceroy in India as a policy of "masterly inactivity." The emir was waiting to see who was winning the war, positioning himself for either eventuality. To the Germans he professed sympathy with the Central Powers. He even asserted that he was willing to lead an attack on India, but preferred to wait for the arrival of German or Turkish troops, which, Niedermayer assured him, would soon be on their way. Whenever the Germans hinted that they might leave if nothing further could be accomplished, the emir urged them to stay. Circumstances might change.

The emir balanced the visits of the mission members with secret meetings with the British agent. He assured the viceroy in Delhi that he would remain beneficently neutral in Britain's favor, entreating him not to be misled by rumors or actions that might have to be taken under duress. The emir followed this up with a complaint to the viceroy that his subsidy increase was too small. Indeed it was insulting to Afghanistan, considering the great service he was rendering to Britain with his neutrality policy. Here he was surrounded by strongly pro-German relatives and court officials and Britain was insufficiently sensitive to his position.

Gradually the German mission members were permitted to deal more or less freely with the people of Kabul and they developed a certain degree of popularity. When they were joined by two dozen Austrians, escaped POWs, Hentig had them build a small hospital "embodying the latest German hygienic principles of light, air, and cleanliness." The mission worked on local hearts and minds. Despite the emir's role as newspaper owner, he tolerated its Pan-Islamist, anti-British, pro-German editorial views. Barakatullah was even the acting editor of the paper for a time. Kazim Bey made friendly inroads into the Turkish community, although he pursued Enver's concept of combining jihad with a Panturanian emphasis looking to the union of the Turkish tribes of Central Asia. Niedermayer presented proposals for reforming the army, which needed small mobile units equipped with a variety of arms. The Germans were good customers in Kabul stores, buying only native goods, and paying cash for them.

The Provisional Government of India and the Draft German Treaty

Suddenly there were significant moves. On December 1, 1915, the Indian leaders of the mission took a dramatic step of their own. They proclaimed a provisional government of India in Mahendra Pratap's rooms at the Bagh-I-Baber Palace, in the presence of their German, Indian, and Turkish mission members and friends. The Provisional Government held itself out as an interim revolutionary regime in exile, prepared to rule an independent India once the British were expelled.

Raja Pratap was declared President of the Provisional Government until the Indian National Congress in India could chose his successor. Barakatullah was named prime minister. A Sikh-turned-Muslim who had made his way to Kabul from India, Maulvi Obeidullah, was proclaimed Minister for Home and Foreign Affairs. Among several Indian exiled "secretaries" to this triumvirate, there were at least two who later held noteworthy posts. Muhammad ʿAlī subsequently obtained an important position at the Third International in Moscow, and Allah Nawaz became Afghanistan's minister in Berlin.

Pratap and his associates hoped that the proclamation of their government-in-exile would finally cause the equivocal emir to summon his people to the jihad, and if not, that he would be swept aside by the passions thus unleashed around him, in his court, and among his people. Indeed for the next two months expectations grew that a declaration of jihad was about to happen. The Indians maintained throughout a friendly relationship with the emir, who pleased them rhetorically even as his actions fell short of what they desired. Everywhere among Afghans, the Germans' public message was freedom, national unity, economic welfare, cultural autonomy, and self-development for Afghanistan. The German posture was one of disinterested help from the benevolent Central Powers who would soon be victorious in the West.

Privately, the Germans and Austrians also had an encouraging month of December 1915, celebrating Christmas in their own fashion in Kabul. It too was enlivened by the emir's personal attention. He took Hentig to his guarded storage room and, for European holiday consumption, presented him with some red wine and cognac left over from the famous Durand mission of forty years earlier.

That same month the emir suddenly told Hentig that he was ready to discuss a German-Afghan treaty of friendship. Hentig believed that this favorable turn had occurred because the emir's brother Nasrullah, the emir's favorite son Amanullah, and the latter's father-in-law, Tarzi, the powerful newspaper editor, had all come down strongly on the German side. The emir cautioned, however, that the treaty would take time, considering all the historical research that had to be done! In spite of what Hentig called "every conceivable objection, each more impossible than the last," work on the treaty now began, with Hentig doing the drafting.

On January 24, 1916, the draft treaty was initialed. It had ten articles. Afghan independence was recognized and friendship with Germany declared. Diplomatic relations were established with Hentig recognized by name as "the Embassy Secretary of the German Empire" in Kabul. Political relations were contemplated "with the peoples" of Persia, India, and Russian Turkestan. To modernize the Afghan military, Germany would provide a hundred thousand contemporary rifles, three hundred artillery pieces, and other equipment. The emir would be paid 10 million pounds sterling. Germany would maintain a regular supply route across Persia for arms and ammunition, and for military advisors and engineers. In case Afghanistan joined the war, Germany would provide all possible help against the Russians and British.

Hentig and Niedermayer both signed the draft treaty in spite of its highly dubious provisions, and in a telegram to the Foreign Office Hentig argued that the draft at least afforded a basis for immediately getting to work. Niedermayer added his estimate of the urgent military requirements—a wireless station, substantial arms shipments, and at least one million pounds in initial funding. He added that the emir had stated that war would begin as soon as twenty thousand German or Turkish soldiers arrived in Afghanistan, and they in turn would have the task of covering the Afghan rear against Russia. Niedermayer informed the General Staff that conditions for an offensive were very favorable, and that the best time for war was the end of April.[22]

Habībullah's judicious maneuvering continued all spring. He kept everyone guessing. He did not intend to find himself on the losing side. Delhi heard rumors of a mysterious letter, allegedly signed by the emir, exhorting frontier chiefs to prepare for a Holy War, the signal for which would be given shortly. In response the alarmed viceroy called a grand jirga of three thousand tribal leaders at Peshawar. They were treated to impressive airplane demonstrations and were told that their subsidies would be increased.

But the British need not have worried. On January 25, 1916, the day after the German draft treaty was signed, the emir summoned the British agent and reiterated his determination to remain neutral. He belatedly replied to King George reaffirming his loyalty. He also knew that the German-Indian-Turkish mission had aroused popular excitement that needed to be deflected. At a durbar four days later, large crowds outside the palace awaited a jihad proclamation. Instead, the emir publicly reaffirmed his neutrality. It was impossible to forecast the war's outcome, he stated, and he asked for unity. Afghans from Kabul to the Indian frontier were generally disappointed, and there were more rumblings about the emir's subservience to the British. His closest relatives regarded his inactivity with open suspicion.

Continually finding new grounds for delay, the emir gradually upped the ante and increased his demands for joining the war. He declared that he would act only if all of India would rise against Britain. He pointed out that before the treaty with Germany could take effect, it had to be signed by both him and the kaiser. This would obviously take quite a lot more time. Meanwhile the treaty was obviously a good insurance policy for the emir, for if its extravagant terms were ever to be met, it would mean that Germany was winning the war.

Worried that British warnings about a coup or assassination might prove correct, the emir gradually began to purge his court of officials known to be close to his brother Nasrullah or his son Amanullah. Without explanation he suddenly recalled emissaries he had sent to Persia to have further discussions with Turks and Germans there about military aid.

Developments in Mesopotamia and Persia itself soon hurt the German cause. The Arab revolt against the Ottoman Empire was a big psychological blow. So was the fall of Erzerum in Eastern Turkey to the Russians. That ended the possibility of a Turkish division reaching Afghanistan. Field Marshal von der Goltz abandoned his plan to lead German-officered Persian volunteers against India, and the German role in Persia itself rapidly declined.

British intelligence seized the opportunity and soon sent Hentig a coded message ostensibly from German sources, transmitted via Herat from a station on the Persian border. "After the capture of Erzerum," it read, "situation has deteriorated. Suggest you discontinue your efforts with the Amir, particularly since other assignments await you." The English spelling of Amir, instead of the German Emir, made it clear, said Hentig, where the message originated.

But the Germans no longer needed British assistance in reaching the same conclusion. "As the weeks passed," Hentig later wrote, "we Germans became reconciled to the Emir's almost insurmountable distrust." The protracted consultations had become tiresome. Hentig and Niedermayer also realized that they themselves might constitute handsome presents from the emir to the viceroy, if it should ever come to that.

"Shortly before the Germans left Kabul toward the end of May 1916," Adamec writes, "Nasrullah made a final attempt to keep them in Afghanistan by offering to act against Habībullah and take over the leadership of the frontier tribes in a war against Britain, but it was too late. The Germans wanted to leave and turn to more fruitful activities."[23]

Their personal roles in the German Great Game in Afghanistan were now concluded, and Hentig and Niedermayer embarked separately on their respective Great Escapes, each of them surviving unbelievable dangers and winning the admiration of friends and enemies alike.

Then and Now: What If?

The German mission of 1915–16, like the American one today, met with daily frustrations of delicate balances and moving targets. Then as now, there were precarious arrangements, implausible alliances, and marriages of convenience. Germans then, like Americans now, faced the challenge of making their national interest interesting to others. There were public debates in the open, and private disputes in the shadows, among elusive adversaries with differing agendas, many of them hidden or half-disclosed.

Visitors were introduced to tentativeness—to the mirages of desert politics and the shell games of uncertain commitments—to personal reinventions and fluctuating loyalties—not to mention the Afghan habit of succumbing to the highest bidder, the culture of changing sides.

In a real sense, the German mission was three years premature. By 1919 the main themes of the mission, if not the main impulses driving it, were bearing fruit in Afghanistan. The seeds of sovereignty and reform, planted by the mission, began to flourish three years later under the auspices of the young King Amanullah, one of the German mission's chief friends, who took power after his father's assassination.

Emir Habībullah had naturally assumed that the victors in Delhi and London would show their gratitude for his virtuoso performance in the service of Britain. In early February 1919 he reminded the viceroy of his services, and formally demanded complete sovereignty and freedom to deal with foreign powers. Ironically, these had been two of the chief recommendations of the German mission three years earlier. But the British were in no mood to listen. They discussed sending another letter from King George as a sufficient reward for the emir's four years of neutrality, while curtly informing him that they would continue to look after Afghanistan's external affairs.

Two weeks later Habībullah was murdered. To this day, no one knows who the perpetrator was. Everyone was blamed—the British, disgruntled Turks, Nasrullah, even some anti-Freemasons. Fortunately there were no official Germans left in Kabul to share in the finger-pointing. The third Afghan War promptly ensued, and after some skirmishes the British finally capitulated, recognizing Afghan independence, which the Germans had so persistently pursued. Defeated Germany was in fact the first to recognize the new sovereign government of Amanullah, who took the title of king.

Writing in 1917, only a year after leaving Afghanistan, Hentig drew attention to the mission's modernizing objectives: "Windows and doors were opened in the closed land, filling them with a new atmosphere of progress and liberty and making this country, perhaps not immediately, but eventually, a center of Asian politics... To strengthen the emerging forces of his own society, to develop and secure its independence on all sides, this is the historical task of Emir Habībullah. If he becomes fully conscious of it, his word will have weight in the future of Asia."[24]

In fact most of the nation-building reforms that the German mission had advocated were seriously undertaken during the next decade under Amanullah, many of them under German auspices. There were constitutional reforms in the direction of a ministerial cabinet. Medical services and hospitals appeared. The first steps were taken toward the emancipation of women and, beginning with the royal family, women began to take off their veils. Teachers from abroad were brought in to organize a serious educational system, open also to women.

Industrialization was promoted with the assistance of foreign experts and companies. German companies like Telefunken and Siemens were taking the lead. Lufthansa started the first airline service from Europe. Cultural development had a distinctly greater secular emphasis. Among the new ventures was the German School in Kabul. At one point it boasted a fellowship named for von Hentig that was devoted to postgraduate study in Germany. By 1929 the Germans were the largest European group in the country, outnumbering the British ten to one.

If the unknown assailant who killed Habībullah in February 1919 had committed his deed three years earlier, while the German mission was in Kabul, developments would have been dramatically different. Either Nasrullah or Amanullah would have succeeded him, and both were staunch champions of the German mission. An Afghan war for independence, successful as it was in 1919, might have had even better prospects three years earlier when British and Indian troops were away in Europe.

Meanwhile, developments elsewhere in Asia kept alive the hopes of that residual part of the German mission remaining behind in Kabul, the Indian Provisional Government. Soon Lenin, Atatürk, Gandhi, and Amanullah had joined Sun Yat Sen on the Asian political scene. Indeed, in 1918, the first year of the new Russia and the last year of the old Germany, Mahendra Pratap personally visited both Leo Trotsky in Petrograd and the kaiser in Berlin, urging them to move jointly against India. But it was too early for Bolshevist Russia and too late for Imperial Germany.

Timing, of course, is everything in politics. In world politics as well governments play the cards they are dealt. In that sense the German mission was a gamble that failed. But it was not a preposterous proposition. It was a close-run operation. It was a serious project in pursuit of serious goals undertaken by serious men. The overall external circumstances were favorable when the mission began. They deteriorated gradually, and the mission was ultimately at the mercy of unfavorable developments far away. As usual, power has its own rewards, and the perception of power was decisive with the one man who counted in Kabul, the emir.

Conclusion

The Afghan venture is a story that can be read on several levels. Adamec's conclusion is a sensible one: "The German expedition was successful insofar as it accomplished some of its objectives. It disturbed Russia and Britain greatly with its activities, and it carried hostile propaganda into an area hitherto the exclusive concern of those two European powers. The expedition came with no more than a message and it nearly succeeded in involving Afghanistan in the war."[25]

Adamec probably did not mean to imply that there was only one message. There were multiple messengers and multiple messages. There was a jihad message from the caliph and Kazim Bey. There was a free India message from Pratap and Barakatullah. There was a German victory message and a professionalization message from Niedermayer for the Afghan military. There was a message of Afghan sovereignty, domestic reform, and nation-building from Hentig. And there was an anti-British message from everybody.

In many ways, the Germans were on the side of the future—on the side of anti-colonialism and self-determination, not only for Afghanistan, but for Persia, India, and even Russian Turkestan. The Germans brought Muslims and Hindus together in their mission, and were in turn the beneficiaries of Muslim-Hindu collaboration, that historically rare phenomenon.

Finally, of course, the mission provided a breathtaking opportunity for heroism and adventure to be staged against a most dramatic background. No matter how gripping or eventful their subsequent careers were to be, Hentig and Niedermayer, for the rest of their lives, were living legends, the German counterparts of Lawrence of Arabia. Niedermayer made a daring escape westward through Turkestan and Persia, wounded, using disguises, at times reduced to begging before he reached friendly lines.

Hentig made a spectacular escape eastward around the world, on foot or horseback, through storms and ice, over the Hindu Kush and the Pamir plateau, avoiding would-be captors for 130 days through Chinese Turkestan and the hot sands of the Gobi desert, across the whole of China to Shanghai, eventually stowing away on an American ship to Honolulu where, after the American entry into the war, he was exchanged as a diplomat and sent via San Francisco, Halifax, and Bergen back to Berlin.

With Hentig's recommendation, Niedermayer was knighted for his services and given the Max Joseph Order, Bavaria's highest. Both Germans went on to colorful and extraordinary careers. So did their Indian partner Raja Pratap, who, after travelling on an Afghan passport for decades, returned to India after independence and was elected to Parliament.

When Hentig returned home, the kaiser personally awarded him with the Hohenzollern House Order. Years later, when he was consul-general in Amsterdam, Hentig occasionally visited his most eminent German constituent, now an exile at Doorn. Once when they were reviewing the Afghan mission, the ex-kaiser opined that if Hentig had only done a quarter of what he did, he really deserved the medal Pour le Mérite. Hentig used this opportunity to explain that the Foreign Office had indeed considered proposing him for that honor. Unfortunately the rules provided that the Mérite could be awarded only if the superior who ordered the mission possessed the order himself, and Chancellor Bethmann-Hollweg did not qualify. "Oh," the fallen monarch cheerfully replied, "one more problem with Bethmann."[26]

Medals aside, Hentig's happiest moment was his triumphal return to Kabul in 1969 on the fiftieth anniversary of Afghan independence. He was the honored guest of King Muhammad Zahir Shah and was given a red-carpet reception by those who remembered him from 1915–16 and by many others who had heard of his legendary exploits. The celebrations were a high point for Afghanistan as well. Alas, no one then guessed that the country was about to descend into three decades of disaster from which it is only now recovering.

Notes

1. Sir Percy Sykes, *A History of Afghanistan*, vol. 2 (London, 1940), 248.
2. Conversation with Prince Louis Ferdinand of Prussia, the kaiser's grandson, Berlin, September 1981.
3. Fritz Fischer, *Germany's Aims in the First World War* (New York, 1967), 126. See also Konrad H Jarausch, *The Enigmatic Chancellor: Bethmann-Hollweg and the Hubris of Imperial Germany* (New Haven, Conn., 1973), 196.

4. Sykes, op. cit., 247–48.
5. Vartan Gregorian, *The Emergence of Modern Afghanistan* (Stanford, Calif., 1969), 217, 220.
6. Ulrich Trumpener, *Germany and the Ottoman Empire 1914–1918* (Princeton, N. J., 1968), 241–42.
7. Friedrich von Bernhardi, *Germany and the Next War*, trans. Allen H. Powles (New York, 1911).
8. V. G. Kiernan, "Tennyson, King Arthur & Imperialism" in his *Poets, Politics, and the People*, ed. Harvey J. Kaye (London, 1989), 105.
9. Emily C. Brown, *Har Dayal: Indian Revolutionary and Rationalist* (Tucson, Ariz., 1975), 189.
10. John Buchan, *Greenmantle* (London, 1916), 19–20.
11. See Peter Hopkirk, *Like Hidden Fire* (New York, 1994, Foreign Office telegram reprint); see also David Fromkin, *The Peace to End All Peace* (New York, 1989).
12. Mahendra Pratap, *My Life Story of Fifty Years* (Dehradun, India, 1947).
13. Mahendra Pratap, "My German Mission to High Asia," *Asia Magazine* (May 1925).
14. Ibid.
15. James Campbell Ker, *Political Trouble in India 1907–1917* (1917; reprint Delhi, 1973).
16. For the entire Hentig journey from Berlin to Kabul and back, see especially: Werner-Otto von Hentig, *Ins Verschlossene Land* (Berlin, 1918 and Potsdam, 1928); as well as his memoirs: *Mein Leben — Eine Dienstreise* (Göttingen, 1962). See also Marion Gräfin Dönhoff, *Menschen, die wissen, worum es geht* (Hamburg, 1976), the chapter on Hentig, 223–34.
17. For accounts of the mission as told by Niedermayer, see: Oskar von Niedermayer, *Afghanistan* (Leipzig, 1924), and *Unter der Glutsonne Irans* (Hamburg, 1925). See also Renate Vogel, *Die Persien-und Afghanistanexpeditionen von Oskar Ritter v. Niedermayer 1915/16* (Osnabrück, 1976). For Hentig's rejoinder and his side of the controversy with Niedermayer, see Hentig's unpublished paper "Der Hadschi Mirsa Hussein im Weltkrieg vor den Toren Indiens" (1976), 1–32, at the Bibliotheca Afghanica. See also the Niedermayer biography by Hans-Ulrich Seidt, *Berlin, Kabul, Moskau: Oskar Ritter von Niedermayer und Deutschlands Geopolitik* (München, 2002).
18. Ludwig W. Adamec, *Afghanistan 1900–1923: A Diplomatic History* (Berkeley, Calif., 1967), 86–87.
19. Ker, 301.
20. Sykes, 248–58.
21. Conversation with Hentig, 1982.
22. Adamec, 94, 182.
23. Ibid.
24. Hentig, conclusion, *Ins Verschlossene Land*.
25. Adamec, 96.
26. Conversation with Hentig, 1982.

Figure 3. Generalmajor Professor Dr.phil. Oskar Ritter von Niedermayer (1885–1948), sometimes called "the German Lawrence," was the military leader of Germany's mission to Afghanistan in 1915/1916; from 1924 to 1931, deputy director and director of the Reichswehr's secret liaison office in the Soviet Union, the "Zentrale Moskau"; professor at the Friedrich-Wilhelms-Universität in Berlin starting in 1936, he became commander of the 162nd (Turk) infantry division of the Wehrmacht in 1942. He died in a Soviet prison in 1948 and was officially rehabilitated by the Russian Federation in 1997.
(Bequest Dr. Friedrich Niedermayer. Archive of the author.)

"When Continents Awake, Island Empires Fall!"

Germany and the Destabilization of the East 1919–1922

HANS-ULRICH SEIDT

In 1919 German military leaders put out secret feelers to Moscow and Kabul through the intermediary of Turkish exiles. Cooperation with Soviet Russia, based strictly on geopolitical and strategic interests, was to shake the British Empire's foundations and bring about a revision of the Treaty of Versailles. The underpinning of these clandestine networks derived from contacts and concepts established during the First World War, particularly the idea of the Islamic "Holy War" — "jihad" — against the West. Viewed within the context of current events, this asymmetrical strategy gains, in spite of its failure, paradigmatic significance.

Reflections at Sea

In early November 1918, several German transport ships set sail from Constantinople across the Black Sea. They carried the remnant of the German Asia units, who fought for four years on the side of the Turks, to ports on the northern coast of the Black Sea. Among the officers leaving the city at the Golden Horn in defeat was Hans von Seeckt, the last chief of the general staff of the Ottoman army.

The sea voyage afforded Seeckt ample time to reflect on the situation. In a memorandum, "Causes of the Collapse of Turkey in Autumn 1918," he noted time and place: "Written on the Black Sea, November 4, 1918." His pragmatic, at times bitter, analysis concluded with a summary evaluation of the operations in the Near East during the end phase of the world war.[1]

In 1918, the Central Powers had effected a strategic shift in their Near East policy. Instead of defending untenable positions in Palestine, the Ottoman army launched an offensive in the Caucasus. These offensive operations in the last months of the war, "the last sign of Turkish war energy," were prompted by broad-based, strategic considerations on the part of the Germans.

By early 1918, Hans von Seeckt had already reached the conclusion that the Ottoman government would sustain, though "unprofessed and unspoken," the loss of its Arab provinces. At the same time, the Ottoman Empire gained a last victory over Russia through the Peace of Brest-Litovsk. The Russian collapse opened tempting perspectives for the leaders in Constantinople. Once again they were able to pursue ambitious aims and follow their illusory visions of extending their dominion over vast areas in the Caucasus and Central Asia.

Seeckt furthered the Turkish ally's grandiose plans since they could be embedded within a long-term, global anti-British concept. As late as November 1918, he held to the view that the German Empire should have supported the Turkish plans more energetically. On November 4, 1918, he noted with regret: "It would have been in the interest of Germany's overall war strategy to give its benevolent support to these fantastic schemes as long as they could be channeled toward an attack against England's weak spot in Iran."

Seeckt remembered with gratitude the Ottoman war minister, Enver Pasha, husband of Sultan Mehmed V's niece, who had been Germany's most reliable partner in Constantinople until the bitter end. "Enver's grasp of the broader questions of war opened him to a consequent pursuit of a train of thought." But history passed over these fantastic ideas and Seeckt noted pragmatically on November 4, 1918: "The shifting fortunes of the world war completely destroyed all these plans and prospects." Nevertheless, a few months later in Berlin, he embarked on the next round of the high-stakes game over the future of Asia and the world.

The Prussian Macedonian

Seeckt, the architect of the Reichswehr and until 1926 its highest-ranking officer, represented the kind of impetuous mixture of spirit and strength, held in bounds through discipline and a classical education, that had been characteristic of the Prussian general staff since the time of Gerhard J. D. Scharnhorst.[2]

As a member of the Alexander Regiment, a unit rich in tradition and named after Tsar Alexander I, Seeckt cultivated a close connection between militarism and tradition. In 1929, during a lecture in Berlin on "Military Leadership in Antiquity," he confessed his dedication to the classical tradition even in bleak times: "The soldier, more than anybody, needs to be educated in spirit and in a broad perspective." Seeckt asserted, "He needs to be inspired by classical models and trained to submit to his fate."[3]

Alexander the Great personified, to Seeckt's mind, ancient military leadership to ideal perfection. "The depth and breadth of the will, that mysterious force, which lifts its gaze beyond the limits drawn over ordinary human beings." He saw the great Macedonian as royal military commander, statesman, and superlative strategist. Alexander invaded the East to lay the foundation of a world empire "along military routes still in use today, marching through deserts and scaling the highest mountains on the way to Kabul and Herat."

Seeckt described in 1929 Alexander's invasion of India in almost the same words he had used in 1918 to express his hope for a successful German advance into India: "Call it fantasy, call it the gift of the seer, when the royal military commander's gaze transcends space and time and he views the land of the future, when he sees, beyond the blue waves of the Mediterranean, beyond the snow-capped mountains, the battlefields before him and his victories, when he sees his enemies and their cities and treasures, and then embarks trusting, either failing or smiling, in his gods."[4]

Seeckt too once stood at India's borders. During his travels to the subcontinent from November 1907 to May 1908, he traced the footsteps of the great Macedonian. On January 7, 1908, he noted in his diary:

"Then a most interesting excursion toward the mountains, across the Indus river, India's ancient border, which Alexander the Great and so many after him have crossed."[5] The border region of India and Afghanistan stirred Seeckt's imagination: "The caravan traffic was fabulous, when I say five hundred camels, it's no exaggeration." The magic of the East cast its spell on him. "Then processions of women under long, blue veils, faces never seen," Seeckt noted in his diary.

Seeckt's "New Reich"

"One might adopt the view of 1866 and leave many border posts intact and yet lay the foundation of a new Reich," Seeckt wrote in 1915 to the respected, influential Prussian aristocrat von Winterfeld-Menkin.[6] The "new Reich" was to be based on trade agreements and customs unions extending over a widespread European area with Berlin as its political center. This was, in his eyes, a *conditio sine qua non* if Germany was to emerge victorious from an inevitable, second global confrontation, the next war, which would decide the new order of the world.

As early as 1915, Seeckt recommended maintaining pressure against British and American overseas possessions after the war and a conclusion of peace. The future empire under German leadership, therefore, had to extend beyond Europe: "The road to Asia must be free. The circle is closing, we must gain dominance over an area from the Atlantic Ocean to Iran, but please, not a "German Reich" within these borders, rather a federation of nations who share our interests and are comfortable within this union."

Toward this goal, Seeckt was already seeking during World War I, a rapprochement with Russia, whose expansionist aims he sought to channel toward the South and East: "The staggering colossus will eventually roll over on its side and England will get to feel its weight in Central and East Asia." Seeckt disapproved of fragmenting Russia as was done at Brest-Litovsk. To his mind, the downfall and dissolution of the Russian Empire favored the global, geostrategic interests of Great Britain and the United States more than Germany's global position.

In the first months of the year 1919, Seeckt viewed the revolutionary excesses in Russia with considerable consternation. However, once Bolshevik power in Moscow was consolidated, he returned to his erstwhile strategic scheme and sought a rapprochement with Lenin's

Russia. In Europe, he envisioned a new partition of Poland, and in Asia, covert German-Russian cooperation against British positions. On February 4, 1920, Seeckt wrote: "Only through a firm confederation with greater Russia will Germany have any chance of regaining its position as a world power."[7] A few days later, on February 20, 1920, the usually cautious and reserved Seeckt presented his ideas at a public lecture in Hamburg: "May the devil get Poland; we should lend him a hand. Our future lies in a union with Russia whether we like its new political order or not."[8] The cooperation with Bolshevik Russia had already been underway since 1919 through secret channels and strange contacts.

Revolutionaries and Exiles

In January 1919, the leaders of the communist Spartacus uprising, Rosa Luxemburg and Karl Liebknecht, were murdered in Berlin by a group of Reichswehr officers. On February 12, 1919, the emissary of the Kremlin, Karl Radek, also fell into the hands of German counterrevolutionaries. But the dangerous revolutionary was spared, for this troubleshooter with Moscow connections was deemed useful to German political aims. Radek was treated as a respected interlocutor. Military leaders, members of the police force, captains of industry, and politicians visited Karl Radek (also known as Karl Skobelsohn), the son of a Jewish petty postal servant from Galicia, in his prison cell in Moabit. Born in 1885 in Lemberg, the Polish city that was then part of the Austro-Hungarian Empire, this brilliant conversationalist had an affinity for the German language and culture.

Figure 4. *Intellectual and Revolutionary:* Karl Radek alias Karl Sobelsohn (1885–1939) was instrumental in establishing Moscow's secret contacts with the Reichswehr and the exiled leaders of the Young Turks. Radek, shown here in a caricature by a friend in 1923, perished in Stalin's GULAG.

Among his first visitors were two of Seeckt's old acquaintances: Enver Pasha and Talaat Pasha, the leaders of the Young Turk movement which had governed the Ottoman Empire since 1908 in the style of a military junta. In November 1918, they fled on a German transport ship to Nikolajev and Odessa, from where they eventually reached Germany.[9]

Radek had previously met Talaat Pasha at Brest-Litovsk, where the Turk sat with German and Austrian officers and diplomats at the victors' table. Now, the once-proud Pasha was a homeless fugitive. He reminded Radek that he, too, was a revolutionary and the son of a petty postal servant. He offered Radek a strategic partnership: The Islamic masses of Asia would be liberated from enslavement to the capitalist Entente by the leadership of the Turkish exiles in alliance with the Bolsheviks.

Talaat Pasha's allusion to their common Western enemies was also an implied justification for the genocide of the Armenians. Did not the Western powers, in collaboration with the Tsarist regime, instigate an Armenian revolt in the rear of the Turkish front? Was it not necessary for the Turkish government to take the most stringent measures? Radek invited the Turks to come to Moscow. Talaat Pasha, however, was unable to follow his invitation. On March 15, 1921, he was gunned down in broad daylight on a street in Charlottenburg. His assassin was an Armenian.

Common Goals and Interests

Radek's invitation to the Turks fit in with Moscow's overall strategic concept that could also be brought into harmony with Seeckt's goals. The Bolsheviks too wanted to revolutionize the Islamic East and eliminate the hegemony of the capitalist West.

German and Bolshevist common interests were evident during the war when the German-financed European Central Committee of Indian Nationalists met in Stockholm on September 4, 1917. The Indian nationalists addressed the "Executive Committee of the All Russian Islamic Union" in Petrograd with approving words: "We Indians welcome the courageous intercession of Russian Muslims on behalf of the oppressed peoples in Asia and Africa. By demanding a determined, firm policy on the part of the provisionary government of free Russia, one that aims at the recognition of the right of self-determination for the peoples of Europe as well as for the peoples of Asia and Africa, they did a great service to the cause of humanity."[10]

Already in early 1918, the lines between Kabul, Moscow, and Berlin were used for revolutionary activities. In March 1918, the Indian revolutionary Kumar Mahendra Pratap, who had been escorted in 1915 to Kabul by the German Afghanistan Expedition, arrived in Berlin. When Emperor Wilhelm II received him on May 6, 1918, the Indian revolutionary suggested the formation of a multi-ethnic, "socialist" army composed of Germans, Austrians, Bulgarians, Indians, and Russians for the liberation of India. When nothing came of this fantastic plan, the Indian went back to Moscow in 1919 to seek support from the Bolsheviks.

Beyond All Fronts

Strange things were happening during the year of chaos 1919. Fritz Tschunke, a German officer, who was to become in the 1930s the director of the influential Ostausschuss der deutschen Wirtschaft, the Eastern Committee of German Industry, recalled, in a letter to Seeckt's biographer in 1940, a strange incident. He was deployed in 1919 as German liaison officer in the Lithuanian city of Kovno. The Bolsheviks stood at the gates, when suddenly two men in civilian clothing in the company of an armed escort appeared in his office. Tschunke, who had served during the world war under Seeckt in Turkey, immediately recognized Enver Pasha, and within a few minutes, he became aware of the situation. Enver's plane had to make an emergency landing on its way from Berlin to Moscow and the Turk was taken into Lithuanian custody.[11]

On board of the plane were maps and documents from the German General Staff. With the help of a German pilot working for the Lithuanians, Tschunke managed to salvage the papers. A few days later, he freed Enver Pasha from Lithuanian detention by way of an adventurous scheme and brought him back to safety on German territory. Tschunke claimed later that Seeckt thanked him personally for obtaining Enver Pasha's release. Nevertheless, the first attempt to get the Turk to Moscow ended in failure.

The next attempt finally succeeded. In the summer of 1920, Ernst Köstring, who had also served with Seeckt in Turkey and later became

German military attaché in Moscow, received the order to take Enver Pasha to the Red Army by way of East Prussia. The right wing of the army troop Tuchatchevski was approaching what was then German territory on its advance on Warsaw.

Köstring and Enver Pasha sailed from Stettin on the Baltic Sea to Königsberg.[12] In East Prussia, Köstring saw himself faced with having to keep a close eye on his protégé, who mindlessly sent open telegrams to his companions in Berlin, asking them to follow him. Shortly before they reached the border, Enver Pasha even sent a registered letter to his wife in Berlin and placed it in an envelope imprinted with the sultan's crown. Köstring was greatly relieved when he escorted Enver Pasha the following night over the green line and handed him over to the waiting advance guard of the Red Army.

Moscow Letters, Berlin Memoranda

On August 25, 1920, Enver Pasha wrote his first letter to Seeckt from Moscow. His knowledge of the German language was good enough for him to formulate sensible political ideas and strategic suggestions without the help of a translator. Enver described the situation within the Moscow political hierarchy. According to his information, the Bolshevik leadership was split into two factions: one wanted to focus on setting up communist revolutionary regimes in Europe, and one advocated an attack on British positions in the East. The option to strike a blow against world capitalism in India, its perceived weakest spot, coincided with Seeckt's own geopolitical thinking. Enver Pasha promised to concentrate his efforts in Moscow primarily on Afghanistan. To this end, he requested several books, particularly Lord Robert's study of 1883 "Is an Invasion of India Possible?" which Seeckt had shown to him before his departure from Berlin. Enver Pasha also asked for certain British operational plans concerning the Indian-Afghan border that were extant in Berlin. The material was to be sent to Moscow together with a radio transmitter and other technical equipment.

Enver Pasha did not place his hopes in Afghanistan without good reason. On February 20, 1919, the Afghan Emir Habibullah was murdered and his third son, Amanullah, seized power in Kabul. He belonged to the Afghan "war party," the same which had assured the

German Afghanistan mission back in 1915/16 of its readiness to launch an assault on India.[13]

In early May 1919, Afghan troops started to engage in war activities. However, the Third British-Afghan War lasted only a few weeks. Whereas the actual fighting ceased at the end of May 1919, the signing of a peace treaty had to wait until December 8, 1921. While this "open" situation lasted, it seemed natural for Enver Pasha in Moscow to put the situation in Afghanistan under close scrutiny. A series of first discussions with the Bolsheviks filled him with heightened expectations even though Moscow's military capability was then limited to defensive operations along the borders of Turkey, Iran, and Afghanistan. Nevertheless, in the spring of 1921, an offensive against the Western Powers seemed quite feasible.

Enver Pasha, the former Ottoman war minister, therefore asked Seeckt, his former chief of staff, for recommendations on how to proceed. He wrote in German: "Since all preparations are now complete, it is possible to launch an offensive in the spring on all fronts. I would like to know your view on this point."

It was clear to Enver Pasha that the defeat of the Red Army near Warsaw had made a reversal of the outcome of the First World War more difficult. And yet, in August 1920, the Red Army still stood at least a theoretical chance of halting the Polish counteroffensive. In a second letter to Seeckt, dated August 28, 1920, Enver Pasha summarized his assessment of the situation. He had been encouraged by a conversation with Trotsky's deputy Skljansky. In order to relieve the pressure on the Bolsheviks, he recommended that Germany start an operation against Poland. He signed the letter with his covert name "Ali."[14]

A few hours later, Enver Pasha was on his way to Baku, the capital of Azerbaijan, in the company of the chairman of the executive committee of the Third International, Grigori Sinoviev. Turkish troops, led by his brother Nuri Pasha, had taken the city during the last weeks of the war in September 1918. So it was in this symbol-laden place that Enver Pasha, assisted by Karl Radek, was to open the "First Congress of the Nations of the East."

Addressing the delegates, Enver Pasha distanced himself from his previous ties with Imperial Germany. But this was nothing more than lip service. When the communist International exhorted the nations of the East to "Holy War against the British imperialists," Enver Pasha

Figure 5. Comrades in Arms: Enver Pasha (center, 1881–1922) and Friedrich Sarre (1865–1945)

knew very well that this coincided with the strategic line his German friends had pursued since August 1914.

German officers in Berlin warmly welcomed Enver's collaboration with the Bolsheviks. As early as September 24, 1919, they founded the "Union of Asia Fighters" at a Berlin restaurant. The main purpose of this organization was collecting and summarizing political and military data as well as putting to use the professional experiences and social connections of its members.[15]

Since December 1919, the Union had been publishing a newsletter that provided well-informed commentaries about the political and military developments in the Middle East. It is hardly surprising that in the December 1, 1920, issue the congress proceedings at Baku received a positive review: "Lenin and Tchitcherin identified with a keen eye the weakest spot in England's position, namely India." The nervous reactions on the part of the British government and military circles were carefully and gratefully noted as well. Two years after the defeat in the world war, the German "Asia fighters" once again saw in the East the rising of a new dawn: "The Congress of Baku should be regarded as the prelude to a life-and-death struggle."[17]

The Union of Asia Fighters also counted among its members Oskar Ritter von Niedermayer, the military commander of the German Iran and Afghanistan mission in 1915/16, who was now adjutant to Reichswehr minister Otto Gessler. In an undated memorandum found among Seeckt's papers, he evaluated the political and military situation in Afghanistan, Turkmenistan, and Iran in light of the Congress of Baku. This memorandum reads like a direct response to Enver Pasha's letters.[18]

Niedermayer, who combined intimate familiarity of the region with academic learning, evaluated the results of Baku with some reticence and skepticism. It was true that targeting India coincided absolutely with the interests of the German Reich, but the presumption of an ideological closeness between Islam and Bolshevism seemed to Niedermayer a political basis that held little promise: "Any attempt to impose Bolshevik rule by force or even a mere confederation on the above-mentioned nations would lead to rather unpleasant experiences."

Instead of rapid revolutionizing, Niedermayer recommended proceeding with caution and never losing sight of the long-term perspective. The destabilization of India needed time and careful preparation. Niedermayer referred back to his own schemes in 1915/16: "I put these plans, together with my overall political, military, and economic exploration of Afghanistan, at the time in writing, unfortunately left behind in Afghanistan in a hiding place! I stand ready to put them at your disposal." Seeckt underlined in red the strategic evaluation that followed: "Today, it is a matter of striking an unsettling blow against England in some area of the Islamic East! Such a strike is possible in Mesopotamia or Iran."

Such a strike could only be successful, however, with the help of the Bolsheviks. Niedermayer's advice, therefore, was to wait: "No decision concerning any action in the above-mentioned countries should be started nervously and prematurely." Again, Seeckt underlined the next few lines in red, "even if the government in Moscow finds itself in whatever desperate situation. Inaction is better here than a wrong move."

In late 1920, Seeckt had another opportunity for a personal discussion with Enver Pasha. Since mid-October, the latter had been in Berlin, where he stayed at the opulent mansion of the archaeologist and director of the Islamic Museum, Friedrich Sarre, who had been a German liaison officer in the Ottoman Empire during the war and felt close to the sultan's family. The mansion in the quiet suburb of Neubabelsberg provided Enver Pasha with an ideal meeting place for his conspiratorial intrigues. He received a steady stream of officers, professors, and diplomats, among them Viktor Kopp, the Soviet attaché in Berlin. In December 1920, Kopp reported in a dispatch to Moscow that Seeckt had discussed with him the build-up of the Soviet armaments industry.[19]

It was only in January 1921 that Enver Pasha left the German capital for good. He returned to Moscow via Vienna and Budapest. The house of his friend Friedrich Sarre still exists, and older neighbors still call the little bridge that leads to Glienicke "Enver Pasha's bridge."[20]

Oriental Games

After Enver Pasha had left Berlin for Moscow in early 1921, Seeckt gathered around him a group of selected officers he called "Special Group R." All had served under him in Turkey, had Russia and Middle East experience, and were now in charge of the Reichswehr's secret contacts with Bolshevik Russia. Head of the group was the chief of the department of the army, Colonel Otto Hasse. Under his command were Major Schubert, Oskar Ritter von Niedermayer, Herbert Fischer, and Fritz Tschunke.[21]

As a result, the ties between Berlin, Moscow, and Kabul were drawn ever closer.[22] On February 26, 1921, Enver Pasha apprised Seeckt of the arrival of a visitor, the Afghan general Mehmed Veli Khan, who was traveling to Europe via Moscow.[23] As early as September 27, 1920, the German attaché in Moscow had reported that a special mission from Afghanistan was on its way to Berlin with the goal of recruiting technical experts for its armaments industries.

On April 8, 1921, the emissaries from Afghanistan arrived in Berlin and were received by Foreign Minister Simon on April 12 and by President Ebert the following day. On April 19, 1921, another letter of recommendation arrived from Enver Pasha. Enver Pasha and Talaat Pasha had not been the only ones who fled Constantinople after the collapse of the Ottoman Empire. Jemal Pasha, former minister of the navy of the Ottoman Empire, brutal military commander in Syria, and third member of the Young Turk troika, had left Turkey for Kabul together with the former prefect of Constantinople, Bedri Bey. It was latter's arrival in Berlin that Enver Pasha was now announcing. Together with Jemal Pasha, Bedri Bey was involved in modernizing Afghanistan's modest armaments industry.

Bedri Bey's mission was to purchase, in Germany and other neutral European countries, machinery for the production of weapons and munitions. To his German interlocutors, he presented an optimistic picture of the situation: Since the Third Afghan War against British India in 1919, Kabul had regained much of its strength. The development of a respectable armaments industry had made great strides.

Yet, Bedri Bey also indicated his increasing distrust of Moscow. The expulsion of the emir of Bukhara, the relentless Sovietization of Central Asia, and the ruthless suppression of the independent republics in the Caucasus seemed proof that the internationalism propagated at Baku was nothing more than rhetoric. The loudly proclaimed, selfless support for the Islamic people was only a thin veil over Moscow's striving for imperial power. Bedri Bey informed his German interlocutors of Kabul's and Ankara's intent to bar all Bolshevist propaganda from Turkish and Afghan territory.

Pragmatic Analyses, Fantastic Plans

In the spring of 1921, while the visitors from Kabul were on their way to Berlin, Oskar Ritter von Niedermayer delivered a secret lecture with the title "Assessment of the Conditions for an Attack on India" at the German ministry of defense, the *Reichswehrministerium*.[24] Another member of the German Afghanistan expedition, Günther Voigt, noted in 1958: "As far as I remember, General von Seeckt was present at the lecture." According to Voigt, not only was the chief of the Reichswehr Niedermayer's mentor, but "Niedermayer was a frequent guest at Seeckt's home."[25]

There was no doubt in Niedermayer's mind that the Indian subcontinent was not yet ripe for revolution. The making of a revolution in India required slow and continuous work on the population; any kind of force or premature action had to be avoided. Most importantly, Indian nationalism first had to be systematically propagated and the religious disparities had to be bridged. Niedermayer was unable to give a precise assessment of the reliability of the Indian army under British command: "But why shouldn't it be possible to poison its spirit through skillfully applied propaganda?"

Afghanistan was to be built into the staging area for anti-British activities: "And then, it's a matter of waiting for the golden opportunity, which will and must come, when England's struggle for retaining her position of world hegemony will have reached a more desperate level. Then the time may have come for taking revenge against England, a country of 50 million, for her presumptiveness of subjugating and exploiting 400 million people around the globe." Niedermayer closed his lecture with the prophetic words: "When continents awake, island empires fall!"

On an attached map, Niedermayer sketched in detail the steps toward an attack on India from Afghanistan. A crucial factor was the water supply for the troops. From 1923 to 1926, Niedermayer's brother Richard, an engineer, was engaged in building a water supply system for the Afghan city of Kandahar. He later wrote a doctoral dissertation on Afghanistan's water problems.[26] Another member of Niedermayer's 1915/16 Afghanistan mission, Kurt Wagner, returned in the mid-1920s to Afghanistan as a representative of German industry.[27] And yet another officer of that expedition, Günther Voigt, acted as a link in the covert German-Russian-Afghan network.[28]

Niedermayer sent Voigt the transcript of his lecture with a request for his comment. Voigt replied on May 20, 1921, with a six-page letter.[28] He paid particular attention to transport and infrastructure problems. Although Niedermayer's deliberations seemed to Voigt in hindsight "rather unrealistic," he expressed his willingness to lend continued support. In the late summer of 1921, Voigt received a telegram calling him to Berlin, where Niedermayer asked him if he was ready to return to Afghanistan via Moscow. His mission was to be threefold: to persuade the Afghan government to form a close alliance with Russia; to further the construction of a road over the Hindu Kush; and to initiate further development of connections between Kabul and Kandahar: "Even if it was not specifically mentioned, it was, nevertheless, clear that these measures were to serve preparations for a Russian attack on India."

Voigt traveled to Moscow with the help of the Soviet trade mission in Berlin. While waiting in a Moscow hotel for a meeting with the Russian emissary to Kabul, he spotted in the lobby two Indian revolutionaries who had been among those escorted to Kabul by the German Afghanistan Expedition. Voigt kept himself in the background: "In order to guard the secrecy of my mission, it seemed to me best to pretend not to recognize the two gentlemen. And they were tactful enough to respect my position."

Voigt had a one-on-one discussion with Foreign Minister Tchitcherin. He also met in Moscow with Jemal Pasha, the Young Turk exile politician and Afghan war minister. The German officer and the Turkish politician conducted their friendly conversation in French; however, Jemal Pasha was not alone: "Besides members of his staff, a young Russian communist was present as well. I had the impression that this young man was not assigned to the Pasha to merely make his stay in Moscow as pleasant as possible, but above all to tail him."

Jemal Pasha offered Voigt a position as officer on his staff. However, after thinking it over, Voigt declined. On October 21, 1921, he informed Tchitcherin in writing of his decision. As member of the Afghan army, Voigt would also have had to report to the Russian emissary in Kabul. He saw himself caught in an irreconcilable conflict of loyalty. "Should I spy on Jemal Pasha in favor of the Russian government? Is that the reason why I was presented in Moscow to the Russian emissary in Kabul?"

When Voigt returned to Germany, he was informed of certain developments that explained his puzzling experiences in Moscow. At the same time as covert contacts between Berlin and Moscow increased, the Young Turk revolutionaries and the Afghan government began dissolving their ties to Moscow. Enver Pasha had been turning away from Moscow since the summer of 1921 when he became increasingly aware that Moscow was sabotaging his goal of a political unification of Central Asia under his rule. After the expulsion of the Emir of Bukhara, the Bolsheviks set up a Soviet government in Central Asia and gave its security organization, the Tcheka, a free hand for ruthless action.

Projects for the Future

Despite these developments, the collaboration between Berlin and Moscow intensified. In April 1921, Viktor Kopp explained to Trotsky in detail the Reichswehr's most important aims, that is, evasion of the armaments control stipulations of the Treaty of Versailles by means of a secret German-Soviet cooperative scheme. The common enterprise was to develop and manufacture fighter planes, weapons, and munitions.[29]

Seeckt's trusted agent Niedermayer began to commute between East and West in the summer of 1921 under the cover name "Dr. Neumann." His travels were quietly approved by the German government, which had been informed by Seeckt in early June 1921 of the most important elements of his strategic plan. The German emissary in Moscow, Wiedenfeld, however, had not been informed. To his surprise, he learned that Niedermayer had been in Moscow for a considerable length of time without his knowledge. Wiedenfeld reported to Berlin: "As I recently found out, Major von Niedermayer, the Reichwehr minister's adjutant, spent several months here, presumably to carry out economic studies." What was going on here? "I was told that his stay was of a strictly confidential nature, but that Chancellor Fehrenbach and Minister Simon were informed of his mission."

Soon the military ties became closer and an agreement was ready for signing. On March 15, 1922, Niedermayer signed, in the name of the army command, a contract with the German airplane manufacturer Junkers for the production of a series of airplanes for Russia. Junkers was to produce, in a Moscow suburb, three hundred metal airplanes annually. The company was also granted the right to carry out transit flights over Soviet territory to Iran and Afghanistan. Even though the ill-fated project eventually caused the bankruptcy of the airplane manufacturer in October 1925, three Reichswehr stations were set up in Soviet Russia in the 1920s. In Lipzek, 400 kilometers south of Moscow, German officers engaged in modern air war maneuvers. In Kazan on the Volga, they tested modern tank weaponry. And near Tomsk, they experimented with weapons of mass destruction like poison gas.[30]

Death of a Revolutionary

In January and February 1922, Central Asian rebels under Enver Pasha's command gained several significant victories over the Red Army. After his break with the Bolsheviks, Enver Pasha had begun to pursue the realization of his fantastic dreams. His future Central Asian empire was to be vaster than the former autonomous emirates of Bukhara and Khiva. He prodded his followers into declaring him emir of all of Turkestan and all trans-Caspian provinces. In May 1922, his forces occupied Ashkhabad. Bolshevist leaders who fell into the rebels' hands were immediately executed on Enver Pasha's order.

On March 19, 1922, the German emissary in Moscow reported that Enver Pasha was supported by Afghan forces fighting with British weapons. Was it possible that British intelligence services operating out of India had prompted Enver Pasha to switch sides? These new developments in Central Asia were no longer favorable to the strategic goals of the Reichswehr leadership. It had not been Seeckt's intention for Enver Pasha to weaken the Bolsheviks in Central Asia when he had sent him to Moscow.

Dr. Nazim, Enver Pasha's emissary, reassured his German friends that he entertained no ties with the British. If his anti-Soviet policies were not unwelcome in London, this was only coincidental and temporary. Enver Pasha's conduct of war was determined solely by the resentment Muslims felt toward Moscow's now obvious policies of conquest and exploitation.

On August 4, 1922, Enver Pasha was killed southwest of Bukhara in the course of a hopeless engagement on horseback with a superior Red Army cavalry division. His sabre-shredded body was placed in a shallow grave and covered with dirt. Jemal Pasha too met with a violent end in the summer of 1922 on his way from Berlin to Kabul. On July 24, 1922, he and two adjutants were gunned down in broad daylight in a street in Tiflis, the capital of Georgia. Was this assassination an act of Armenian revenge? Or did Jemal Pasha fall victim to the Tcheka?

Hans von Seeckt warmly remembered Enver Pasha, whom he had received in his home in Berlin shortly before the latter's final departure for Moscow. Sought by the Western Powers as a war criminal, pushed out of Turkey's political life by Mustafa Kemal (Atatürk), Enver Pasha was politically cut off from his homeland. Free of all political ties, driven by delusions of grandeur, he followed in the end a dream, the union of the Turkic peoples of Central Asia under his rule. When Seeckt told a Turkish compatriot of Enver Pasha's death, he replied with a shrug of the shoulders: "Que voulez-vous, c'est la fin d'un révolutionaire."[31]

Fatal Connections

Enver Pasha's lonely death marked the end of the partnership of Germany's military leaders and the Young Turk movement that had started before the First World War. Kemal Pasha (Atatürk), the founder of modern Turkey, always kept his distance from Enver Pasha's and his German friends' adventurous schemes. Kemal Pasha's pragmatic policy focused on Turkey's national interests, avoided a partnership with Hitler's Germany, and led his country into the Atlantic Alliance.

The Reichswehr's secret cooperation with Turkish and Bolshevik revolutionaries remained an episode. First criticized by German liberals during the Weimar Republic and later even by Adolf Hitler, the idea of weakening the British Empire by creating unrest in India and the Islamic world was the fantastic scheme of only a small group of experts. While the Hitler-Stalin Pact was in effect from 1939 to 1941, some of them tried to revive the idea of a German-Soviet-Afghan axis. But these attempts failed to gain support. Not only did Stalin show no interest, Hitler too, even during the Second World War, never took these anti-British machinations seriously. He abhorred, for ideological reasons alone, the idea of siding with people of color in a fight against British rule.

However, after 1945, as the Cold War was heating up, Moscow's partners in East Berlin were only too willing to lend support to Soviet operations. In concert with their comrades in Moscow, East German diplomats and military experts stirred up unrest in Egypt and Iraq, in Libya and Afghanistan. An analysis of this German-Soviet connection is a challenging task. The question of continuity or discontinuity of German Middle East policy remains open to further investigation and new answers.

Notes

1. Hans von Seeckt, "Die Gründe des Zusammenbruchs der Türkei im Herbst 1918," Bundesarchiv-Militärarchiv Freiburg, in *Nachlaß Hans von Seeckt,* BA-MA, N 247/50.
2. On Seeckt and the German General Staff see the studies by John W. Wheeler-Bennett, *The Nemesis of Power. The German Army and Politics 1918–1945* (New York, 1969); and Hans Meier-Welcker, *Seeckt* (Frankfurt am Main, 1967). Seeckt himself wrote several books in a highly stylized, classical language: *Antikes Feldherrntum* (Berlin, 1929); *Moltke. Ein Vorbild* (Berlin, 1931); *Gedanken eines Soldaten* (Berlin, 1935).
3. Seeckt, *Antikes Feldherrntum,* 5.
4. Ibid., 11. On May 2, 1918, in a letter to his friend von Winterfeldt-Menkin, Seeckt used similar language: "When I was standing on the railroad tracks to Tiflis and Baku, my thoughts took wing over the cotton fields of Turkistan. They scaled the Olympic Mountains, and if—as I must hope—the war will continue for a long time, we will finally knock on the gates of India." Cited in Winfried Baumgart, "Das 'Kaspi-Unternehmen'—Größenwahn Ludendorffs oder Routineplanung des

deutschen Generalstabs?" *Jahrbücher für Geschichte Osteuropas,* NF, 18, no. 1 (1970): 47–126.
5. Hans von Seeckt, *Aus meinem Leben 1866–1917. Unter Verwendung des schriftlichen Nachlasses im Auftrage von Frau Dorothee von Seeckt herausgegeben von Generalleutnant Dr. hc. Friedrich von Rabenau* (Leipzig, 1938), 49.
6. Seeckt to von Winterfeldt-Menkin, October 29, 1915, cited in Meier-Welcker, *Seeckt,* 712–16.
7. Meier-Welcker, *Seeckt,* 295.
8. Ibid., 324.
9. Otto-Ernst Schüddekopf, "Karl Radek in Berlin. Ein Kapitel deutsch-russischer Beziehungen im Jahre 1919," *Archiv für Sozialgeschichte* 2 (1962): 87–166; Marie Louise Goldbach, *Karl Radek und die deutsch-sowjetischen Beziehungen 1918–1923* (Bonn, 1973); Dietrich Möller, *Karl Radek in Deutschland. Revolutionär, Intrigant, Diplomat* (Cologne, 1976).
10. National Archives Washington, Captured German War Documents, T 149/400.
11. Fritz Tschunke, "Befreiung Enver Paschas aus litauischer Gefangenschaft" in *Nachlaß Hans von Seeckt,* BA-MA, N 247/175.
12. Hermann Teske, *General Ernst Köstring. Der militärische Mittler zwischen dem Deutschen Reich und der Sowjetunion 1921–1941* (Frankfurt am Main, 1965), 47.
13. Enver Pasha to Seeckt, Moscow, August 25, 1920, in *Nachlaß Hans von Seeckt,* BA-MA, N 247/195.
14. Ludwig W. Adamec, *Afghanistan's Foreign Affairs to the Mid-Twentieth Century. Relations with the USSR, Germany, and Britain* (Tucson, Ariz., 1974), 42–51.
15. Enver Pasha to Seeckt, Moscow, August 28, 1920, in *Nachlaß Hans von Seeckt,* BA-MA, N 247/195.
16. *Mitteilungen des Bundes der Asienkämpfer* (Berlin), December 1, 1919.
17. Der Kongreß von Baku, *Mitteilungen des Bundes der Asienkämpfer* (Berlin), December 1, 1920.
18. Undated memorandum by Oskar Ritter von Niedermayer about the situation in Afghanistan, Turkistan, and Iran, in *Nachlaß Hans von Seeckt,* BA-MA, N 247/204. On Niedermayer see Christoph Jahr, "Generalmajor Oskar Ritter von Niedermayer," in *Hitlers militärische Elite,* vol. 1, *Von den Anfängen des Regimes bis Kriegsbegin,* ed. Gerd R. Überschär (Darmstadt, 1998), 178–194. Hans-Ulrich Seidt, "From Palestine to the Caucasus. Oskar Niedermayer and Germany's Middle Eastern Strategy in 1918," *German Studies Review* 24, no. 1 (February 2001): 1–18.
19. Manfred Zeidler, *Reichswehr und Rote Armee 1920–1933. Wege und Stationen einer ungewöhnlichen Zusammenarbeit* (Munich, 1993), 51.
20. Interview with Dr. Jens Kröger, curator, Islamisches Museum, Berlin, March 14, 2001.
21. Zeidler, *Reichswehr und Rote Armee,* 53.
22. On the contacts between Berlin and Kabul in 1921, see *Mitteilungen des Bundes der Asienkämpfer,* May 1, 1921. British intelligence officers tried to track the secret contacts between German officers, Russian revolutionaries, and Turkish exiles. On their view of a German-Jewish-Muslim conspiracy against British global interests see the studies by John Fisher, "The Interdepartmental Committee on

Eastern Unrest and British Responses to Bolshevik and Other Intrigues Against the Empire during the 1920s," *Journal of Asian History* 34, no. 1 (2000): 1–34; and "Major Norman Bray and Eastern Unrest in the Aftermath of World War I," *Asian Affairs* 6 (2000): 189–97.

23. Enver Pasha to Seeckt, Moscow, February 2, 1921, and Moscow, April 19, 1921, in *Nachlaß Hans von Seeckt*, BA-MA, N 247/195.
24. Oskar Ritter von Niedermayer, "Geheim! Beurteilung der Militärgeographischen Verhältnisse eines Angriffs auf Indien. Vortrag gehalten im Februar 1921 im Reichswehrministerium," in *Nachlaß Günther Voigt*, Bibliotheca Afghanica/ Schweizer Afghanistan Institut (BA-SAI), Bubendorf/Switzerland.
25. Voigt to Richard Gehrcke, Tübingen, January 1, 1958, in *Nachlaß Günther Voigt*, BA-SAI.
26. Richard Niedermayer, "Das afghanische Bewässerungswesen" (Diss., Danzig, 1926).
27. Francis R. Nicosia, "'Drang nach Osten' Continued? Germany and Afghanistan during the Weimar Republic," *Journal of Contemporary History* 32, no. 2 (1997): 235–57.
28. Günther Voigt, "Rückblick auf meine Rußlandreise 1921/1922. Zu meinen Lebzeiten nur mit meiner ausdrücklichen Genehmigung zu veröffentlichen!" in *Nachlaß Günther Voigt*, BA-SAI.
29. Voigt to Niedermayer, Münster, May 20, 1921, in *Nachlaß Günther Voigt*, BA-SAI.
30. On the secret cooperation between the Reichswehr and the Red Army, see Wipert von Blücher, *Deutschlands Weg nach Rapallo* (Wiesbaden, 1951); F. L. Carsten, *The Reichswehr and Politics 1918–1933* (Berkeley, 1973); Julius Epstein, "Der Seeckt-Plan," Der Monat 1, no. 2 (1948/49): 50–55; Gerald Freund, *Unholy Alliance: Russian-German Relations from the Treaty of Brest-Litovsk to the Treaty of Berlin* (London, 1957); Olaf Groehler, *Selbstmörderische Allianz. Deutschrussische Militärbeziehungen 1920–1941* (Berlin, 1992); Gustav Hilger, *Wir und der Kreml* (Frankfurt am Main and Berlin, 1956); Cecil F. Melville,*The Russian Face of Germany. An Account of the Secret Military Relations beween the German and Soviet Russian Governments* (London, 1932); Aleksandr M. Nekrich, *Pariahs, Partners, Predators: German-Soviet Relations 1922–1941* (New York, 1997); Helmut Speidel, "Reichswehr und Rote Armee,"*Vierteljahrshefte für Zeitgeschichte* 1 (1953): 188–92; Hermann Teske, *General Ernst Köstring. Der militärische Mittler zwischen dem Deutschen Reich und der Sowjetunion 1921–1941* (Frankfurt am Main, 1965); Zeidler, *Reichswehr und Rote Armee*.
31. Seeckt, "Erinnerungen an Enver Pascha," in *Nachlaß Hans von Seeckt*, BA-MA, N 247/178.

Figure 6. Dr. Fritz Grobba, 1886–1973

"The Jinnee and the Magic Bottle"

Fritz Grobba and the German Middle Eastern Policy 1900–1945

WOLFGANG G. SCHWANITZ

The subject of this essay is an evaluation of German Middle Eastern policy from 1900 to 1945 in light of a recently discovered retrospective account by one of its key players. For a quarter century, Dr. Fritz Grobba was the foremost German envoy to the Middle East. As a dragoman and a lawyer, he was raised in two traditions. First, the German Middle Eastern policy was only secondary to policies concerning Europe and America. Thus, it was a tool of politics to prevent undesirable coalitions in Central Europe by keeping the Eastern Question open and placing Berlin in the position of mediator. Grobba applied this principle as a minister to Kabul, and to a lesser degree in Baghdad and ar-Riyād. There he leaned more toward finding a genuine German Middle Eastern peace policy. The personal conflict in which he thus found himself was partially alleviated when Berlin changed course to a primary Middle Eastern war policy after 1939. Then, Nazi policy makers were ready to sacrifice (after the projected fall of Moscow) two of the main pillars of German Middle Eastern policy: the maintenance of the status quo and the renunciation of territorial claims in the region.

In his capacity as Foreign Office Plenipotentiary for Arab Affairs and head of the Arab Committee, Grobba also applied the second tradition, the use of Islam for political aims. He released weekly talks for Arabic broadcasts from Germany to the Middle East and coached Grand Mufti Amīn al-Husainī in declaring a Holy War against the Allies. Thus Grobba uncorked a magic bottle of warfare under cover of religion. Although he did not distance himself from Nazi ideology after the war, he criticized the German Middle Eastern policy. Upon his release as a Soviet prisoner of war in 1955, he found a world divided by the Cold War. As the West contained the spread of totalitarian regimes, he decided to share his experiences with the West Germans and the Americans. Through this knowledge transfer to Washington, the foremost German diplomat in the Middle East became involved in German Middle Eastern policy once again. Here is a chronology of salient points in Dr. Grobba's life:

07/18/1886	Born in Gartz/Oder, Pomerania
09/02/1973	Died in Bonn, Bad Godesberg
1908–1913	University of Berlin, Law and Oriental Languages (Arabic, Turkish)
1913	Jerusalem, dragoman — Dragomanatseleve — at German Consular General
1914–1918	Palestine, commander of an Arab POW unit, Kressenstein's orderly
July 1921	Second State Examination, becomes a civil servant, rank of vice consul
09/06/1922	Berlin, enters Foreign Office, Wilhelmstraße, Department of Law
01/29/1923	Foreign Office, changes to Department of Oriental Affairs
12/16/1923	Kabul, envoy ad interim, establishes the first German Diplomatic Mission
10/01/1926	Joins the Department III (Persia, Afghanistan, India) of the Foreign Office

03/24/1932	Baghdad, becomes the first German envoy to Iraq
02/13/1939	Jidda, becomes the first German Envoy to Saudi Arabia
09/06/1939	Returns to Berlin after break of relations; serves with Wilhelm Keppler
May 1941	Special envoy to Iraq, travels Berlin-Baghdad-Berlin, from May 6 to June 6
Feb. 1942	Berlin, Plenipotentiary of the Foreign Office for the Arab Countries; coach of exiled Grand Mufti of Jerusalem who calls for a jihad
12/24/1942	Berlin, loses position and gets order: "No engagement in Arab politics"
02/13/1943	Paris, German Archive Commission, tries Arab politics again
06/10/1944	Berlin, Foreign Office, receives his early retirement
1944–1945	Dresden, joins Saxon government, responsible for war industry
1945	Meiningen, public prosecutor, Russians imprison him as spy
1955	Returns from the Soviet Union to West Germany
1956	Stuttgart, writes supplement to "German Exploitation of Arab Nationalist Movements in World War II" as requested by the former general Franz Halder
07/29/1957	His eighty-two page supplement is ready: "P-207" is now 300 pages long
03/03/1958	Guest of King Saʿūd, intends to establish a German-Arab Society in Bonn

GERMAN ORIGINAL

GERMAN EXPLOITATION OF ARAB NATIONALIST MOVEMENTS IN WORLD WAR II

MS#P-207

HISTORICAL DIVISION
HEADQUARTERS, UNITED STATES ARMY, EUROPE
FOREIGN MILITARY STUDIES BRANCH

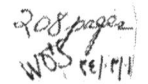

Figure 7. The cover sheet of "MS#P-207" by former Generals Walter Warlimont and Hellmuth Felmy to which Fritz Grobba added his supplement in 1957 for the U.S. Army.

1959	Moves to Bonn, Bad Godesberg, as informal advisor
Sept. 1963	Last trip to Iraq, Syria, and Lebanon
1967	Memoirs, *Men and Power in the Orient*, published in Göttingen

What was the state of literature? Besides a few works and Grobba's memoirs published in the 1960s,[1] only a handful of studies have appeared since. The most important of these is a book of essays by Uriel Dann that deals with Grobba's mission to Afghanistan, Iraq, and Saudi Arabia.[2] Francis R. Nicosia has written the best foreign overview so far on Fritz Grobba.[3]

Edgar Flacker published his source work in *Fritz Grobba and Nazi Germany's Middle Eastern Policy*.[4] A French point of view is expressed in Chantal Metzger's *L'Empire colonial français dans la stratégie du Troisième Reich*.[5] There are also revelations about looted gold transactions by Nazi Germany with Turkey[6] and new studies by Gerhard Höpp[7] that touch on the German Middle Eastern policy (Middle East include the Near East).

Nevertheless, a research gap remains. A comprehensive modern study of the Middle East and Nazi Germany based on Near Eastern and European sources is still missing. Such a work should not only cover German policies with regard to Arabs, Jews, Turks, and Persians, but it should also take due account of German Middle Eastern paradigms and guidelines,[8] and the Middle East policy of the great power of the twentieth century, the United States. This book remains to be written.[9] There are no new Arabic source studies that cover the policies of Middle Eastern countries with regard to Nazi Germany based on Middle Eastern records, although various of case studies were published by Israel Gershony,[10] Wajīh ʿAbd as-Sādiq ʿAtīq,[11] and Fahd Bin ʿAbdallah as-Simmārī in the 1990s.[12]

Today, the gleaning of European archives for Fritz Grobba is nearing its end. Fresh insights are to be expected from Middle Eastern archives, especially those of Iraq, Syria, Saudi Arabia, Turkey, Egypt, and Israel, as well as collections in the United States, including the captured enemy property in the National Archives with unique German records.

This essay focuses on German Middle Eastern policies, Fritz Grobba's life, the origin, contents, and circumstances of his knowledge transfer to the United States in 1957 which can be considered as his most important reflection in retrospect. I also discuss here the allied reactions to Grobba's activities. Important records have been discovered recently.

German Middle Eastern Paradigms and Guidelines at 1900

The German Middle Eastern policy had its origin in the period after the founding of the German Empire in 1871. Chancellor Otto von Bismarck outlined Germany's essential foreign policy position before the Parliament in 1888:[13]

a) Situated in the heart of Europe, Germany was vulnerable to multiple warfronts at one time.

b) A particular threat existed for Germany from possible coalitions between neighboring states like France and Russia [we may add Great Britain here].

c) Germany always needed to take care not to provoke others to invade it.

The main geopolitical problem was this: by maintaining a level of power sufficient to oppose her three potential adversaries, Germany might have provoked them into viewing German power as too great for each of one of them alone. The arms race among the four major powers in Europe created lasting instability. The one in the middle felt threatened by possible coalitions that needed to be disrupted to prevent a multiple-front war. To this end, Bismarck regarded the Eastern Question on the periphery of Europe as a welcome means of disrupting undesirable coalitions surrounding Germany. The Eastern Question at that time boiled down to which European power would get what out of the declining Ottoman Empire. If we take Bismarck's words and the policy of Emperor Wilhelm II, we find guidelines of German Middle Eastern policy in 1900 as standard explanations for problems and approaches to solve them:

1) The web of peace for a German world policy was to be put up at the edges of Europe.

2) By keeping the Eastern Question open, Berlin placed itself in a position from which to manipulate the coalitions of its adversaries and to mediate its neighbors' disputes at the periphery.

3) The two main pillars of German Middle Eastern policy center on maintaining the status quo in the Middle East and renouncing any acquisition of colonies or territories in the region.[15]

But the most striking paradigm of German Middle Eastern policy at the beginning of the twentieth century was that, although it was a very direct, active policy, it was secondary and non-imperial. In the hierarchy of policy-making factors, German European and American policy always ranked first, and the German Middle Eastern policy was primarily a means for disrupting antagonistic European coalitions through manipulating the Eastern Question. This was to change during World War I.[16]

Middle Eastern Guidelines in the Republic of Weimar and Nazi Germany

Allied with the Ottoman Empire during World War I, Berlin's primary Middle East war policy was directed against France, Russia, and Britain. The German Foreign Office or Wilhelmstraße (named for the street on which the German Foreign Office was located) developed a special strategy of inciting people against their rulers by "Islamic revolts." The mastermind of this dual concept, "war by riots" in the hinterland and "war by troops" on the front, was Max von Oppenheim, whose bureau was hosted by the Foreign Office.[17] At the same time, Fritz Grobba, a young lieutenant and intellectual in his late twenties, was gathering valuable experiences in Palestine as commander of an Arab unit of prisoners of war.[18]

With Germany's defeat and the dismemberment of the Ottoman Empire, the situation changed drastically.[19] The League of Nations regulated the Eastern Question without regard for Berlin's world policy or German participation in the French and British Mandatory regimes.

The German Foreign Office returned to a secondary German Middle East peace policy upholding the status quo and renouncing territorial claims in the region. Germany's interests in the Middle East were purely economic and cultural. However, Germany did become a critical factor in promoting national independence in the areas of the European empires. New countries like the Republic of Turkey appeared.[20] Others, like the Kingdom of Egypt, were greatly disappointed by the Mandatory regime of old European powers in the former Arab parts of the Ottoman Empire like Palestine. As anti-Semitism was on the rise in Europe, the Balfour Declaration promised a national homeland for Jews in Palestine. The conflict intensified in that area.

In 1923 Grobba advanced to the position of German envoy to Afghanistan. He became the classic case of a diplomat who used Kabul as a basis for a secondary Middle East peace policy. His primary concern was not then developing the bilateral aims of Germany and Afghanistan but changing his host's relations with third parties, like Soviet Russia, Great Britain, and India, in the German interest.[21]

In the 1930s other newly independent countries appeared, like the monarchies of Saudi Arabia and Iraq. But after the ending of the Caliphate they all lacked an "Islamic umbrella," a greater union that the Ottoman Empire used to provide. Again it was Fritz Grobba who became the first German envoy to Baghdad in 1932. Ten years later, he advanced to first Plenipotentiary of the Foreign Office for Arab Countries, having also been appointed envoy to Saudi Arabia in 1939. By 1943, however, his promising career met with a sudden end because of intrigues.

How did the guidelines of the Nazi German Middle Eastern policy change in this period?

1) Berlin pursued once again a secondary Middle East policy in its search for world domination, ready to sacrifice the previous pillars, those of upholding the status quo and of renouncing all territorial acquisitions in the region. From 1941 to 1943, Germany, in alliance with Italy, changed to a primary Middle East war policy directed against the main Allies, Great Britain, the United States, and the Soviet Union.

2) The Middle East was regarded as a war zone, but not as a zone for German settlements or colonies. At first Hitler left this region to Mussolini. In the case of a German-

Italian victory, they would establish a dictatorship over the region. There is no doubt that had the plan succeeded, Jews in the Middle East would have met with the same fate as those in Europe. In a second step in 1941, Hitler approved preliminary designs on the Middle East, to be developed after the fall of Moscow. Germans planned a Greater Arab Union that would be dependent on Germany and Italy.

3) Germany again advanced the concept of Islamic Holy War, a jihad, by instigating revolts among Arabs and other Muslims against the British, French, and Russians. With the help of leaders like the Grand Mufti Ḥājj Amīn al-Husainī, the Germans recruited some Muslim troops.

This secondary and primary Middle Eastern policy was the frame for Grobba's mission to the Middle East. A learned and devoted civil servant, he had a great affinity for the local population, especially Turks and Arabs, among whom he made many friends. Besides being an admirer of their history, culture, and civilization, he was able to adapt the Foreign Office rules and games to good advantage at his posts in the Middle East. He was consulted not only by German military leaders, but also by leaders in Egypt, Iraq, Saudi Arabia and Palestine. In the thirties he had already gained an almost legendary stature in the region, as Dr. Günther Pawelke, his deputy in Baghdad, has testified.[22]

The Origin of Fritz Grobba's Supplement to "P-207" after World War II

To examine the circumstances under which Grobba wrote the supplement (hereafter also briefly called study) to the manuscript "German Exploitation of Arab Nationalist Movements in World War II" (see its cover sheet, figure 2) it is necessary to return to the literature discussed above. There are two main groups of sources, records from administrations in Germany and other countries until 1945, and published or unpublished sources produced by the former actors in memoirs and diaries. Many of these papers, which appeared after World War II, were compiled either as evidence for the Nuremberg tribunals or with the aim of diffusing the facts. In general, the published memoirs are similar to the human memory that dislikes unpleasant things out of the past. Fritz Grobba's memoirs of 1967, *Men and Power in the Orient*, are no exception. But his study, written ten years earlier, shows far more accuracy and offers insights that are not in his memoirs.[23]

This unpublished, unique record is free of any direct political purpose, for it was written in 1957 long after the close of the trials. Thus, unlike Grobba's memoirs, the study was not meant to influence public opinion. On the contrary, his manuscript was for internal use. An explanation of its origins makes it clear. His diplomatic career came to a sudden halt in 1943 and he was transferred to the German Archive Commission in Paris. Since he tried there again to engage himself in Arab politics, especially to influence the Algerians to establish a committee for the liberation of their country from the French, a *hai'at at-tahrīr*, he was swiftly removed to Berlin in 1944, and later to Dresden. There he worked in Saxony's war industry.

After the war, newspapers called for persons with legal training and without a Nazi record to be engaged as lawyers. Since Fritz Grobba had not been a member of the Nazi party, he responded to the call and served as public prosecutor in the town of Meiningen, but the Russians imprisoned him and deported him to their country. When he returned in 1955 at the age of sixty-nine, he was asked by the former general Franz Halder to write a political commentary on an essay entitled "German Exploitation of Arab Nationalist Movements during World War II." Halder, a former chief of the General Staff who had been dismissed by Hitler in late 1942 and had published a book *Hitler as a General* in 1949, was then employed by the Historical Division of the U.S. Army in Europe. One of his projects was to solicit contributions from German officers for the Army's Foreign Military Studies Branch.

With regard to the Middle East, Halder had already engaged the former generals Hellmuth Felmy and Walter Warlimont to write about Germany's exploitation of Arab nationalist movements during World War II. Felmy was the chief of staff for German Middle Eastern affairs,[24] and Warlimont was one of the chief planners at military headquarters. The two finished a 208-page report in 1955 while Grobba was still a prisoner in Soviet Russia. After his return, as soon as his condition permitted, Fritz Grobba wrote an 82-page commentary as a supplement to the generals' report. It includes valuable additions and clarifications, wrote Franz Halder in his foreword to the supplement (see the foreword to document 2).

The now 300-page manuscript on how the Germans exploited Arab nationalists during World War II—or vice versa—by the former outstanding German diplomat and the two former generals passed on to the U.S. Army,[25] called there "MS # P-207," and has remained unpublished until today.[26] Moreover, its existence is still widely unknown.[27] Besides the three main papers, this document "MS # P-207" contains:

- Additional supportive material;[28]

- Letters by witnesses, for instance soldiers of Middle Eastern origin in the German army or service like Fauzī Qāwuqjī;

- Several key documents,[29] maps,[30] timetables;[31]

- Overviews of sources and names of the interviewed participants, among them Arabs like Mahmūd Rifāʾī of Baghdad; several members of German intelligence services like Hans Antonius, Leopold Bürkner, Hans Freund, Paul Leverkuehn,[32] Edgar Scholtz, Bernd Schulze-Holthus;

- Other evaluations of former generals like Hasso von Wedel, and of the former diplomats Joachim von Geldern, Günther Pawelke, Rudolf Rahn, Ernst Woermann.[33]

The circumstances under which they told Felmy and Warlimont their stories were those of the postwar geopolitical configuration of the Cold War with new power players in the Middle East, such as the United States, the Soviet Union, and China.[34] There was no intention of publishing these accounts. Fritz Grobba wrote his part after the Suez crises. The Suez war showed for the first time that conflicts in the Middle East could lead to World War III through the use of weapons of mass destruction, including ballistic nuclear missiles.[35]

Thus, it is not surprising that these former German generals and veteran Orient experts became unique sources for the West in the fight against totalitarian regimes in the divided Europe and their spread to the Middle East. There are indications that Grobba served as advisor to the West German intelligence service, the Bundesnachrichtendienst.

We will know this for sure in the future, for there are still some top-secret folders on Dr. Fritz Grobba in the Political Archive of the German Foreign Office to be declassified. Other sources, especially those held by the West German intelligence service, are still out of the reach of researchers.[36]

Fritz Grobba's Retrospective of 1957 and His Activities during World War II

When Fritz Grobba wrote his political commentary on Felmy's and Warlimont's texts about the "German exploitation of Arab nationalist movements in World War II," his memory was better than it was ten years later when he wrote his memoirs, *Men and Power in the Orient*.

It is worthwhile to take a closer look at three of the main points he makes in the study of 1957. First, Grobba maintains that the Arab nationalist movement was essentially pro-German. When the Arabs were not granted their independence as promised after World War I, they placed their hopes on Germany. Arabs and Germans saw in the British and French their common enemies (according to the slogan *'adū 'aduwī sahbī*—the enemy of my enemy is my friend).

However, in Grobba's eyes, this relation was clouded by German anti-Semitism and racial approaches, which complicated his diplomatic mission.[37] Fritz Grobba's complaint against racial doctrines was merely practical, inasmuch as they impeded his mission to the region. But he was not a member of the Nazi party (since he had been rejected as a Freemason). Nevertheless, he pursued the Nazi foreign policy guidelines effectively and did not distance himself from Nazi ideology even twelve years after the end of the war, despite more knowledge of the Holocaust. At least, he had the chance to do so in his study. Thus, the question remains whether he did grasp the anti-human nature of approaches to the foreign policy that divided humankind into "higher" and "lower" races.

Fritz Grobba frequently emphasized his basic disagreement with Berlin's Middle Eastern policy. He explained: "The rejection of every unilateral German initiative in the Arab region was due to the fact that Hitler's enemies in the Foreign Office worked against any expanding the war to the Middle East. In part, they didn't recognize the opportunity there, and in part they obstructed it."[38] Moreover, he noted, he always looked for a German Middle East peace policy that would be guided by genuine German *and* Middle Eastern interests, whereas Berlin saw the region merely as a secondary means for its primary Central European world policy.[39]

Francis R. Nicosia rightly remarked: "For Grobba the Middle East was an end in itself, an area in which he wished Germany to promote her exports and investments, show respect for British interests, place less emphasis on promoting Zionist emigration from Germany to Palestine, and more on publicly supporting Arab nationalism, and show much less deference to Italian ambitions. The German government, on the other hand, viewed the region as a convenient means to reach more important goals in Europe."[40] This is an expression of the main conflict between the primary policy—Europe and the world—and the secondary policy toward the Middle East.

This is also a continuation of Bismarck's traditional Middle Eastern policy. It was basically a secondary policy, though an active and direct one. But it was a policy subordinated to more important priorities like Europe, the United States, and Asian powers like Japan. Fritz Grobba was anchored in that tradition, but he opposed it later. He saw many possibilities of a primary bilateral policy toward the newly independent countries. And he criticized European empires in the Middle East in the era of imperialism and the following Mandatory regime. He went also through two major shifts to a primary Middle Eastern war policy during both world wars.

As a man who was at home in Arabic as well as in Turkish, Grobba bemoaned the foreign minister's misperception of Arab nationalist movements. How could Joachim von Ribbentrop have handed the Arab region over to the Italians as he did in the Tripartite Pact of September 27, 1940, he asked. This Middle Eastern envoy wrote: "Hitler and Ribbentrop displayed total disinterest for Arab aspirations, Hitler by rejecting the Grand Mufti's request for recognition of the independence of the Arab countries, and Ribbentrop by concluding a pact with Count Ciano designating the Arab countries as a priority sphere for Italian interests... It can be said that in the Second World War the Arab movement made more concerted attempts to exploit Germany than did Germany to exploit the Arab movement."[41] This was his central conclusion (see his final remarks in document 3).

Then, Fritz Grobba underlined, since Hitler was at the peak of power after the fall of Paris 1940, he would have done better to engage British troops at their softest spot, in the Afro-Asiatic region. All this "war by troops" and "war by riots" aimed at using Islam for military and political aims. Grobba claimed, it went on with the help of Arab nationalist leaders as the Grand Mufti of Jerusalem Hajj Amīn al-Husainī and the exiled Iraqi Prime Minister Rashīd ʿAlī al-Kailanī, the Iraqi whose short reign in Baghdad was the "missed chance" for Germany to organize the next war on British influenced territory and at the same time cutting off the route to India.[42]

In short, Russia as the next theater of war was a mistake; the Middle East would have been a better choice. Fritz Grobba explained his thesis: "The Iraq conflict offered Germany a unique opportunity to gain a foothold behind the British frontline in the Middle East from which to launch a very effective pincer operation against Egypt and the Caucasus. Successful German operations in Iraq and Egypt would have opened the way to India and, by posing a serious threat to India, would have created favorable conditions for an agreement with England.... This opportunity was not recognized in time by influential policy makers at the Foreign Office and the Army High Command, and was, due in part to their opposition to Hitler, consciously not seized upon. The lack of understanding of the Middle East on the part of high-level German military leaders and the opportunities arising from exploiting the indigenous movements for the German war strategy had already come to the fore in the First World War."[43]

Moreover, Fritz Grobba revealed details of the Foreign Office's payments to Muslim nationalists like Amīn al-Husainī and Rashīd ʿAlī al-Kailanī. For them the Foreign Office released a declaration of German sympathy for the Arab independence on October 21, 1940.[44] The Foreign Office paid or established several Islamic institutions like the Pan-Islamic weekly *Islam* in Switzerland, the Central Islamic Institute in Berlin, and the Dresden-based "Mullah School" for the training of Islamic leaders for troops and for the planned Greater Turkestan.[45]

Basically, the talk of the "missed opportunity"[46] in the Middle East was an old theme from World War I as Germans wondered why they had lost the war. Some used to argue that having attacked the heavily fortified French at Verdun in 1916 was the big mistake. Instead they should have turned against weaker spots in Southeastern Europe to advance to the borders of India. Nevertheless, Germany continued its policy of using Islam for jihad.[47] In this regard Hitler acknowledged in his final days: "A bold policy of friendship with Islam," he lamented, "had still been possible until 1941, stopping the war against England: London could manage its Empire, and Berlin would eradicate Bolshevism."[48]

However, Grobba was also responsible for this Middle Eastern policy.[49] But after 1939 Germany had no longer diplomatic representations in the Arab region. The only areas that remained open to Germany were Turkey, and after the fall of France, the Vichy-controlled territories like Syria,[50] and, for a short time during the spring of 1941, Iraq.

When Fritz Grobba returned to Berlin from Baghdad, he drafted several foreign policy plans for the Arab region in his capacity, from February 1942 on, as plenipotentiary for Arab countries and head of the Arab Committee. Within the Foreign Office, the Arab Committee issued weekly guidelines for German radio broadcasts in Arabic. Here is an example of his style: "British propaganda is failing," Fritz Grobba argued at the end of 1942. "His Majesty's Ambassador to Madrid, Sir Samuel Hoare, praised the Anglo-Saxon crusaders against the infidels and he spoke ill of Sultan Salāh ad-Dīn." These words of the supreme Christianity, Grobba claimed, hurt not only the feelings of Muslims as allied soldiers, but also of all Muslims. One should only remember, he declared, how the British behaved in the Middle East and that they are today friends of the anti-religious Bolshevists: "Who still trusts Hoares words?"[51]

With such inflammatory Arabic broadcasts, Fritz Grobba used Islam for German propaganda. Whether it made an impact on the Allies can be gauged from two American documents. The U.S. coordinator of information originated the first document (see document 1, "Axis propaganda in the Moslem World"). This secret service was a forerunner of the Office of Strategic Services (OSS). The agency was concerned with the German-Arabic broadcasts of "Radio Zeesen," named after a village near Berlin.[52] As shown, the Arab Committee of the Foreign Office determined the content of the Arabic broadcasts. Therefore as head of the committee, Grobba was responsible for the contents. I shall return later to the second document produced by the OSS from American-British files.

The U.S. coordinator of information drew this conclusion about the German propaganda in the Muslim world at the end of 1941: "The Arabs are united on one general purpose, to free their world from the domination of French and British masters. Some Arabs are blinded to Italian imperialism and to German domination of Europe by their anxiety to get rid of the foreign control. This arises not only from a desire to play all European powers off against each other but from a naiveté which assumes that anyone who is against their masters is a friend of the Muslims. They fail to realize that, in case of a British defeat, there would be a substitution of Axis for the British or the French domination."

Regarding the targets of the propaganda, the Americans distinguished sentiments and feelings on which the Germans relied. Therefore, the anti-British sentiment has two causes: The British support of Jews in Palestine and of other minorities for the apparent purpose of dividing and ruling the Arab states and is the reluctance of Britain to grant independence to mandated territories. This made it easy for Axis propaganda to stir up Arab nationalist sentiments. On the other hand, the anti-American sentiment resulted from expressed sympathies of American officials with political Zionism in Palestine and America's increasingly close alliance with Britain. All these factors, the Americans concluded, were fully exploited by Radio Zeesen in broadcasts to the Near East and India.

In the anti-Jewish feeling, maintained the American coordinator, anti-Semitism had an important effect on the Arabs. There could be no doubt that the situation created by the Zionist program in Palestine caused the position of Jews to deteriorate throughout the Arab world. There were too many Jews in Palestine and abroad who adhered to this attitude, according to William B. Ziff:[53] "The Jews are entering Palestine by divine right and intend to make the Arabs go back to the desert where they came from." Radio Zeesen had recently been reading anti-Jewish passages from the Koran, emphasizing that the Jews are the enemies of Islam.

The American analysis of the German-Arabic propaganda also elaborates on anti-French and anti-Bolshevik feelings. All this, the co-ordinator of information concluded, appealed to conservative Muslims from Morocco to India. The acquisition of independence by Iraq and Egypt only after years of rebellion convinced Arabs that force was the only means by which they could extract from the British what they regarded as their rights. An illustration of the strength of this attitude was the Arab population's support of the Mufti Amīn al-Husainī, who was the apostle of force against the British. What success the Axis powers had in playing to that state of mind could be judged from the fact that the Mufti was now in Berlin. Recently Radio Zeesen had been playing up the alleged suppression of Muslim minorities in Russia (a British ally at the time); another curious anti-British blast from Zeesen accused the British of being pagans like pre-Islamic Arabs and thus the natural enemies of Islam. The announcement that Britain was stripping Arab countries and India of food is often repeated by Zeesen, which added that Britain meant to sacrifice millions of Indian and Arab lives in a vain attempt to resist the Axis. All in all, we can see here that Grobba's Arab Committee had an impact, especially through the German-Arabic broadcasts into the Muslim world.[54]

I turn now to the second document that illustrates here the impact of Fritz Grobba's activities to the Allies. A secret communication, it was circulated within the OSS. It reflects the indirect impact of Grobba's propaganda and the Allies' reaction. The most critical time for the Middle East was between mid-1940 and mid-1942. British troops capitulated in at-Tubruq and General Erwin Rommel advanced with his German-Italian troops into Egypt. Then, the (Anglo-American) Joint Psychological Warfare Committee discussed the problem of how to use Islam and its leading figures for warfare in North Africa.

One member of the Warfare Committee suggested enlisting the legendary leaders ʿAbd al-Karīm of Morocco and Idrīs as-Sanūsī of Libya and Tripolitania. He reminded the members of the Warfare Committee that in World War I German propaganda was not totally unsuccessful, at least as far as stirring up trouble among the Muslim Berber tribes who resisted Spanish and French penetration is concerned. According to the document, the Warfare Committee concluded: "Under the tutelage of the United Nations, and more especially that of the United States, these two [Arab leaders, ʿAbd al-Karīm and Idrīs as-Sanūsī] can make the Mediterranean safe for the Allies. Equally important is the influence that such a move will have throughout the Muslim world. From India to the Atlantic, Allah will be praised, and the Allies will receive the plaudits and the support of the faithful."[55]

The head of the OSS, William J. Donovan, approved further investigation into this project, whereas General Kroner pointed out the possible far-reaching effects, especially the possibility of a Christian-Muslim war. Thus, General Wedemeyer, chief of the Strategy and Policy Group of the War Department at the Pentagon, was very reluctant to submit the proposal of using the two Arab leaders to General Dwight D. Eisenhower. It was only when intelligence of the Mufti Amīn al-Husainī's service to the Axis became known that the OSS looked for a counterpart to the Mufti on the allied side. But this was not an easy task since not every Arab leader could have claimed direct descent from the Prophet Muhammad, as the Mufti did. Moreover, the former American Military Attaché to Cairo referred to the Mufti in mid-May 1941 as a religious authority and the "greatest leader of the Arab peoples alive." General Bonner F. Fellers, who was also an advisor to the OSS, did evaluate the possible results of the Mufti declaring a Holy War for the Axis: it would be an anti-Jewish, not a religious war. Amīn al-Husainī was a religious figure turned political, concluded the General.[56]

But the discussion within the OSS and the suggested choice of ʿAbd al-Karīm as a potential asset for the Allies brought up a really big question: "Will he be of use to the war effort, or will his release be like that of a Jinnee out of the magic bottle?" The German Islam policy as a part of the Middle East policy and Fritz Grobba's propaganda apparently pushed the Allies toward a matching policy, not only defining a nonreligious war in religious terms, but adopting a concept similar to that of "war by proxy." Fortunately, it did not come to that, nor did such a policy determine the Allies' actions. Max von Oppenheim's jihad concept, born in World War I and forwarded by him again in 1940, was further developed by Fritz Grobba for using Islam for political aims. It remained, at least until 1945, a concept made in Germany.

Conlusions

German politicians used the Eastern Question for their secondary peace and primary war policies in the Middle East. It was also a tool for Berlin to gain a central position from which to manipulate the alliances of other European neighbors, thus to mediate or facilitate their disputes in that region. The policy was based on three main pillars: Maintenance of the status quo, renunciation of any territorial acquisitions, and the diplomacy of mediation.

The politicians in Berlin came to realize that a peace web in the "German world policy" would have to be established at the edges of Europe, especially in the Balkans and in the Middle East. Nevertheless,

Kaiser Wilhelm's policy, including his scheme to use Islam to instigate a war by troops and war by riots, failed. It was a ruthless policy that would incite others through religious propaganda without much German effort or expense.

This was the kind of thinking in which Fritz Grobba was educated. A devoted envoy to the Middle East for twenty-five years, he pursued a more subtle approach toward using Islam for political purposes. But his efforts did not pay off. As before, Muslims remained in World War II thinking subjects. While some followed his tactic, the best[57] kept aloof from the proposed proxy war by minds, troops, and riots. Grobba drew about this a frank, and to a certain degree self-critical picture in his report for the U.S. Army in 1957. But he widened the magic bottleneck, tempting the Allies to do the same. That Jinnee would eventually turn against them: Natives directed the same tool against the infidels. But the resistance of the Allies, including natives, spared the Middle East from a brutal experience.

Some questions and tasks remain. What did the Americans do with the studies gathered by Franz Halder? Did Fritz Grobba's knowledge have an impact? Did it in some way touch or influence the new shaping of the American Middle Eastern[58] policy after the Suez war? Furthermore, how did West Germany use Grobba's experiences in building her Middle Eastern institutions and intelligence services in the fifties and sixties?

On the other side of the divide, how did the East Germans react to this policy and to Fritz Grobba's new activities, such as his attempt to establish a German-Arab Friendship Society in 1958[59] or his visits to several Arab capitals, among them Baghdad in September 1963? Did the Israelis watch him closely, and was there even any kind of cooperation, as some suggested?[60] How influential was Grobba's legacy for the German Cold War in the Middle East, for the main conflict there, and for the role of Islam in the foreign policy?

For Fritz Grobba, a primary German Middle Eastern peace policy was never realized. The Republic of Weimar had to obey the Treaty of Versailles, and Nazi Germany ultimately switched to a primary war policy aimed at world hegemony. After 1945 the chances for a primary peace policy vanished with a global Cold War and with shooting wars in the Middle East. Both Germanies were occupied, not sovereign states free to pursue a unilateral Middle Eastern policy. Whereas Bonn followed a Washingtonian Middle Eastern policy, East Berlin toed the line of the Kremlin. Both power blocs made the Middle East a battlefield for unsolved European problems.[61]

Since the fall of the Iron Curtain in 1989 and with Germany and Europe unified, there is, for the first time since 1871, a chance for a genuine primary German Middle Eastern peace policy. But it is uncertain whether or not the capabilities will developed for military intervention. Challenges to Berlin's new approach to the Middle East and conflicts with Washington are very likely. In a positive sense, Berlin has to reposition itself in Europe and towards the transatlantic alliance.

The field is still open to researchers. For example, a comprehensive study remains to be written on the United States, the Middle East, and Nazi Germany that will also shed light on a period of acute German awareness of the Orient and the Middle East, the German Orient founding years between 1884 and 1914.[62] This was a time when Germany intensified its relations to the Middle East at all levels.

The study "P-207," in which Fritz Grobba and two former generals, Hellmuth Felmy and Walter Warlimont, outlined their Middle Eastern experiences should be edited and made available in print. As Franz Halder underlined, the two former German generals had this message for the U.S. Army in the mid-1950s: An effective Middle Eastern policy requires experienced experts with insider knowledge based on their knowledge of regional languages, developed and ready means of intervention, and a well-placed secret service.

It is not unlikely that Fritz Grobba was asked to write a similar report during his ten-year imprisonment in the Soviet Union. If this report could be located somewhere in Moscow, a comparison could be made between his report to the Russians and that to the Americans.

Finally, it is high time for a biography of Dr. Fritz Grobba that will take full account of Middle Eastern sources and of the life of his remarkable deputy in Baghdad, Dr. Günther Pawelke. He was also not a member of the Nazi party and became in the early fifties the first West German Ambassador to Cairo.[63] Their lives would provide a unique glimpse into German Middle Eastern policies between 1886 and 1976, from Imperial Germany to the Weimar Republic to Nazi Germany and to the Federal Republic. Both were raised in the German tradition of not seeking colonies or making territorial claims in that region, but working to maintain the status quo. Thus, Germany stands out among the European powers. Moreover, it mediated disputes between her neighbors over areas on the periphery of Europe.

Grobba faithfully executed this Middle Eastern policy within the changing frameworks of a secondary peace and a primary war policy. As a devoted civil servant with great affinity for the people and culture of the Middle East, his struggle for a genuine primary peace policy was never realized. Instead he played a key role in promoting a concept of proxy war by Islamic riots and units, or war by revolution in the enemy's hinterland, that was truly made in Germany.

When Generals Felmy and Warlimont concluded their study MS # P-207 in late 1955, the veteran Orient expert of the German Foreign Office and former envoy to Iraq, Dr. Fritz Grobba, had just returned to West Germany from imprisonment in the Soviet Union. His absence had been painfully noted during work on the study since it was clear that, due to his personal experience, he must have the most profound knowledge of the political circumstances of the subject matter. Because he was in poor health after ten years of imprisonment, it was only in the spring of 1956 that it was possible to interview him.

As soon as his condition permitted, Dr. Grobba took on the task of reviewing the report by Generals Felmy and Warlimont from a political perspective and to supplement it where necessary. The result of his work has been added in its original version to the study MS # P-207 as a supplement. Besides the material in the list of sources, the author had available to him personal notes that had been safeguarded in Berlin during his imprisonment. However, it is hardly surprising that his commentary, in part, bears the mark of very personal character.

Document 2. Foreword by former General Franz Halder to Fritz Grobba's supplement of the study "MS # P-207" by former Generals Felmy and Warlimont for the U.S. Army, translated by Brigitte M. Goldstein.

According to its original conception, the study MS # P-207 was to touch on political matters inasmuch as they helped to make clear the concept "Arab nationalist movements" in order to highlight the atmosphere in which the inadequate and unsuccessful military efforts on the part of the Germans were undertaken. Dr. Grobba's original report essentially remains within this framework and includes valuable additions and clarifications from his personal experiences to the facts uncovered by Generals Felmy and Warlimont. It explains especially the lack of interest and understanding on the part of the highest-level German leadership for the Arab question and shows the personal and organizational inadequacies of the German leadership. Here it is necessary to bear with an occasional discussion of details that reaches far beyond the subject and is colored by a very personal perspective. The details the author contributes to the Arab point of view are very informative with regard to furthering an understanding of the internal tensions within the Arab world and the Arabic national character as manifested in the actions of the main players involved.

The critical reader will, under the impression of these descriptions, be able to meet the depiction of the reticence on the part of the policy-making German agencies and personalities with some understanding of the Arab question and will regard the author's overall assessment as laid down in the first paragraph of his concluding observations (next page [document 3, "Grobba's final remarks"]) with some reservations. The statement by General Warlimont (page 60) cited in the supplement, that none of the studies on the operations of the German army or those of the Tank Commander Rommel mention anything about a possible exploitation of the Arab nationalist movements, is quite true. But it must be added that the Higher Command of the Wehrmacht (OKW) under Hitler's influence had reserved for itself all decisions on broad policy questions and jealously guarded against any intrusion into its sphere of any proposals and suggestions by Rommel's Tank Command (AOK).

Signed: Franz Halder [1957]

Document 2, continued

The Iraq conflict offered Germany a unique opportunity to gain a foothold behind the British frontline in the Middle East from which to launch a very effective pincer operation against Egypt and the Caucasus. Successful German operations in Iraq and Egypt would have opened the way to India and, by posing a serious threat to India, would have created favorable conditions for an agreement with England. Churchill writes about the Iraq conflict: "Hitler certainly rejected a brilliant opportunity to gain a great prize in the Middle East with a minimum of investment."[1]

This opportunity was not recognized in time by influential policy makers at the Foreign Office and the Army High Command, and was, due in part to their opposition to Hitler, consciously not seized upon. The lack of understanding of the Middle East on the part of high-level German military leaders and the opportunities arising from exploiting the indigenous movements for the German war strategy had already come to the fore in the First World War. The then German commander of the Sinai front, General Kreß von Kressenstein, writes in his book[2]: "How much we still lack at the beginning of the war any recognition that the modern war is fought not alone by soldiers, but also through a close cooperation of all departments, can be seen from the fact that nobody at the German embassy in Constantinople informed me, before I took over my command in the Arabic provinces, that an Arab question existed which influenced to a high degree the internal politics of Turkey, and that I too did not think about requesting the information from the embassy."[2]

And Churchill writes in his book about the First World War that Falkenhayn had made a fateful error at the end of the summer of 1916 by attacking the strongest enemy in its strongest spot (Verdun). If he had instead turned against his weak opponents in Southeastern Europe, he could have advanced to the borders of India with 15 to 20 divisions, whereby he would have breached the blockade of Germany, tied down entire British and Indian armies in Egypt, Mesopotamia, and India, and could have spread

Document 3. Fritz Grobba's final remarks in his supplement to "MS # P-207" [1957], translated by Brigitte M. Goldstein.

the glory of the German eagle and the feeling of coming changes among the peoples of Asia.[3]

With regard to the Second World War, General Warlimont states in his report: "As all the more peculiar, it remains to note the fact that in the numerous surviving studies of the operations of the High Command of the Army as well as of Tank Commander Rommel no single mention is made anywhere of the Arabs' sympathies for the German cause, let alone of the exploitation of the Arab indigenous movement."[4]

The chief of the foreign counterintelligence department, Admiral Canaris, due to his opposition to Hitler, failed to provide the German High Command with information that could have served as a basis for strategic planning.

The policy-making authorities of the Foreign Office were only interested in a policy with regard to Europe and North America, not in the Middle East, let alone in the the Arab world. Furthermore, State Secretary Weizsäcker, Under State Secretary Woermann, and Ambassador Hentig, as opponents to Hitler, also opposed the expansion of the war to the Arabic sphere.

It is true that "no German Lawrence appeared who would have been up to the great task on the basis of personal knowledge and strength."[5] But the following must be taken into consideration:

1. Lawrence as a personality is very controversial;[6]

2. Lawrence's importance was more in the area of literature than in the military and political;

3. Lawrence had a wealth of gold and arms at this disposal without which he would not have been able to make any headway among the Bedouins of Hedjaz;

4. Behind him stood the intelligent and powerful Churchill, while the German civil servants who spoke in favor of the Arabs were called "amateur

Document 3, continued

diplomats" by State Secretary Weizsäcker and "Arabomans" by the Under State Secretary.[7]

Hitler and Ribbentrop displayed total disinterest for Arab aspirations, Hitler by rejecting the Grand Mufti's request for recognition of the independence of the Arab countries, and Ribbentrop by concluding a pact with Count Ciano designating the Arab countries as a priority sphere for Italian interests.[8]

The Arab movement emerged from the Second World War greatly strengthened. Several Arab countries, which were still under the Mandate or colonies, gained their independence at the end of the war (Syria, Lebanon, Jordan, Tunis, and Morocco). Egypt freed itself from British military occupation. A strong bond for the Arab movement constitutes a common hostility toward Israel, the common interest for Algeria in its fight for independence, and the feeling of solidarity with Nasser.

The Arabs' sympathies for Germany meanwhile were further strengthened, since the Germans were the Arabs' brothers in arms during the Second World War, and since German blood was shed on Arab soil.

It can be said that, during the Second World War, the Arab movement made more concerted attempts to exploit Germany than did Germany to exploit the Arab movement.

Notes:

1. Cited in Franz von Papen, *Der Wahrheit eine Gasse*, p. 540.
2. "With the Turks to the Suez Canal," p. 31.
3. Winston S. Churchill, *The World Crisis, 1916–1918*, part I, p. 79.
4. Warlimont, p. 154.
5. Ibid., 181,
6. Compare Richard Aldington, *The Case of T. E. Lawrence*.
7. Von Weizsäcker, *Erinnerungen*, p. 335, 35.
8. Ibid., 65; Warlimont, p. 133.

Notes

1. For the state of the literature see Wolfgang G. Schwanitz, *Gold, Bankiers und Diplomaten. Zur Geschichte der Deutschen Orientbank* (Berlin, 2002), 16–158.
2. Yehuda L. Wallach, "The Weimar Republic and the Middle East: Salient Points," in *The Great Powers in the Middle East 1919–1939*, ed. Uriel Dann (New York, 1988), 271–73; Andreas Hillgruber, "The Third Reich and the Near and Middle East, 1933–1939," in ibid., 274–82; and Bernard Lewis, "Epilogue to a Period," in ibid., 419–25.
3. Francis R. Nicosia, "Fritz Grobba and the Middle East Policy of the Third Reich," in *National and International Politics in the Middle East*, ed. Edward Ingram (London, 1986), 206–28; see also: Francis R. Nicosia, "'Drang nach Osten' Continued? Germany and Afghanistan during the Weimar Republic," in *Journal of Contemporary History* 32, no. 2 (1997): 235–57.
4. Edgar Flacker, *Fritz Grobba and Nazi Germany's Middle Eastern Policy, 1933–1942* (London, 1998); see also his bibliography 376–82.
5. Chantal Metzger, *L'Empire colonial français dans la stratégie du Troisième Reich 1936–1945* (Brussels, 2002), 2 vols.
6. Wolfgang G. Schwanitz, "Research Project on the History of the German Orientbank," *DAVO-News* (Mainz) 10 (September 1999): 61–62.
7. Gerhard Höpp, "Der Koran als 'Geheime Reichssache.' Bruchstücke deutscher Islampolitik zwischen 1938 und 1945," in *Gnosisfroschung und Religionsgeschichte*, ed. Holger Preißler and Hubert Seiwert (Marburg, 1994), 435–46; Gerhard Höpp, "Araber im Zweiten Weltkrieg—Kollaboration oder Patriotismus?" in *Jenseits der Legenden: Araber, Juden, Deutsche*, ed. Wolfgang Schwanitz (Berlin, 1994), 86–92; Gerhard Höpp, "Der Gefangene im Dreieck. Zum Bild Amin al-Husseinis in Wissenschaft und Publizistik seit 1941. Ein bio-bibliographischer Abriß," in *Eine umstrittene Figur, Hadj Amin al-Husseini, Mufti von Jerusalem*, ed. Rainer Zimmer-Winkel (Trier, 1999), 5–23; Gerhard Höpp, *Mufti-Papiere. Briefe, Memoranden, Reden und Aufrufe Amin al-Husainis aus dem Exil, 1940–1945* (Berlin, 2001).
8. For a discussion of guidelines and paradigms see Wolfgang G. Schwanitz, "Paradigms of the Near East policy in Bonn and East Berlin," *DAVO-News* (Mainz) 13 (February 2001): 51–55. I was inspired by L. Carl Brown's remarkable book and I tried to apply some of the rules he sets down to Germany with regard to the Middle East. See L. Carl Brown, *International Politics and the Middle East* (Princeton, N.J., 1984).
9. Wolfgang G. Schwanitz, "The U.S., the Third Reich and the Near East: The Case of Germany and Egypt," *DAVO-News* (Mainz) 8 (September 1998): 91–94.
10. Israel Gershoni, "Confronting Nazism in Egypt. Tawfīq al-Hakim's Anti-Totalitarianism 1938–1945," *Tel Aviver Jahrbuch für deutsche Geschichte* 1997: 121–50.
11. Wagīh ʿAbd as-Sādiq ʿAtīq, *Al-Jaish al-Misrī wa al-Almān fī athnaʾ al-Harb al-ʿAlamīya ath-Thanīya* [The Egyptian Army and the Germans during World War II] (Cairo, 1993).
12. Fahd Bin ʿAbdallah As-Simmārī, *Al-Malik ʿAbd al-ʿAzīz wa Almānīya 1926–1939* (King ʿAbd al-Azīz and Germany 1926–1939) (Beirut, 2001).

13. Heinz Wolter, ed., "Bismarck im Reichstag, 06.02.1988.," in *Otto von Bismarck. Dokumente seines Lebens 1815–1898*, ed. Heinz Wolter (Leipzig, 1989), 401–402.
14. For an explanation of the Eastern Question with the main focus on internal regional factors in the declining Ottoman Empire before and during World War I and on Germany's role see Efraim Karsh and Inari Karsh, *Empires of the Sand. The Struggle for mastery Mastery in the Middle East 1789–1923* (Cambridge, U.K., 1999). For a diplomatic history with main focus on the Great Powers and on extraregional factors see Gregor Schöllgen, *Imperialismus und Gleichgewicht. Deutschland, England und die orientalische Frage 1871–1914* (Munich, 2000).
15. Respecting the colonies or similar territories of other powers has been a longstanding Prussian tradition as can be seen from an order given by Friedrich Wilhelm von Brandenburg in 1680. See Ulrich Van der Heyden, *Rote Adler an Afrikas Küste* (Berlin, 2001), 15; Axel Fichtner, *Die völker- und staatsrechtliche Stellung der deutschen Kolonialgesellschaften des 19. Jahrhunderts* (Frankfurt am Main, 2002), 63–92.
16. For an overview see Donald M. McKale, *War by Revolution. Germany and Great Britain in the Middle East in the Era of World War I* (Ohio, 1998).
17. Compare "Die Nachrichtenstelle für den Orient und Max Freiherr von Oppenheim," in *Weltgeschichtliche Mosaiksplitter. Erlebnisse und Erinnerungen eines kaiserlichen Dragomans*, ed. Karl Friedrich Schabinger, Freiherr von Schowingen (Baden-Baden, 1967), 115–55.
18. For overviews about POW and case studies see Gerhard Höpp and Brigitte Reinwald, eds., *Fremdeinsätze. Afrikaner und Asiaten in europäischen Kriegen, 1914–1945* (Berlin, 2000).
19. L. Carl Brown, ed. *Imperial Legacy: The Ottoman Imprint on the Balkans and the Middle East* (New York, 1996).
20. For the special role of Turkey see Bernard Lewis, *The Emergence of Modern Turkey* (New York, 2002).
21. Fritz Grobba, *Männer und Mächte im Orient* (Göttingen, 1967).
22. But see the quite different picture that Grobba's notorious rival, Werner Otto von Hentig, drew in his review of Grobba's memoirs: "Ein Korb von Ibn Saud. Als Diplomat für Kaiser und Hitler im Nahen Osten," *Die Zeit*, 03.29.1968.
23. I wish to thank Udo Grobba of Bad Homburg for his kind explanations regarding the life of his father given to me in late August 2002.
24. Oberkommando der Wehrmacht [German High Command], Weisung [Order] 32, Dienstanweisung für Sonderstab F. (General der Flieger Felmy) [Service Order for Special Staff F.], Führer Headquarters, June 21, 1941, signed Chef des Oberkommandos der Wehrmacht, Wilhelm Keitel: "Special Staff F is the central organization responsible for all questions regarding the Arab world. It is to be consulted in all planning and strategic measures in the Arab areas."
25. U.S. National Archives II, MD (USArchII), Record Group (RG) 338, Historical Division, Headquarters, U.S. Army Europe, Record of the U.S. Army Commands, Foreign Military Studies, FMS, Mss. P-207, "German exploitation of Arab nationalist movements in World War II" by Franz Halder (introduction, 1955, 1957), Hellmuth Felmy (study 1955), Walter Warlimont (study, 1955), and Fritz Grobba (supplement, 1957), 300 pp. As a general rule, the English- and German-language

versions of the Foreign Military Studies (FMS) manuscripts for the Ethint-, A-, B-, and C-series are available on microfiche. For the P-, and T-series manuscripts, only the English-language versions are available. For the English-language version of P-207 see USArchII, RG290, 35/34/02, Box 77, 117 pp. Whereas this study of Warlimont and Felmy is available in English and on microfiche (indicated by the letter P), Grobba's supplement is not available in English nor on microfiche.

26. A first overview on "P-207" see Wolfgang G. Schwanitz, "Nahostpolitische Retrospektive Dr. Fritz Grobbas (1886–1973)," *DAVO-Nachrichten*, (Mainz) 14 (August 2001): 53–56.
27. That "MS # P-207" ("MS" for "manuscript") with Grobba's supplement is fairly unknown was seen at the German-American conference at the panel "Germany and the Middle East, 1919–1943" in Washington, D. C. in late 2001. See my report in *Orient* 42, no. 4 (2001): 585–90. Even a thorough source study on Grobba does not contain "P-207." See Edgar Flacker, *Fritz Grobba and Nazi Germany's Middle Eastern Policy, 1933–1942* (London, 1998); see his bibliography 376–82. For the only published mention on the role of Franz Halder and the existence of such studies made in the mid-fifties for the U. S. Government see "Franz Halder's Historical Division" in Wilhelm von Schramm, *Der Geheimdienst in Europa 1937–1945* (Munich, 1980), 29. He did not reveal his source, but wrote that all such studies remained unpublished. I am very grateful to Tim Mulligan of the National Archives II, and to Hans-Ulrich Seidt of the German Embassy in Washington, D. C., for their kind help in locating related studies, including "P-207." Martin Kröger mentioned recently Grobba's supplement: Martin Kröger, "Max von Oppenheim: Mit Eifer ein Fremder im Auswärtigen Dienst," in *Faszination Orient. Max von Oppenheim: Forscher, Sammler, Diplomat*, ed. Gabriele Teichmann and Gisela Völger (Köln, 2001), 107–39.
28. Supportive documents: 1. X-411: Werner Otto von Hentig's Report on Syria (Top Secret: Greater Arabia and the Situation in Syria), February 26, 1941, 6 pages.; 2. Rahn Report about the German Mission to Syria, May 9 to July 11, 1941. C-043: Report Greiner about the Supreme Command; 4. C-043: Eastern nationals in the German Army.
29. Orders given by Hitler with regard to the Near East and Middle East: "Führer-Lagebesprechungen" 1942 (deutscher Zusammendruck); "Führerweisungen," Weisung Nr. 30: "Mittelmeerkrieg: Unterstützung des Irak und der Araber 1941 (Mittlerer Orient), 23.05.1941," Nr. 32, and order "Special Mission of General Felmy."
30. "Orientierungsmappe Mittlerer Osten," August 1941 (OKL/5)."
31. "Zeittafel May 6, 1941 to February/May 1945," 101–106.
32. Paul Leverkuehn, *German Military Intelligence* (London, 1954); see also Paul Leverkuehn, *Der geheime Nachrichtendienst der deutschen Wehrmacht im Krieg* (Frankfurt am Main, 1964).
33. See the names of co-workers in "Verzeichnis der Mitarbeiter," "MS # P-207," V–VII.
34. For the situation in the Middle East until 1955 see Fritz Steppat, "Regionale Sicherheitsbestrebungen im Mittleren Osten," in his *Islam als Partner* (Würzburg, 2001), 15–54.

35. Wolfgang G. Schwanitz, "West- und ostdeutsche Bemühungen um das Aswân-Hochdamm-Projekt und die Nationalisierung der Sueskanalfirma 1956," in *125 Jahre Sueskanal. Lauchhammers Eisenguss am Nil*, ed. Wolfgang G. Schwanitz (Hildesheim, 1998), 218–240.
36. For the general archival situation see Mary Ellen Reese, *Der deutsche Geheimdienst. Organisation Gehlen* (Berlin, 1992).
37. USArchII, RG 338, FMS, "P-207," Fritz Grobba, "Die deutsche Ausnutzung der arabischen Eingeborenenbewegung im Zweiten Weltkrieg," with an introduction by General Franz Halder, "Supplement" (Stuttgart, 1957), 17.
38. USArchII, RG 338, FMS, "P-207," Grobba, ibid., 37–38, 81; "However, Hitler opponents State Secretary von Weizsäcker, Undersecretary of State Woermann, and Ambassador von Hentig were opposed to an expansion of the war to the Arab areas."
39. USArchII, RG 338, FMS, "P-207," Grobba, ibid., 81: "The policy makers at the Foreign Office were only interested in Europe and North America, not in the Middle East, let alone the Arab world."
40. Nicosia, *Fritz Grobba*, 224.
41. USArchII, RG 338, FMS, "P-207," Grobba, ibid., 81–82.
42. For the Axis powers and India see also Jan Kuhlmann, *Subhas Chandra Bose und die Indienpolitik der Achsenmächte* (Berlin, 2003).
43. USArchII, RG 338, FMS, "P-207," Grobba, ibid., 79.
44. Gerhard Höpp, "Nicht aus 'Alî zuliebe, sondern aus Hass gegen Mu'awîya.' Zum Ringen um die 'Arabien-Erklärung' der Achsenmächte 1940–1942," *Asien, Afrika, Lateinamerika* 27 (1999): 569–87.
45. USArchII, RG 338, FMS, "P-207," Grobba, ibid., 69, 73.
46. For a plausible argument against the "missed chance" see Andreas Hillgruber, *Third Reich and Middle East*, 274–82.
47. For Jihad in general see: Rudolph Peters, *Jihad in Classical and Modern times* (Princeton, N. J., 1996). In particular see Herbert Landolin Müller, *Islam, gihâd (Heiliger Krieg) und Deutsches Reich* (Frankfurt am Main, 1991).
48. Jochachim C. Fest, *Hitler. Eine Biographie* (Berlin, 1997), 1011.
49. For Grobba's positions in the hierarchy of the Foreign Office and Middle East related commissions see USArchII, T120, roll 28, serial 41, frames 28202ff.; Politische Abteilung, U.St.S.Pol.Nr.959, Aufzeichnung über Fragen des Vorderen Orients, Geheim, Berlin, 06.11.1941, Anhang "Sonderaufträge für die Angelegenheiten des Vorderen Orients" (Keppler, Grobba, von Hentig, and colleagues).
50. USArchII, RG 338, Chief of Military History, Foreign Studies Branch, DC, X-411, Hentig Report on Syria, Greater Arabia and the situation in Syria, February 26, 1941.
51. USArchII, T120, roll 392, serial 930, frames 297916ff., special files of Envoy Ettel who was attached for services to the Grand Mufti of Jerusalem, Arabien-Komitee, Gesandter Dr. F. Grobba, 38. Meeting, December 3, 1942, topics of the talks November 26 to December 2, 1942, topic 9: "The Christian Thesis of English Propaganda," 5–6.
52. Radio Zeesen was the German shortwave broadcasting station near Berlin-Königswusterhausen. The Propaganda Ministry had supervised the station since April

1933; in September 1939 it came under the direction of a department of the Foreign Office headed by Ernst Wilhelm Bohle. It had several transmitters in Athens and Tunis from 1940 to 1942. Among the Arab native speakers was also Habīb Bīrgība, later the president of Tunisia. See also Herbert Schröder, *Ein Sender erobert die Welt* (Essen, 1940).

53. The text here, see the following footnote, mentions William B. Ziff's book, *The Rape of Palestine* (New York and Toronto, 1938).
54. For an American analysis of the content of the German Arabic broadcasts guided by Grobba see USArchII, RG 165, Box 3061, Coordinator of Information, Washington, D.C., December 23, 1941, "Axis Propaganda in the Muslim World," 6 pages.
55. USArchII, RG 218, Box 59, Joint Psychological Warfare Committee, 'Abd al-Karim of the Rif, JPWC 21st meeting, 03.08.1942, secret note from Secretary A.H. Othank, August 1, 1942, discussions, memoranda to Generals Handy and Smith, and investigation request to O.S.S., the Joint Chiefs of Staff, secret, Washington, D.C., August 4, 1942.
56. USArchII, RG 165, Box 3055, To Secretary of War, State Department, "Amin el Husseiny and a Muslim Holy War" by Bonner F. Fellers, confidential, Cairo, May 19, 1941. Compare it with the description of the Grand Mufti for Hitler: USArchII, T120, roll 63, serial 71, frames 50682 ff., "Der Großmufti von Jerusalem," Berlin, November 28, 1941, signed Grobba, four pages.
57. Israel Gershoni, "Egyptian Liberalism in an Age of 'Crisis of Orientation': *Al-Risāla*'s Reaction to Fascism and Nazism, 1933–39, *International Journal of Middle Eastern Studies* 31 (1999): 551–76. For mixed feelings among Egyptian officers like Anwar as-Sadat see also Bernard Lewis, *A Middle East Mosaic* (New York, 2000), 314–16.
58. Bernard Lewis, "The United States, Turkey and Iran," in *The Middle East and the United States. Perceptions and Politics*, ed. Shaked Haim and Itamar Rabinovich (New Brunswick, N. J., 1980), 165–80.
59. For the German-Arab Society of East Berlin see Wolfgang G. Schwanitz, "Streng vertraulich? Aus den Akten der Deutsch-Arabischen Gesellschaft 1958–1969," in *Berlin-Kairo: Damals und heute.* (Berlin, 1991), 85–104.
60. Brentjes saw an early cooperation between the secret services of Israel and the Federal Republic of Germany, on the German side often with the same cast of characters as the one active before 1945 with an old spirit; see Burchard Brentjes, *Geheimoperation Nahost. Zur Vorgeschichte der Zusammenarbeit von Mossad und BND* (Berlin, 2001). For the Middle East-related continuity of personnel at the Foreign Office before and after 1945 see my review "Biographical Encyclopaedia of the German Foreign Office, 1871–1945," *Orient* 43, no. 1 (2002): 120–23.
61. For the topic on making the Middle East a battlefield for unsolved European problems during the Cold War, see for the German case Wolfgang G. Schwanitz, *Deutsche in Nahost 1946–1965: Sozialgeschichte nach Akten und Interviews* (Frankfurt am Main, 1998), vols. 1 and 2.
62. For an explanation and timetable of Deutsche Orientgründerjahre see August Bebel, *Die Mohammedanisch-Arabische Kulturperiode* (Berlin, 1999), 8, 52, 180–83, 188.

63. Wolfgang G. Schwanitz, "Doppelte deutsche Gesandte in Kairo 1953–1963," in *Misr wa Almāniya fī al-Qirnain at-tāsiʾa ʿashr wa al-ʾIshrīn fī dhauʾ al-Wathāʾiq* [Egypt and Germany in the Nineteenth and Twentieth Centuries as Reflected in the Archives], ed. Wajīh ʿAbd as-Sādiq ʿAtīq and Wolfgang G. Schwanitz (Cairo, 1998), 158–215; for Pawelke see also *DAVO-News* December 2002: 16, 62–63.

Figure 8. The Ibn Saʿūd: King ʿAbd al-ʿAzīz (1880–1953), who built the kingdom of Saudi Arabia

German-Saudi Relations and Their Actors on the Arabian Peninsula, 1924–1939

UWE PFULLMANN

Overall Conditions

By actors I mean here all the persons who were politically and economically active exercising an important influence on the development of German-Saudi relations. On the Saudi side was the reigning actor King ʿAbd al-ʿAzīz II (1880–1953), who figures in the popular literature generally under the not quite correct clan name Ibn Saʿūd. Germany was not among European countries with a distinct interest in the Near East. In contrast to the traditional colonial powers Great Britain and France, Germany, because of the late date of its founding as a unified nation in 1871, established its influence in the region toward the end of the nineteenth century. In doing so, German business circles concentrated primarily on the Ottoman Empire, whose possessions in Asia were regarded as absolutely necessary for the expansion of German influence. A high point in this development was the construction of the Hijaz and Baghdad railroads.

Even though the Ottoman Empire's support of the Central Powers—Germany, Austria-Hungary, Bulgaria, and at first also Italy—did not derive from absolute necessity, it was the end result of decades-long military contacts between German and Ottoman officers. This active policy of economic penetration and political influence ended with the German surrender at the end of World War I in 1918. Regarding German policies toward Arab lands, it is impossible to speak of continuity from Imperial Germany to the Weimar Republic and the Nazi regime, in part because of the late awakening of Arab nationalism. This is the subject of investigation of the present essay.

German-Saudi relations from 1924 to 1939 can be divided into four periods. In the first phase, 1924 to 1929, both sides put out unofficial feelers. The second phase extended from the conclusion of the German-Saudi Friendship Treaty in 1929 to the opening of a German consulate in Jidda in 1931 until its dissolution in 1934. The third phase, 1934 to 1937, was characterized by renewal of unofficial contacts. In the fourth phase, 1937 to 1939, German prestige in the region rose because Germany regained a position as a world power under the Nazis. King ʿAbd al-ʿAzīz II's assumption of power in the Hijaz marked the beginning of German-Saudi relations. The king did not play as active a role during the First World War as Grand Sharīf Husain and his sons, who were favorably disposed toward Germany. As Winston Churchill, the British colonial minister at the time, put it: "This Arab potentate gained support, not so he would do something in return, but so that he would do nothing." The hope that a stable government in the Hijaz and considerable profits from pilgrimages would increase the demand for German products prepared the ground for economic relations between Germany and Saudi Arabia.

Germany considered British interests in its Middle East foreign policy, which was guided by concerns that any reduction of British hegemony in the Near East might decrease Great Britain's moderating influence on the demands for reparations by France and Belgium. This basic direction of German foreign policy persisted until 1937. This was the reason for the German Foreign Office's clear, political restraint in the Near and Middle East. The Saudi government's insolvency in the wake of the world economic crisis at the end of the 1920s caused the almost complete collapse of German-Saudi economic and political relations. The German consulate in Jidda was closed in early 1934.

The German actors in the region operated against this general background. Their economic interests were narrowly delimited by these general political conditions. Nevertheless, several of the German actors tried to overcome the obstacles in order to inflict on Germany's former opponents in the First World War as much damage as and wherever possible. Germany's primary interests remained limited to Continental Europe, despite offers of oil concessions. Also within this time period, the Hashemite-Saudi conflicts were decided in favor of the Wahabi ruler ʿAbd al-ʿAzīz II, who strengthened his preeminence on the Arabian Peninsula with the conquest of the Hijaz. Arab actors were primarily concerned with importing arms and technology from Germany as well as with gaining international recognition of the countries they represented. Generally unknown even today are, for example, reports from the last months and weeks of the Hashemite kingdom of Hijaz. Here is a new in-depth examination of the interstate relations between the double kingdom of Hijaz and Najd—that is, its successor state Saudi Arabia—and Germany, which extend from arms deliveries and oil concessions to the very subjective, but very intimate and informed, reports by the German engineer Kurt Krokowski. In 1993 an essay appeared in Arabic about German archive documents pertaining to German-Saudi relations.[1] The writings of Helmut Mejcher are another informative source.[2]

The End of the Hashemite Kingdom of Hijaz

The end of the First World War introduced far-reaching political changes to the Arabian Peninsula. France and Great Britain divided the Arab prey left over from the bankrupt Ottoman Empire under the guise of Mandate rule. On September 26, 1924, Ibn Saʿūd's soldiers occupied the town of al-Hadda, a pilgrim station before Mecca. The notables of the town, ulema and merchants, demanded, in the morning of October 2, 1924, that King Husain abdicate in favor of his son ʿAlī. At first, Husain had no intention of abdicating. In typical despotic manner, he abused the deputation and chased them from his house. The customs director of Jidda, Muhammad Tawīl, the only man whom Husain still trusted, telephoned Husain and urged him to abdicate. The delegation that had been chased from the palace meanwhile stirred up public opinion against Husain; they mobilized the street against the unpopular ruler. The crowd in front of the government building grew larger and louder. Husain now realized that his time in Mecca had expired. He abdicated in the evening of October 3 and designated his oldest son ʿAlī as his successor. Husain loaded his possessions and the British subsidies paid in gold sovereigns and left for Jidda.

One of the first actors in the period of 1924 to 1925 was the German diplomat Hans-Joachim von Bassewitz (b. 1898). In August 1925, he was engaged in conversations with King ʿAlī in Jidda and was thus one of the few eyewitnesses to the end of the Hashemite kingdom of Hijaz. This is how he characterized the last ruler: "King Ali, the oldest son of King Husain, is in his forties, he is gifted with inexhaustible work energy and a quick mind, very well educated, his manners are very gracious and, on closer acquaintance, he displays pleasant character traits. He lacks both the strength and the brutality as well as the avarice which are attributed to his father; he is popular among his entourage and the people, he has personal courage and understanding for the modernization of the country. Meanwhile he is still an absolute ruler—and behind him the grandees of the country."[3] Bassewitz traveled in Turkey, Egypt, and Hijaz. From 1926 on, he was the secretary of the German Oriental Society.

Another German and retired major of the aviator corps, Hans Steffen, gave this estimate of the strength of the Hashemite Hijaz army: 1,500 soldiers and 2,500 Bedouins.[4] His Berlin company for airship articles and war materiel delivered war materiel worth 500 thousand gold marks to King ʿAlī's army.[5] He also advised Husain's Turkish officers in matters of military war strategies. His "Notes about Arabia" are very interesting as they describe the last weeks of Jidda besieged by Sultan[6] ʿAbd al-ʿAzīz:

> We had in the city about 3,000 Yemenite soldiers (mercenaries) and 3,500 Bedouins from Hijaz and Transjordan. The department of the general staff under a former Turkish general staff officer was totally incompetent. To begin with, I had the town fortified according to modern principles. Ibn Saoud attacked twice and was repelled each time with heavy casualties. His Bedouins stood no chance against field fortifications. Then I suggested going on the counterattack and I worked out a plan of attack. The conditions in the besieged town were unbearable. Hundreds of inhabitants died every

day in epidemics. I myself contracted malaria, dysentery, and scurvy. Any health care had to wait for weeks. The soldiers went unpaid. An attack remained their only salvation. But the king did not dare make the move. He forcibly prevented my departure on an Arab sailboat. I managed to send a radio telegram via a steamboat passing Jidda to King Husain in Aqaba. I described my situation and requested to be relieved and his help. Two weeks later, Husain sent one of his steamboats to come and get me—at the same time with the order to familiarize myself with the coastline of Hijaz along the way. I left Jidda and stopped over in the ports of Rabigh (Rābigh), Jambo (Yanbuʾ al-Bahr), and el Wejd (al-Wadj) in order to undertake, during shorter or longer stays, excursions on horseback with the help of Bedouin tribes to the inner coastline.[7]

Steffen spent three weeks in al-ʿAqaba where he and King Husain worked out plans for a new campaign against Sultan ʿAbd al-ʿAzīz II. He was to be attacked from the north by an army with modern equipment. But this did not come about. British intelligence received messages of Husain's activities and the British government dispatched two warships to al-ʿAqaba which took Husain into exile on Cyprus.

First German Contacts with ʿAbd al-ʿAzīz

German relations with the new ruler of the Hijaz began on an unspectacular note. The determining factor for seeking economic contact with ʿAbd al-ʿAzīz II, who had been proclaimed king in December 1925, was the expectation that stable rule and the sizable income from the pilgrim traffic would raise the demand for German industrial products. The first inquiries with the Foreign Office concerning customs tariffs revealed the dilemma that not a single official German representative was present in the area of the actual Arabian Peninsula, south of the Jordan River. Even though the German embassies in Cairo and Addis Ababa, the general consulate in Jerusalem, and the consulate in Beirut issued reports about the Arabian Peninsula, a lack of information was still quite apparent. Unofficial Saudi representatives also sought contacts with Germany, of which it was rightly assumed that it was not pursuing any political goals in the area at that time. Shakīb Arslān,[8] a confidant of ʿAbd al-ʿAzīz II, sought the assistance of the former German minister resident in Istanbul, Max Freiherr von Oppenheim, in introducing the Saudi overtures into the official channel of the German Foreign Office, which Oppenheim did by forwarding Arslān's letter to the Foreign Office.

The answer makes clear the dilemma of German foreign policy in the 1920s: the fear of losing Great Britain's goodwill in the restructuring of European politics and the undermining of some of the terms of the Treaty of Versailles. Thus, Herbert von Richthofen wrote to Max von Oppenheim: "Herewith return of Chékib Arslan's letter with many thanks. The dispatch of a bacteriologist to Djidda would coincide with my wishes; I would try everything here to make the matter as pleasant as possible from our side as well. I much prefer starting out with a bacteriologist to IBN SAUD [ʿAbd al-ʿAzīz II], than with a consul. The individual would have to be really carefully selected."[9] And yet, the officials of the Foreign Office delayed recognition of ʿAbd al-ʿAzīz II on grounds that no official representative had approached the Foreign Office. As a result, Germany was left out during the European travels of Emir Faisal in October and early November 1926.[10] German officials therefore sought to explore possibilities for establishing official contacts with Saudi authorities through other friendly governments. The Swiss government's recognition of ʿAbd al-ʿAzīz II as ruler of the kingdom of Hijaz and sultan of Najd was reason enough to seek more information, and the Orient department of the Foreign Office charged German diplomats to find out in particular whether the Swiss Federal Council sought prior contacts with other powers, especially with England. For its own, internal, confidential information, the Foreign Office added that it had so far avoided a decision concerning the question of recognizing ʿAbd al-ʿAzīz II, because the question had been raised at the Office through middlemen, whose authorization to negotiate the matter seemed rather doubtful.[11]

The fact that German officials expressed so much interest was most of all a result of the desires of the German export economy, which received increasing orders and wanted to be represented in this expanding market. Obstacles to establishing diplomatic relations derived from the fact that the Saudi authorities lacked all experience in the areas of diplomacy and international law. Thus the envoy Friedrich Max Weiss wrote in a private letter to Herbert von Richthofen that the "activities of consuls and diplomats in Djidda are taking place without lawful grounding; they are tolerated, the Soviets popular (because of money)."[12]

The Swiss answer to the inquiry of the Foreign Office made clear the reservations that Europeans, with a long tradition of law, had toward the appearance of a new state. Indeed, the Federal Council answered that Swiss recognition of the government in Hijaz was prompted indeed by the entry of the Hijaz into the world postal association. The application was made by the plenipotentiary of ʿAbd al-ʿAzīz II, Hasan "Voefki" Bey. In addition, the Swiss Federal Council had made inquiries with London concerning the authenticity of the Hijaz representative's identity papers.

Meanwhile, Switzerland had no intention of setting up a diplomatic delegation in ʿAbd al-ʿAzīz's realm. On February 22, 1927, Hajj Muhammad Nāfiʿ Shalabī, a student at the Berlin Technical Institute and native of Syria, held a lecture at the German Association for Islamic Studies about a pilgrimage to Mecca and the sacrificial service on Mount ʿArafāt. Among those present at the lecture was Fritz Grobba, the German envoy to Iraq. Grobba's report indicates that according to Shalabī's point of view "Ibn Saud does not want to create a pan-Arab empire, he rather wants to pursue pan-Islamic tendencies." The offer of the Syrian throne to his son was also to serve this purpose. Grobba registered with keen attentiveness the reception of guests from Germany. "He and his presumably German[14]... traveling companion are said to have been very well received by Ibn Saud and been treated as guests. [...] They are said to have been asked frequently why Germany had not yet recognized Ibn Saud. The lecturer said he intended to participate in the pilgrimage this year again and hoped that he could bring some kind of official message to Ibn Saud. It can therefore be rightly expected that he will approach the Foreign Office with such a request."[15]

Marginal notes indicate that the Foreign Office had a problem with this kind of unconventional contact initiation whose unofficial character was quite obvious. The interest of the Foreign Office in the Hijaz under ʿAbd al-ʿAzīz was due to the German export industry's desire for opening new markets.[16] Excerpts of the voluminous reports by Weiss, the German envoy posted to Addis Ababa, concerning the demand for automobiles and tires, among other things, were passed along to the German automobile and tire manufacturers, who received them with great interest.[17] The Sharqīya Company (Being the Company of Explorers and Merchants in the Near and Middle East), was recommended as negotiating partner of German industry. Founded by Harry Sanct Bridger John Philby, the company, whose directors, located in London, were First Lieutenant A. St. John Cooke, Sir C. Butler, Major R. E. Fisher, H. L. Bromhead, and T. D. Cree, had its headquarters in Salisbury House at the London Wall. The composition of the board leads to the assumption that Sharqīya was not only involved in business transactions, but also served intelligence purposes.

The Germans too were skeptical about Philby's intentions: "It is hardly thinkable that a man with his past and ambitions should now be satisfied with the role of businessman in Jidda. He is, no doubt, there to observe the course of events and to remain close to his contact men around Ibn Saud. If this gentleman now reveals his Germanophile heart to our envoy Weiss, we should remember that, only five years ago in a book about Arabia, he found it appropriate to call us Germans Huns."[18] The lack of a diplomatic representation in Jidda forced the Foreign Office to seek information from other governments concerning customs tariffs, trade practices, and references.[19] The extraordinarily high customs tariffs fluctuated between 75 percent for tobacco, 25 percent for all woven silk fabrics, silk threads, and partial silk, 20 percent for carpets, iron, medications, red corrals, spices, coal, and so on, 17 percent for gasolin,e and 10 percent for rice, flour, grains, and other foodstuffs.[20] Initial successes in the export trade with the Hijaz led the Foreign Office to regard the region more closely. Thus, the Adam Opel Bicycle and Automobile Manufacturer was able to advise the German delegation in Addis Ababa that they were able to sell, via the firm S. Bahafzallah, two 4 PS-Four-Seat Opel Vehicles to Jidda.[21]

At first, a peculiarity of German-Saudi relations was the low interest in Germany in the dual kingdom of Hijaz and Najd. The high political esteem in which ʿAbd al-ʿAzīz II and his relative independent-mindedness were held led in due course to a rethinking on the part of the Foreign Office. The defining moment for this was, no doubt, the signing of the British-German treaty of May 20, 1927, which recognized ʿAbd al-ʿAzīz II as ruler of the Hijaz, though it left unsolved the territorial question of al-ʿAqaba-Maʾān. This reevaluation also had repercussions for German-Saudi relations. Recognition of ʿAbd al-ʿAzīz II as ruler of the Hijaz removed all fears of a potentially detrimental effect on

German-British relations. The treaty was met with loud protests by the Hashemite governments in the British Mandate areas.

Leopold Weiß, alias Muhammad Asad, Enters the Near Eastern Stage

Another German-speaking actor in Arabia during the interwar period was Leopold Weiß. He was born in 1900 in Lemberg into a Jewish family. Weiß reported about a meeting with Harry Philby, who had been living in Jidda as a merchant since 1926. Philby had resigned from his last official position as adviser to the Transjordanian government "disgusted, as he says, by the British Foreign Office's constant going back on its word, and at the same time, he tendered his resignation from the Indian Civil Service from where he originally hailed."[23] Leopold Weiß converted to Islam in 1926 and made his way to Mecca and Medina as Muhammad Asad; he was allowed to continue his travels to Riyad, where he was received by ʿAbd al-ʿAzīz II. The high esteem in which Weiß was held by the king is supposed to have prompted Harry Philby to convert to Islam as well. Weiß reports about his pilgrimage in 1927 to Mount ʿArafāt. According to his estimates, the number of foreign pilgrims reached about a hundred thousand.[24] Nothing had changed at this time regarding the trade policy's dependence on the pilgrimage. Weiß wrote a detailed report concerning this aspect to the Foreign Office.[25] In his report, Weiß also exhorted the German export trade sector to pay closer attention to the Hijaz and Najd.

According to this report, economic life in the Hijaz was dominated by Arab and Indian firms, among them twenty-one of larger size. Weiß was also active for a long time as Near East correspondent of the *Frankfurter Allgemeine Zeitung*. From 1927 to 1932, he made five pilgrimages to Mecca. Weiß alias Muhammad Asad went to India in 1932. After the partition of the country, he gained a confidential position with the new Pakistani government. He died there, highly regarded, in 1992.

Carl Rathjens Visits the Hijaz

The attempt by the German traveler Dr. Carl Rathjens[26] to obtain a visa for the Hijaz was unsuccessful at first since "the king makes such decisions in person and was for the time being in the Najd. Someone closely familiar with the Hijaz confirmed that entry was hardly ever granted lately for security reasons even for highly recommended Egyptians."[27] In the years 1927–28, Carl Rathjens was on a South Arabian expedition with Hermann von Wissmann, the results of which were published under the title "Rathjens–von Wissmann South Arabian Travels." In November 1929, Sharīf Ibrāhīm, the Moroccan general consul in Jidda, suggested to Rathjens an excursion through the Hijaz, Najrān, and Yemen. Sharīf Ibrāhīm, a lieutenant colonel during the First World War, had been a commander of Allied forces besieging Medina. He had been representing French interests in Arabia for thirty years. Pure courteousness and civility should not be excluded as a motive for this suggestion, but it is likely that he meant to arouse British distrust for German efforts in the Near East. The fact that Rathjens managed to obtain a visa after all should probably be attributed to the good offices of ʿAbd al-ʿAzīz II to further the renewal of contact with German companies. The king's efforts to quiet the internal Saudi opposition to his modernization plans required new sources of money and product deliveries. These efforts were finally sealed in 1929 with a Saudi-German friendship treaty. Rathjens noted the following: "My dear Baron (Max von Oppenheim) — my first assault on the Hijaz was repelled. [...] I managed to at least land in Jidda in the daytime. For the time being, Ibn Saud closes off his country completely against all European influences and does not admit any Europeans. Philby has been ready for two years with packed crates and still awaits permission to enter the country. I was able to film all sorts of things in Jidda despite prohibition and confiscation of all filming equipment. Thanks to the help of the Dutch consul [Daniel van der Meulen] we were also 80 km from Jidda in the Wadi Fatima, and 15 km from Mecca."[28] The cause of Rathjens' travel difficulties was the Ikhwān unrest near the Iraqi border.

The Modernization of the Twin Kingdom of Hijaz and Najd

At about the same time, Hāfiz Wahba, the foreign policy advisor of ʿAbd al-ʿAzīz II, published in the Egyptian press an invitation to German businessmen to become involved in the Hijaz. "You should not take it as flattery when I assure you: we like dealing with Germans. While other foreigners often come with a hidden political agenda, the Germans are only looking for economic advantage. We have had good experiences with them. The director of our ice factory in Jidda is a German engineer, and we recently assigned the roofing of a 700-meter-long street in the same city to a German entrepreneur."[29]

The forced modernization of the country met with resistance from the ulema. A short time before, a large number of British automobiles was delivered to King ʻAbd al-ʻAzīz.[30] Philby too was preoccupied with the enormously expanding automobile market and saw himself cheated out of a dealer's commission by Mercedes-Benz. Daimler-Benz was ordered to review the matter and to come to an agreement with Philby. However, Daimler-Benz rejected any kind of demand for a commission since the sale of the automobile was not made from Stuttgart but through a London dealer. As Daimler-Benz found out later on, the London dealer bought the vehicle under dealer conditions and when Philby later made claims to a commission in a letter, the directors of the automobile manufacturer regretted to let him know that they were unable to honor his claim since the purchase was made through a London dealership.[31] Typical for the German-Saudi relations was the high value of economic interests. But political goals and considerations held clear priority over economic considerations.

Arms Deliveries for the Druze Uprising in Syria

In the spring of 1926, Amīr Shakīb Arslān, the representative of Syrian interests at the League of Nations, contacted Hans Steffen and requested an arms delivery in order "to revive the almost defeated uprising of the Druze. I rejected the Arabs' idea to ship arms and munitions through Palestine, Syria, or Turkey to Jabal ad-Druze as out of the question and made the counter suggestion to unload in the port of Rabīgh and to transport the materiel from there, with the help of Ibn Saʻūd's camel caravan, and under his protection, through the desert to the Druze. The suggestion was accepted and then carried out by me. A few weeks later, specially selected materiel went to Rabīgh, was unloaded in the early morning hours and transported from there by several caravans of about fourteen hundred camels, which Ibn Saʻūd made available according to plan, 1,000 km through the desert to Jabal ad-Druze. This march was accomplished in four weeks. The Druze rose again and France was forced to quickly detach a considerable number of forces from Morocco in order to put down this second uprising."[32]

The support of the Druze was by no means altruistic. They occupied the key positions in Syria's grain production. King ʿAbd al-ʿAzīz felt encircled by the Hashemite Mandate areas of Transjordan and Iraq and sought to gain influence in Syria with a submissive ethnic group. However, his ally, who had been defeated by massive French troop contingents, did not get to know ʿAbd al-ʿAzīz's much praised generous hospitality.

The Druze Sultan al-Atrash was forced, after the defeat of the uprising, to go into Saudi exile. The British traveler Eldon C. Rutter described his fate: "After we had left the Wadi's-Sirhan, we passed al-Nabaq and al-Haditha, two small settlements, occupied by Druze refugees. In al-Haditha, I met the Druse chief Sultan Pasha al-Atrash, who lived in a ragged tent in abject poverty. We made our way through the green hills of Balqa and on February 5, 1930, we reached Amman where I separated from my last guide."[33]

In 1927, the already-mentioned Steffen was invited to a visit with Ibn Saʿūd in Jidda. The two met in the spring of 1928, first in Jidda and then in his camp near Shamasī (Shamasī near Mecca does not exist but there is a section of Riyad by that name), close to Mecca. The topic of discussions between Steffen and ʿAbd al-ʿAzīz II was the reorganization of the pilgrimage (for raising his money), armaments questions, and the establishment of a connection between Ras Tafari, the then-regent of Abyssinia, and ʿAbd al-ʿAzīz II, as the so-called standard bearer of the national Arab question.[34]

From 1928 on, the German engineer Kurt Krokowski sent regular letters with political and business contents to the German delegation in Cairo, which were, for the most part, passed on to the Foreign Office despite reservations. Krokowski wrote to Cairo: "Thus he (the king) is thinking particularly of the construction of a railway line Jidda-Mecca (85 km), of which it is expected that it will transport annually hundreds of thousands, probably mostly pilgrims, and many goods to Mecca. After completion of this railway, he is also considering the construction of a railway from Rabīgh to Medina."[35]

ʿAbd al-ʿAzīz II owed his seizure of power in part to the fact that the Hijaz nomadic tribesmen rejected the further development of the Hijaz railway, since it had a negative effect on the basis of their economic existence. Even though the railway was not put back into operation, the transportation of pilgrims on vehicles broke the tribes' back and caused the Ikhwān uprisings, which were put down in 1929 in the battle of Sabīla. The Ikhwān opposition was supported by Ibn Saʿūd's brother Muhammad, who sought to promote his own son, Khālid, as successor to the throne. The connection of a rival for the throne from within the same family and tribal resistance against the king's efforts of modernization gave the Ikhwān uprisings a dangerous dynamic.

In 1928, Hans Steffen participated in the arming of ʿAbd al-ʿAzīz's army. The Foreign Office was swamped with inquiries from German companies, among them the Association of the Armaments and Munitions Industry,[36] for addresses of wholesale merchants in the Hijaz.

The German-Saudi Friendship Treaty of 1929

The engineer Kurt Krokowski, meanwhile, tried, through multiple submissions, to persuade the Foreign Office to set up a diplomatic representation in Jidda. Krokowski himself sought to obtain a position as consular agent in Jidda.[37] The reply from the Foreign Office to the delegation in Cairo concerning this push was kept rather terse. The delegation was informed that, for the time being, there was no intention of opening a professional consulate or a consular agency in the Hijaz.[38]

However, the political contacts that had been established meanwhile led to a rethinking among professional diplomats. The matter of the establishment of a German foreign delegation in the Hijaz was now deemed important enough to merit reconsideration by the Foreign Office. The argument advanced was that the absence of a German representation in the Hijaz might gradually lead to an economic disadvantage there if German economic interests could only be inadequately realized.[39] The budget commission of the Foreign Office was advised to reexamine the possibility of a professional delegation in Jidda since at the moment they depended on Krokowski's "subjectively tinted reports."[40]

The first official diplomatic contacts with the kingdom of Hijaz, Najd, and territories belonging to it began with a letter from Fūʾād Hamza (acting director of the kingdom's Foreign Office) to the Foreign Office of September 29, 1928.[41] In March 1929, Germany and the kingdom of Hijaz, Najd, and territories began negotiations for a friendship treaty, article two of which provided for the establishment of diplomatic relations at a propitious moment. The plenipotentiaries on the Saudi side were Hāfiz Wahba and Shaikh Fauzān as-Sābiq, on the German side, the envoy to Egypt, Dr. Eberhard von Stohrer. The negotiations for the treaty did not go smoothly since the Saudi representatives objected to all expressions like "most favored nation," "privileges," and the like. Counselor Enno Littmann was also consulted during the discussions. Shortly before the conclusion of the negotiations, Herbert von Richthofen sent a telegraph to the German delegation with the directive: "Concerning article two: deletions requested by the Hijaz representatives not desirable, especially since only a little while ago, Persia, which cancelled existing treaties with all European nations, has expressly granted us "most favored status" in a new treaty.... However, please do not permit the treaty to fail over this."[42]

On April 26, 1929 (16 dhū'l-Qaʿda 1347 AH), the friendship treaty was signed by Stohrer, Wahba, and as-Sābiq. The conclusion of the friendship treaty with the kingdom of Hijaz was preceded by careful inquiries in London. "I request to inform senior officials in the Foreign Office and to make clear the following: Since we are aware of England's overwhelming interest in the Hijaz we did not want to be remiss in confidentially informing the British government about this matter. The logical consequences of our correspondence would in all likelihood constitute the conclusion of a very generally kept friendship treaty with the Hijaz."[43] The German ambassador's reply was not long in coming: "I informed Sir Ronald Lindsay today of the correspondence concerning the recognition of the kingdom of Hijaz and the conclusion of a trade treaty with it. Lindsay was pleasantly touched by the information and thanked me repeatedly with warm words. Factually he declared that he had not the slightest objections to the plans as presented. However, he did not seem to put too much value in the results of a trade treaty since conditions in the Hijaz are, as he says, still very disorderly."[44]

The text of the treaty was first published in June 1929 in the *Islam Echo* of the Islamic press agency of Hajj Muhammad Nafiʿī Shalabī, however, with several errors.[45]

A short while thereafter, two ships, the *Falkenfels* and the *Weissenfels,* were unloaded in Jidda. On board were three thousand rifles and three million rounds of ammunition for Ibn Saʿūd, shipped by the firm Steffen & Heymann, part via Hamburg and part via Antwerp. About this shipment Krokowski, the "man on the spot," wrote: "Unloading during the day was done in a way that the goods were covered with sugar sacks, while at night, unloading proceeded without particular measures. One day before the arrival of the *Falkenfels*, a British man-of-war apparently arrived in order to observe the unloading. The English are supposed to run motorboat patrols to observe at night every sailboat in which rifles and munitions were transported."[46] The firm Sulaiman A. Gabil in Jidda tried to gain some advantage from this arms trade by reporting the unloading of the arms deliveries to the British consulate. In a letter to the Foreign Office, Hans Steffen, co-owner of Steffen & Heymann, reported that the goods were "newly manufactured in a Polish rifle factory in Warsaw. The transport did not traverse German territory."[47] Whereupon the German Foreign Office informed the embassy in Cairo that the insurance of the shipment through Lloyds of London followed the agreement with the British Foreign Office. There was no reason, therefore, to keep the delivery a secret from the English. In a confidential report, Steffen let it be known in Cairo that he did not intend to use the aid of Kurt Krokowski in similar deliveries should they arise in the future, since the latter was not well regarded by the Hijaz government because of illegal dealings in alcohol.[48]

In August 1930, the friendship treaty between Germany and the dual kingdom of Hijaz and Najd was published in the *Reichsgesetzblatt*[49] with the following appraisal: "The largest part of the Arabian Peninsula was thereby united in one hand and, at the same time, was moved closer to one of the world trade routes, that is, the Red Sea. For us too, the country gained in importance.... The treaty has been purposely kept short and contains more programmatic agreements about the treatment of possible future diplomatic and consular representatives on the basis of mutuality and according to the principles of international law. It contains, furthermore, arrangements concerning the housing of the citizens of both countries and the exchange trade on the basis of most favored nation. The treaty contains, due to its nature as a friendship treaty, no time limitation."[50] On November 6, 1930, the ratification document was exchanged in Cairo between Germany and the kingdom of Hijaz. The ratification of the friendship treaty was announced in the *Reichsgesetzblatt* (Imperial Record).[51]

The Establishment of a German Consulate in Jidda in 1931 and Amīr Faisal's Visit to Germany in 1932

Whether the continued discussion about the Caliphate accelerated the recognition of ʿAbd al-ʿAzīz II as ruler of the Hijaz cannot be determined from the German files. It is certain, however, that ʿAbd al-ʿAzīz's advisor urged him not to take this step, especially in view of the example of King Husain. In the wake of the conclusion of the friendship treaty between Germany and the Hijaz, an optional German consulate was set up under the merchant Heinrich de Haas, whose political activities, however, were negligible. The consulate's only political significance was in connection with Amīr Faisal's prospective European travels in the course of which he also was to visit Germany. De Haas sent the following telegram to Berlin at the end of March: "Mission headed by Vice-King Faisal plans to pay official visit there sometime in May. He requests confirmation via telegram, that is, an invitation to pass along. Further instructions for me."[52]

The Foreign Office instructed the diplomats in Cairo to inquire with the Hijaz representative about the purpose of the visit. Dieckoff stated furthermore: "Since the purpose of the visit might also seek to further financial requests, it would be, in the current financial situation, rather inconvenient."[53] At about the same time, ʿAbd al-ʿAzīz's representative in Cairo petitioned the German legation for German pilots and mechanics. The Germans were, at first, quite willing to fulfill ʿAbd al-ʿAzīz's wishes: "However, the respective pilots would have to declare themselves ready, not only to serve civilian traffic, but, in case of war, also as military pilots. I told the agent (Fauzān as-Sābiq), that it might be possible to find German pilots who, in return for appropriate payment, would be ready to come to the Hijaz. However, the first condition would be, of course, that the prospective applicants would be informed about the type of aircraft in question. I declared an engagement for war purposes not appropriate; at least, in such a case, the German government would not be able to play the role of intermediary. The further course of the conversation made clear that the agent, that is, his government, was primarily interested in finding suitable pilots for the purpose of war."[54]

The German diplomatic delegations followed with particular attention the movements of Vice-King Faisal's European travels, begun in April 1932. In London, for example, Faisal visited the factory of the

Morris Automobile Company, the port of London, and the Mansion House, the official residence of the Lord Mayor.[55] Meanwhile, the Foreign Office made preparations for Faisal's visit to Germany. In a memorandum concerning Faisal's reception, the following topics of conversation were taken into consideration: "Among German scholars who have traveled in Arabia would be particularly Professor Euting of the University of Strasburg, who informed the scholarly world about interesting pre-Islamic inscriptions in Hijaz and Najd on the basis of his travels in 1884. It would be desirable that further exploration of these monuments remains the exclusive domain of German scholars."[56]

Also mentioned was Heinrich August Meißner-Pasha, who supervised the construction of the Hijaz railroad between 1900 and 1908 as well as the Sinai railroad during the First World War. An addendum to these notes contained economic projects in which the interests of German industry found expression.

1) Necessity for expansion of the port of Jidda;...open docks, interspersed with coral reefs

2) construction of rail line Jidda-Mecca

3) pilgrim traffic, automobile traffic, very expensive

4) construction of hydroelectric dams? For collection of winter rain

5) gold mining, expansion of the carpet industry, Arabian province Asir famous for its cotton industry.[58]

On May 20, 1932, Vice-King Faisal arrived at Tempelhof airport in Berlin from Den Haag. On order of the Reich President, he was greeted by Oswald Baron von Hoyningen-Huene (1885–1983), the ministerial counsel. Also present were the chief of protocol, Envoy Gottfried Count von Tattenbach (1875–1961), and other representatives from the Foreign Office.[59] Fūʾād Hamza Bey petitioned the German government for a credit of 300,000 to 400,000 pounds sterling and offered, in case of an accord in principle with the loan request, special guarantees and concessions for the gold mining and petroleum resources into German hands,[60] which had recently been discovered by an American expert[61] near the Persian Gulf and the Red Sea.[62] However, Germany found itself unable, due its own difficult financial situation and the reparations payment, to satisfy the Saudi credit requests.[63] A financial engagement on the part of the German government with Arabia would have given France and Belgium reason to demand even more energetically the collection of reparations payments and would, at any rate, make it easier for them to push for the application of more forcible means.

Faisal's visit to Berlin, from May 20 to 24, 1932, contained the following program:

Friday   Tour of the UFA [German film studio] pavilion on Nollendorfplatz with the film *Der Kongreß tanzt*;

Saturday   Visit to the Zoological Gardens and the Aquarium and reception with Reich Chancellor Heinrich Brüning; in the evening, a dinner with the chancellor;

Sunday   Tour of the castle of Berlin and the Reichstag, in the afternoon an automobile race on the AVUS, and in the evening a visit to the Winter Gardens;

Monday   Tour of the Siemens factory as well as private events with the Arabian colony; in the evening, attendance at a performance of *Die schöne Helena* at the Grand Theater.

In the morning of May 24, Faisal continued his journey to Warsaw in a salon carriage of the German Reichsbahn (State Railway).[64] On May 26, 1932, the acting Saudi Foreign Minister Yūsuf Yāsīn paid a visit to the German consul in Jidda at the behest of ʿAbd al-ʿAzīz to express the latter's warm thanks to the German government for the friendly reception granted his son. On this occasion mention was also made, besides a loan guarantee on the part of Germany (underwritten by the Hermes Financial Company) for the delivery of German goods, of the question of a recommendation for suitable pilots. "Concerning this last question, I should urge extreme caution in the eventual selection. Furthermore, I respectfully request, if possible, not to leave any people behind before I have had an opportunity to see them for myself in Germany and to orient them about the precise local conditions. In my opinion, it would be a mistake, with consideration of the English, to send any German pilots at all to this place."[65]

At about the same time, Harry Philby, after having successfully traversed the al-Rubʿ al-Khālī, was in London on a lecture visit, where he was approached by the representative of the U.S. oil company Socal with the suggestion to petition King ʿAbd al-ʿAzīz for a petroleum concession. Philby declared his willingness to do so. "He returned to Saudi Arabia with a secret monthly honorarium of 1,000 dollars for advancing the oil company's interests and participated in negotiations between Socal and the king's representatives, which took place in Jidda in February 1933. After three months of tough negotiations, during which Harry Philby functioned as intermediary, the Socal representative and ʿAbdullah Āl Sulaiman, the king's finance minister, reached a compromise. The final agreement, calculated in pounds sterling since the British currency was the only one accepted in the Near East, provisioned that the oil company paid 30,000 pounds to the king as a down payment and an annual 5,000 pounds as a lease."[66] In May 1933, a treaty was correspondingly concluded between Socal and ʿAbd al-ʿAzīz II. The United States, which was not under suspicion of being an imperial colonial power in the Near East, received the concession. Harry Philby, who had left his country Great Britain because of his "socialist" ideas, exercised considerable influence on King ʿAbd al-ʿAzīz II and vice versa. The diminishing prospects both for a solution to the frustrating payment difficulties as well as for a potent moneylender soon led to a cooling of Saudi-German economic contacts. The German creditors were soon rudely excluded.

The Kurt Krokowski Affair

One reason for Heinrich de Haas's reservation in the matter of the pilots was an incident, with grave consequences, that had taken place three weeks before and became the Krokowski Case. The German engineer Kurt Krokowski was accused of having attempted to toss a bomb at the airport of Jidda. "On the second of the month, Mrs. Krokowski was informed that, on the previous evening, her husband had been flogged in the presence of the king and was now in prison.... I immediately contacted the acting foreign minister, Yussuf Yassin, and was immediately received. I requested an explanation about Mr. Krokowski."[67] A short while later, de Haas was granted permission to visit Krokowski in prison. Krokowski, who was barely in a condition to answer questions, swore that he was innocent. At the same time, King ʿAbd al-ʿAzīz issued an order to transfer Krokowski to a hospital.

"I protested the very rough treatment meted out to Mr. K. and asked if the king had been informed about the incident. I was assured that the king was familiar with all the details. Yassin told me furthermore that the king had decided to banish Mr. K."[68] In the following, the Saudi government moderated its claims against Krokowski and declared itself ready to bear the costs of his journey abroad. "I am unable to give an explanation of the direct reason for this order. Mr. K. had been employed by the government as a pilot and was supposed to fly to Djizan last September and bombard the rebellious tribe in that area. However, shortly after his departure, he returned and took a nose-over on landing. The two mechanics were severely flogged back then and banished due to the conviction that it was sabotage and they were all responsible for the mishap. I managed, for the time being, to protect Mr. K. from any kind of punishment, but I presume that the past incident was the main reason for the present castigation. Mr. K. has been in the country for five years; however, despite his knowledge of land and people, he did not know how to gain the people's good will. He frequently treats them in a rude and insulting manner.... He was also very indiscreet when the king or one of his ministers was the subject of conversation.... In sum, it is my opinion that the government's patience ran out and this castigation was in retaliation for a lot of small and big offenses."[69]

The fact is certain that the incident at the airport of Jidda had been prepared for a long time and could not have taken place without the king's express approval. Krokowski, who carried on, at the same time, a lively business through a trading company founded by him, the DEHANI (German Trade Establishment), and was owed considerable sums of money by the Hijaz government, described the likely background as follows: "He answered me verbally,... that I was flogged because, in a report to my government (I presume letter no. 5721 of February 2, 1932), I made remarks about the local conditions which presumably presented the Hijaz government in a bad light. I replied that I had every right to warn my countrymen and my government. Besides, it all corresponded to the truth ... I was at the house of Mohamed al Fazal, [who] asked me whether I had written the article in which it was said the king had 270 wives.... The reason for our expulsion [Krokowski was in Jidda with his wife] was thus very clear; it was the letter which, of course, had nothing good to say about the government, ... fraud here and there, a double standard in making payments, lack of meeting responsibilities, and so on. I have no idea how this letter might have gotten into the hands of that government; at any rate, I was speechless."[70]

It would probably be correct to seek the source of the indiscretion with the German Consul de Haas. However, the fact remains that Krokowski and de Haas regarded each other as competitors in the economic sphere and that Krokowski would have liked to take on the position of consular agent himself, but did not have the desirable social background that de Haas had. Heinrich de Haas was in 1932 still very optimistic in his estimate of the creditworthiness of the Hijaz government, while Krokowski continuously warned the Foreign Office about the poor payment attitude of the Hijaz. The payment moratorium declared by ʿAbd al-ʿAzīz on November 9, 1931, finally vindicated Krokowski. In a letter of his "German Trade Establishment," Krokowski commented on a manifesto from the Hijaz government:

> The debts and salaries will be paid to each creditor without favoritism *(has not happened yet)*.
>
> - Improvement of health care in the country *(the doctors all flee because of non-payment of salaries, hospital is closed; medications almost non-existent ...)* and of the pilgrims
>
> - improvement of traffic roads *(one road was actually improved, namely the connection between two palaces in Mecca)*.
>
> *Page two of the manifesto:*
>
> Our doors are open to everybody. We will take care of everybody ourselves. *(Even this declaration is untrue, for physicians are prohibited from emigrating and the way the government takes care of everybody can be seen among the poor soldiers who in part have to go begging inasmuch as the British government has not returned them home. These people did not get 40 percent of the salaries due and are without means of subsistence)*. Riyad, Jamaʿa 28, 1350.[71]

Of particular interest in Krokowski's drastic estimate of the situation is his mention of the presence of foreign soldiers, who were likely involved in combating the Ikhwān rebels. Krokowski sent urgent warnings to the Chamber of Commerce, the Center for Foreign Trade, the Hansa steamship company, the German Economic Service in Berlin, the Economic Association in Nuremberg, and the Reich Chancellery against business dealings with the Kingdom of Hijaz: "The economic situation of this country, which lives off pilgrims, has deteriorated this year to such a degree that one has to count on heavy losses of considerable amounts of money for European companies. If the government had only some degree of honest intention, then the matter would be half as bad. But the government has proven on various occasions that it never takes its promises seriously. Goods were taken from the customs office without payment."[72]

Krokowski also debated unambiguously the matter of the German Consul Heinrich de Haas:

> I advocated back then, with great emphasis, the establishment of a German consulate here, in order to better represent our German interests.... Unfortunately, all hopes received a strong slap in the face. The German Consul arrived here as a merchant under optimistic preconceptions, which have constantly run aground to this day. The optimistic expectations of this gentleman exceed to this day all expectations, as I believe, to the detriment of German companies.... Again, the German got the short end of the stick by making offers that can never be credited and, in view of the present conditions, can never be balanced.... The young Mr. Dietrich, a merchant with the firm Job, Hansen, Hamburg, does his best as deputy consul, but here nobody gives a hoot about reminders from a deputy.... The Italian is almost always here, the German is constantly traveling.[73]

As marginal note to this report, the German envoy to Cairo, most likely following the information from Heinrich de Haas, added a negative evaluation of Krokowski: "The author is a dubious personality! He is a former chauffer and is said to be living now primarily from the 'tax income' of his wife. His submissions about the economic conditions in Jidda are either wrong or exaggerated."[74] However, Krokowski's warnings were to be borne out: "Of the five-month back payment of salaries to the soldiers and bureaucrats not a penny has been paid. How can the Consul claim that 40 percent had been paid? This is a falsehood that contributes to the deceiving of the business world. The soldiers were left without clothing, some of them wander about now begging for bakshish or inasmuch as they came from the Sudan, they were returned to the Sudan by the British government (IN ALL HONESTY) without cost."[75]

It is certainly not wrong to assume that these reports led to the assault against Krokowski. Kurt Krokowski set his claims against the Hijaz government with the Foreign Office at 303.07.04 pounds sterling (303 pounds, 7 shillings, 4 pence) and demanded for the physical injury suffered 400 pounds sterling in gold. In a letter to the Saudi State Secretary Fū'ād Hamza, the presenting legation counsel Kurt Prüfer (1881–1959) wrote: "During your visit to Berlin I availed myself of the opportunity to inform Your Excellency of the intention of the German Government to accredit their Minister in Addis Ababa simultaneously to His Majesty King Ibn Sa'ūd. Before taking the necessary steps to this end, the Foreign Office would, however, highly appreciate it if the Krokowski case could in the meantime be settled in a manner acceptable to both sides, so that our Minister need not trouble the Hijaz Government with this invidious affair on assuming office."[76] Prüfer further emphasized in his letter that the treatment of Krokowski was not in harmony with the principles set down in the friendship treaty of 1929 and that the accusations against Krokowski rested on a misunderstanding. The government of the Hijaz meanwhile was not ready to accept these preconditions of the Foreign Office. The Saudi government attempted, at the same time, to again recruit German pilots for the flight school in the Hijaz (Jidda).[77] In a draft treaty that the Foreign Office had worked out for four pilots (Count Schaessberg, Robert Mossbacher, P. D. Harnack, and Karl Schlenker), the salary for the pilots was set at 1,500 Reichsmark and at 1,200 for the mechanics/flyers, and corresponding modes of payments and insurance premiums were suggested.

At the same time, Fū'ād Hamza was offered the purchase of training aircraft from the Junkers airplane manufacturer.[78] But apparently, the Saudi government was not ready to meet the contractual demands of the Foreign Office which were deemed too high. As a result of the desperate financial condition in the Hijaz, the majority of German companies were left without any compensation. The Krokowski affair made clear that German officials formed an exclusive club by background, education, and class conceit, a fact that at times clouded the view on what was really going on. Thus it was outright short-sighted to view reports by an insider like Kurt Krokowski in a negative light. With a little bit of foresight, it would have been possible to establish an invaluable source of information. The Krokowski affair coincided with the beginning of the world economic crisis. With these outright rude methods, bothersome creditors were forced to leave Saudi Arabia. Although physically unharmed, the German honorary consul Heinrich de Haas, too, soon had to throw in the towel.

World Economic Crisis and the End of the Consulate in 1934

Heinrich de Haas, the German Consul, admitted at the end of 1932: "The total claims of German companies amount to about 150,000 Reichsmark. The information concerning the fund for debt liquidation as contained in the memorandum is incorrect since I presume that parts of these funds have been used to meet the excessive costs of the campaign against Ibn Rifada, who was supported by the Transjordanian Emir ʿAbdullah, as well as for the suppression of the present rebellion in Asir. Whether the government will be able to pay off its debts in the coming year depends entirely on the number of pilgrims who will arrive here for the next pilgrims' meeting, about April 2, 1933."[79]

Thus, the claims by Büssing (Vereinigte Nutzkraftwagen Aktiengesellschaft) of Brunswick alone amounted to 1320.10.3 pounds in gold, for which all Büssing received were treasury notes without backing. The strategy employed by Saudi businessmen and the government of the Hijaz to obtain urgently needed goods on a credit basis and then to devalue the claims through monetary coercive measures worked only within limits. The Büssing firm wrote to the Foreign Office: "The finance ministry of the Kingdom of Saudi Arabia, Mecca, was to establish a spare parts warehouse with the firm Khalid El-Gargani in Jidda, which has applied to become our representative. We would open up this spare parts warehouse inasmuch as we receive sufficient security from the above-mentioned firm as well as the finance ministry of the Kingdom of Saudi Arabia."[80]

The Saudi government's insolvency as well as unwillingness to meet its financial obligations finally led to the almost complete break of German-Saudi economic and diplomatic relations. Creditors who insisted on being paid again and again had to be satisfied with promises of payment later. Finally even the honorary consul, Heinrich de Haas, was expelled for this reason. As of December 31, 1933, he liquidated his firm de Haas and Company. He cited as a reason the fact that the finance minister, Khālid Āl Hūd al-Qarqānī, had told his business partner as well as the manager of de Haas that, due to a written report from "Bengali," he could no longer work with me. "Another reason, which was decisive for me, was the fact that despite great efforts on the part of my business friends and myself, despite my open sympathetic attitude toward the government, I was unable, in the course of my three-year stay, to get the government to keep its promises and fulfill its responsibilities toward me.... The supposed report about me is, in my opinion, another attempt to steer clear of meeting the responsibilities incurred toward me."[81]

Heinrich de Haas's hopes of profiting from the economic upturn that the founding of the Saudi-Arabian state bank and the construction of a rail line from Jidda to Mecca were expected to bring were disappointed, since neither project was realized. In addition, on the basis of the payment moratorium of 1931, the treasury notes issued in late 1933 were not honored. With this disappeared the actual economic-political reason for the existence of the consulate in Jidda. At the same time, Heinrich de Haas informed the Foreign Office that he had definitely decided not to return to Jidda.[82] The dissolution of the consulate in Jidda was made public in a circular letter dated January 9, 1934, and addressed to the various authorities. This marked the end of the first German diplomatic representation in Saudi Arabia.[83] The former Consul de Haas had to wait until 1938 for payment of the money owed to him. In an exchange that took place on November 5, 1938, in Baghdad, Fritz Grobba pointed out these circumstances to Yūsuf Yāsīn, ʿAbd al-ʿAzīz's private secretary: "During this exchange, I had to remind the sheikh that the debt the Saudi-Arabian government owed the former German consul in Jidda, Heinrich de Haas, was still outstanding, and I declared that it might facilitate the establishment of the diplomatic relations which King Ibn Saud desires if this matter were taken care of."[84] Yāsīn assured me that in 1938 and the following year, de Haas's claims in the amount of 2,000 pounds sterling would be met.

The following conclusion can be drawn: German-Saudi relations were first and foremost based on economic relations. The world economic crisis spelled the end of the German export economy in Hijaz and also put an end to many ambitious Saudi projects. The consulate, which was minimally funded (200 Reichsmark for the rent of a house[85]), was abandoned with the end of Consul Heinrich de Haas's business activities. For the Saudis, Germany was a desirable business partner, since Germany pursued no political ends in Saudi Arabia until the end of the thirties and, until the closing of the consulate, in contrast to Great Britain, France, and Italy, had no means of force (for example, warship) to employ in collecting from recalcitrant Saudi debtors as Great Britain, at least, was wont to do. The planned German arms deal with Saudi Arabia on the eve of the Second World War has been well researched.[86] Hans Steffen too was traveling in Iraq in 1938, as the representative of the German Iraq Consortium (Rheinmetall, Krupp, BSW, and Otto Wolff), in order to place the Iraqi armaments program under German control. Nothing is known about the subsequent fate of Hans Steffen.

Following the closing of the consulate in Jidda in early 1934 and non-payment of German deliveries, a break in German-Saudi relations occurred that lasted until 1937. The year 1937 means, in historical terms, the recovery of Germany as a world power and with it a shift in the worldwide balance of power in favor of the Axis powers of Italy, Germany, and Japan to the detriment of the British Empire. The ruler of Saudi Arabia, ʿAbd al-ʿAzīz, with his nose for shifts in power, saw here a possible chance to break out of the British policy of containing his realm in the north, east, and west of Saudi Arabia. As in 1928, ʿAbd al-ʿAzīz took the initiative in seeking Germany's help and its weapons-technological know-how to change the status quo in the Near East and to expand his hegemony over the rulers on the Gulf, in North Yemen, and the Hashemite lands. ʿAbd al-ʿAzīz II followed with great interest, and no doubt also with sympathy, the rise of Germany in Europe and the world.

The U.S. military attaché in Berlin, Major Truman Smith, reported on June 15, 1937, that the Saudis were interested in German arms.[87] It is quite correct, therefore, to speak of Saudi Arabia as wooing Germany at that time. In January 1939, the Swastika flag was hoisted over Pilgrim Hotel, the temporary seat of the envoy Grobba in Jidda. Grobba presented King ʿAbd al-ʿAzīz with a silver model of a Ju 52 [Junker airplane]. In early February 1939, Grobba was presented with counter gifts (*kūfīya*s [headdress], *ʿiqāl*s [headband], etc.).[89] On June 17, 1939,

Hitler received Saudi Arabia's special envoy Khālid Āl Hūd al-Qarqānī, who remained in Germany until September 7, at the Berghof in Berchtesgaden.[90] Among the topics of conversation with Hitler were, besides the exchange of courtesies, first and foremost the weapons deliveries desired by Saudi Arabia. "According to King Ibn Saud's request and following an internal preparatory inquiry with the economic department, our aid will for the time being be limited to a relatively rather modest credit of about 1.5 million Reichsmark, which will be used for the immediate purchase of eight thousand rifles and eight million rounds of ammunition as well as the construction of a small munitions factory in the interior of the country. Added to this will be light anti-aircraft guns and tanks."[91]

The weapons were to be delivered within fourteen to eighteen months.[92] The visit met with great public interest in the world. Coinciding with Khālid Āl Hūd al-Qarqānī's visit with Hitler, rumors were heard about "an ultimatum from Ibn Saud to Great Britain," which were in all likelihood put into circulation as targeted misinformation. According to this report, Foreign Minister Faisal is said to have addressed a series of demands of the British government, among other matters, concerning Palestine. Werner von Hentig wrote following an inquiry with Khālid Āl Hūd: "The king is neither by nature nor by position able to present England with such an ultimatum."[93] Speaking to the British press, Khālid Āl Hūd categorically denied the German-Saudi negotiations and, concerning the alleged ultimatum, he declared: "We are good friends of England." His visit with the "Führer" was a return visit to Dr. Grobba's visit with ʿAbd al-ʿAzīz.[94] The king was apparently not very happy that the exchange of his special envoy with Hitler had aroused so much attention. Fritz Grobba, for his part, sent a telegram to Berlin with the request to pay as little attention as possible to Khālid Āl Hūd's visit, "since Ibn Saud places greatest value in keeping the negotiations inconspicuous."[95] The negotiations over weapons deliveries, meanwhile, dragged on, for "the matter of credit as well as of the arms deliveries were treated by Hitler's Germany in such a dilatory manner that in all likelihood no rifles or only negligible amounts reached the Arabian Peninsula before the outbreak of the war."[96]

Fritz Grobba's hopes to set up an alternative base in Jidda at the beginning of the war were not realized. Even though it is not likely that Ibn Saʿūd broke off diplomatic relations as early as September 11,

1939, as Josef Schröder claims,[97] it is, nevertheless, incontestable that Grobba's presence in Jidda was unwelcome and that he was forced to return to Berlin. British policy of resolve since May 1940, under the new Prime Minister Churchill, also meant the removal of Harry Philby from King ʿAbd al-ʿAzīz's surroundings, since Philby had been spreading defeatist propaganda in which he predicted the victory of the Axis Powers. However, it is more likely that the opposite was true. Harry (since 1932 ʿAbdullah) idolized the Saudi ruler unconditionally, so it is more likely that ʿAbd al-ʿAzīz influenced Philby in a pro-Nazi direction. Philby was interned in England during the war and returned to Saudi Arabia in 1946. ʿAbd al-ʿAzīz had him picked up in Cairo in one of his airplanes.

Saudi Arabia remained formally neutral until February 28, 1945, when it declared war on Germany, but was in fact on the British side. Nevertheless, German Muslims have made creditable reports about German warships (especially submarines) docking in Saudi Arabian ports during the Second World War, in order to use the customary time limit of twenty-four hours for repairs.

The following conclusions can be drawn. Consideration for Great Britain's interests in the Near East played a foremost political role on the German side. Thus German efforts were concentrated on expanding economic relations with Arabia, specifically with Saudi Arabia. It was only in the later part of the 1930s that an appreciation of King ʿAbd al-ʿAzīz II's relatively independent role gained importance in the Arabian policy of Nazi Germany. ʿAbd al-ʿAzīz II, for his part, placed the greatest priority on being recognized as king of the Hijaz as well as securing financial aid in order to safeguard his power and the desired succession to the throne (that is, his son Saʿūd IV). Germany, which had few political interests in the region and was not incriminated by a colonial past, was initially seen as the most suitable partner, but was left out in the cold in 1932 in favor of the United States. Only the politically unstable situation in the late 1930s led to Saudi Arabia's "wooing" of Germany, as mentioned above, and the widely known weapons deal.

GERMAN-SAUDI RELATIONS AND THEIR ACTORS ON THE ARABIAN PENINSULA

Notes

1. Fahd as-Simmārī, "Nadhra ʿala wathāʾiq arshif Būtsdam al-mutaʿallaqa bi-Taʾrīkh al-Mamlaka al-ʿArabīya as-Saʿūdīya fī ʿAhd al-Malik ʿAbd al-ʿAzīz," *ʿAlam al-Kutub*, (Riyad) 14, no. 6 (November/December 1993); Simārī, *König Abdulaziz und Deutschland: Eine historische Studie der saudi-deutschen Beziehungen 1926–1939* (Beirut, 1999).
2. Compare among others Helmut Mejcher, *Die Politik und das Öl im Nahen Osten* (Stuttgart, 1980), 1990; Mejcher, "Saudi-Arabiens Beziehungen zu Deutschland in der Regierungszeit von König ʿAbd al-ʿAziz Ibn Saud," in *Der Nahe Osten in der Zwischenkriegszeit 1919–1939: Die Interdependenz von Politik, Wirtschaft, und Ideologie*, ed. Linda Schatkowski Schilcher and Claus Scharf (Stuttgart, 1989), 109–27; Mejcher, Germany's Relations to the Near and Middle East, 1934–1938," in *German Near and Middle East Association (Jubilee) Report* (Hamburg, 1983/84).
3. Bundesarchiv Berlin (hereafter BArch), R 901/43 514, Foreign Office, Bl. 294 Rs, Hans-Joachim von Bassewitz to Herbert von Richthofen.
4. BArch Berlin, R 901/43 514, Bl. 320, Hans Steffen to Foreign Office.
5. Ibid., Bl. 186, notes of Hans von Saucken to von Podewils, March 10, 1925.
6. After conquering the Shammar Emirate of Hāʾil in November 1921, ʿAbd al-ʿAzīz II assumed the title "Sultan" at a tribal meeting.
7. BArch Berlin, R NS 10/394.
8. Shakīb Arslān (1869–1946), a Druze emir and Pan-Islamic politician, had very good connections with influential German players, such as Max von Oppenheim. During the Second World War, Arslān, at the initiative of the Foreign Office, worked on an Arabic translation of Hitler's *Mein Kampf*. See Gerhard Höpp, "Araber im Zweiten Weltkrieg—Kollaboration oder Patriotismus," in *Jenseits der Legenden. Araber, Juden, Deutsche*, ed. by Wolfgang Schwanitz (Berlin, 1994); also Gabriele Teichmann and Gisela Völger, *Faszination Orient. Max von Oppenheim – Forscher, Sammler, Diplomat* (Cologne, 2001).
9. Political Archive of the Foreign Office (hereafter PA of Foreign Office), Bonn, no. R 78 384, Bl. L 323 212, Herbert von Richthofen to Max von Oppenheim, Berlin, July 8, 1926.
10. During this journey, Faisal thanked the governments of Great Britian, the Netherlands, and France for their recognition of his father as king of the Hijaz. He returned to the Hijaz from Marseilles on the *Macedonia*. Compare ibid., Bl. L 323 229–30, and *al-Ahrām*, November 4, 1926.
11. Ibid., Bl. L 323 232, Heinrich de Haas, Foreign Office to German Embassy in Bern, Berlin, 2.
12. Ibid., Bl. L 323 238, Friedrich Weiss to Herbert von Richthofen, Addis Ababa, October 10, 1926.
13. Ibid., Bl. L 323 243, Müller to Foreign Office, Bern, February 11, 1927.
14. The Italian Embassy passed along, in early November, to the Reichskommissar for Guarding Public Order a letter in which a certain Bruno Kramer Shalabī was accused of having received money from the Soviet Embassy which he used for "active propaganda among Oriental students in Berlin" as well as "a fierce and

unjustified hate campaign" against Italy in the *Islam Echo*. An investigation by department IA found that Kramer had met Shalabī in 1926 during a hike through Asia Minor and accompanied him that same year on a pilgrimage to Mecca. The German had meanwhile become a member of the Islamic community and—according to the denunciation—an opponent of the Syrian in his dispute with the imam of the community, Khairī. At any rate, Shalabī was now described by the police presidium of the Reichskommissar as idle and money-hungry and was accused of having transmitted material about the current uprisings in Asia Minor to the Russian Embassy and the IAH. Gerhard Höpp, *Arabische und islamische Periodoika in Berlin und Brandenburg* (Berlin, 1994), workbook no. 4, 39.

15. PA of the Foreign Office, Bonn, no. R 78 384, Bl. L 323 256 and 257, Fritz Grobba to Foreign Office, Berlin, February 23, 1927.
16. Ibid., Bl. L 323 321–33, Friedrich Weiss to Foreign Office, Addis Ababa, April 10, 1927.
17. Ibid., Bl L 323 290–93.
18. Ibid., no. R 78 384, Bl. L 323 261, Bertram Moritz to Foreign Office (Diel and Fritz Grobba), Berlin, April 6, 1927.
19. Ibid., Bl. L 323 297, Ministry of Buitenlandsche Zaken to Foreign Office, den Haag, Foreign Office, March 29, 1927.
20. Ibid., addendum to B 530 of June 7, 1927.
21. Ibid., Adam Opel Bicycle and Automobile Manufacture to German Embassy Addis Ababa, Rüsselsheim, June 27, 1927 (German Embassy log no : 1148).
22. Compare BArch Berlin, film no. 17 529, Bl. L 323 340–42. Compare also the pseudonymously published work by R. Donkan, *Die Auferstehung Arabiens* (Leipzig, 1937) as well as his travelogue about Riyad: Leopold Weiß, "Heart of Arabia," in *Living Age* (New York), 339 (September 1930), 69–72. Compare also the photographs taken by Leopold Weiß in 1927 of the pilgrims' road to Mecca: PA of the Foreign Office, Bonn, no. R 78 384, Bl. L 323 294, and the accompanying travelogue by Weiß, in ibid., Bl. L 323 290–93.
23. BArch Berlin, R 901, film no. 17 528, Bl. L 323 279, Friedrich Weiss to the Foreign Office, March 11, 1927. In the thirties, Philby was definitely highly regarded in the German press. He was called the "white raven" while mention was made of his supposed return of his medal to London and refusal of the pension to which he was entitled as an official of the India Office. Compare BArch Berlin, R 49.02 (German Institute of Foreign Studies), no. 3496, Bl. 12.
24. PA of the Foreign Office, Bonn, no. R 78 384, Bl L 323 291.
25. Ibid., Bl. L 323 321 and 322, Friedrich Weiss to Foreign Office, Addis Ababa, April 10, 1927.
26. Rathjens was born on March 10, 1887 in Elmshorn (Holstein) and died in 1966. He became an assistant at the Zoological Museum in 1911 and a short while later an associate of the Colonial Institute. In 1908, he visited Abyssinia, and from 1912 to 1913 he traveled around the world. He later traveled to Albania (1924), Tripolitania (1925), Lapland (1926), Jidda and Yemen (1927–1928 and 1931), North Africa (1929), and Egypt and Yemen (1934–1938). Besides reports about geomorphology, ethnography, and archaeology, he also published travelogues.
27. Ibid., Bl. L 323 362, Eberhard von Stohrer to Foreign Office (telegram), Cairo, November 25, 1927.

28. PA of the Foreign Office, Bonn, no. 78 384, Bl. L 323 362, Eberhard von Stohrer to Foreign Office (telegram) Cairo, November 25, 1927.
29. Compare PA of Foreign Office, Bonn, no. 78 384, Bl L 323 361, *Deutsche Allgemeine Zeitung*, November 23, 1927.
30. From late 1926 to early 1930, almost fifteen hundred automobiles were imported to the Hijaz and Najd. Ibid., no. R 92 146, Germany Embassy, Washington to Foreign Office, September 9, 1930 (no. 1358), Commerce Reports, 1930, no. 35.
31. Ibid., Daimler-Benz to Foreign Office, Stuttgart, February 15, 1928.
32. Ibid., Bl. 180ff.
33. Eldon Rutter, "A Journey to Hail," *Geographical Journal* (London) 80 (October 1932): 331.
34. Compare PA of the Foreign Office, Bonn, Bl. 181ff.
35. Ibid., Bl. 323 458, Schaefer-Rümelin to Foreign Office, Cairo, September 5, 1928 (Report of the German Citizen, Kurt Krokowski to the embassy).
36. Ibid., von Düring to Foreign Office, December 7, 1928. The cooperative was referred to the firm Steffen & Heymann, Berlin W 35, Blumeshof 17, which had already delivered arms to the Hashemite King ʿAlī in 1924/25.
37. Ibid., no. R 78384, German Embassy in Cairo to Foreign Office, March 27, 1929 (no. 222).
38. Ibid., Foreign Office to German Embassy Cairo, Berlin, September 26, 1929.
39. Ibid., no. R 78 386, Bl. 2 and 2 Rs, German Embassy Cairo to Foreign Office, Ramleh, October 18, 1929.
40. Ibid., Bl. 3.
41. Ibid., no. R 78 387, Fūʾād Hamza to Foreign Office, Mecca, September 29, 1928.
42. Ibid., Bl. L 323 554 Herbert von Richthofen to German Embassy Cairo, telegram nos. 39 and 40, April 24, 1929.
43. Ibid., Bl. L 323 522–23, draft letter of Foreign Office to German Embassy in London, Berlin, November 19, 1928.
44. Ibid., Bl. L 323 534, Stamer to Foreign Office (telegram), London, November 23, 1928.
45. Ibid., Bl. L 323 603, Muhammad Naṣ́ī Shalabī to Foreign Office, Berlin, July 5, 1929.
46. Ibid., Bl. L 323 614, Schaefer-Rümelin to Foreign Office, Cairo, August 29, 1929.
47. Ibid., Bl. L 323 620, Hans Steffen to Foreign Office (Fritz Grobba), Berlin, September 20, 1929.
48. Ibid., Bl. L 323 623, Foreign Office (Fritz Grobba) to the German Embassy in Cairo, Berlin, September 25, 1929.
49. Compare Reichsgesetzblatt, part 2, 1930, issued in Berlin, Law Concerning the Friendship Treaty between the German Reich and the Kingdom of Hijaz, Najd, and attached areas, of July 28, 1930, pp. 1063–65.
50. Ibid., Bl. L 323 671–72, Notes, no. 30, August 13, 1930.
51. Compare Reichsgesetzblatt, part 2, 1930, issued in Berlin, December 9, 1930, no. 41, p. 1274.
52. PA of the Foreign Office, Bonn, no. R 78 398, Bl. L 324 199, Hans Heinrich Dieckhoff to the German Embassy in Cairo, Berlin, April 1, 1932.
53. Ibid.

54. Ibid., no. R 78 398, Bl. L 324 212, Eberhard von Stohrer to Foreign Office, Cairo, April 5, 1932 (no. 223). In this connection it is interesting to note the planned attempt of two German sport pilots, Dr. Schulte and Dr. Simmer, to fly over the Hijaz. Consul de Haas commented that he urgently advised against this plan, for the Hijaz government, out of consideration for the English pilots active in the Hijaz, was not likely to give permission for flyovers to pilots of other nationalities; the plane would inevitably be shot at. PA of the Foreign Office, Bonn, no. R 78 383, Bl. L 323 190, Berlin, December 14, 1931.
55. Ibid., no. R 78 398, Bl. L 324 247, Konstantin Alexander Freiherr von Neurath to Foreign Office, London, May 11, 1932.
56. Ibid., no. R 78 398, Bl. L 324 256, Notes for the reception of Emir Feissal, vice-roy of Mecca.
57. Compare Uwe Pfullmann, *Durch Wüste und Steppe*, 295–97.
58. Ibid., Bl. L 324 265, Addendum to notes for the reception of Emir Faisal, vice-roy of Mecca.
59. Compare BArch Berlin, no. 17 530, Bl. L 324 258, file note, May 20, 1932.
60. The fact that a correct estimate of the extent of the Saudi oilfields was already extant in the mid-1930s is shown in the following citation: "Ibn Saud was waiting to allocate exploration concessions this long until old English rights expired last year [1934], since he did not want the imperialistically dangerous English, French, and Italians to participate in opening up his country. The explorations of the American Californian Standard Oil Company, which received the concessions, yielded the amazing result that the Arabian Peninsula must be considered the epicenter of the entire Near Eastern oil deposits and the fields of the English company in Iraq and southern Iran must be regarded as merely marginal." Ibid., no. R 92 144, Veltenbriefe, Fischstick to Schlieper, July 22, 1935.
61. The American engineer Karl Saben Twitchell is said to have been charged by ʿAbd al-ʿAzīz in October 1931 with exploring for oil and iron ore deposits. De Haas reported: "Since his demands are extraordinarily high and he also did not know how to gain the trust of the natives, he fell into disgrace and returned to Yemen about four weeks ago." Ibid., no. R 92 148, Heinrich de Haas to Foreign Office, Jidda, March 30, 1932. Compare also Karl Saben Twitchell, *Saudi Arabia*, 3rd edition (Princeton, 1958).
62. Compare BArch Berlin, no. 17 530, Bl. L 324 268, Prüfer to Foreign Office, May 21, 1932.
63. Ibid., Bl. L 324 273–77, Foreign Office to German Consulate in Jidda, May 31, 1932.
64. Compare PA of the Foreign Office, Bonn, no. R 78 398.
65. Ibid., Bl. L 324 282, German Consulate Jidda to Foreign Office, May 27, 1932 (no. 22/32).
66. Compare *The Arabian Peninsula*, Time-Life Books with photographs by Pascal and Maria Maréaux, 6th edition (Amsterdam, 1991), 95.
67. PA of the Foreign Office, no. R 78 402, Heinrich de Haas to Foreign Office, Jidda, May 5, 1932 (no. 17/32), page 1 of the report.
68. Ibid., page 2 of the report.
69. Ibid., pages 3 and 4 of the report.

70. Ibid., no. R 78 402, Report about the ambush on the engineer and pilot Kurt Krokowski, page 9.
71. Ibid., no. R 92 130, Kurt Krokowski to Foreign Office, Jamaʻa 28, 1350. Mail received at the Foreign Office: February 20, 1932.
72. Ibib., Kurt Krokowski to Foreign Office, Jidda, March 3, 1932, page 1 of the report.
73. Ibid., page 2 of the report; compare also no. R 92 143 (fraudulent company in Hijaz), Kurt Krokowski to Foreign Office, Jidda, July 27, 1930, letter sign 4448.
74. Ibid., page 1 of the report.
75. Ibid., page 3 of the report.
76. Ibid., no. R 78 402, log - no. III 02483, Prüfer to Fu'ad Hamza, Berlin, 4 August 1932, page 2 of the letter.
77. Ibid., no. R 78 383, Bl. L 323 191–96, Fū'ād Hamza to Foreign Office (Prüfer), September 12, 1932.
78. Ibid., Bl. L 323 201–206, draft treaty.
79. Ibid., no. R 78 402, Heinrich de Haas to Foreign Office, Jidda, November 27, 1932.
80. Ibid., Büssing-NAG to Foreign Office, Berlin, January 3, 1934.
81. Ibid., Heinrich de Haas to Foreign Office, Berlin, November 4, 1933, pages 1 and 2 of the letter.
82. Ibid., no. R 78 397, notes of Schmidt-Rolke to Prüfer, Berlin, November 4, 1933.
83. Ibid., internal department circular, Poensgen, Berlin January 9, 1934.
84. Ibid., no., 104 795, Bl. L 385 474, Fritz Grobba to Foreign Office, Baghdad, January 20, 1938 (no. 142).
85. This reimbursement had been granted effective April 1, 1932. Compare PA of the Foreign Office, Bonn, no. R 78 397, file: no. I B (II Asia 116), Busch, Berlin, April 7, 1932.
86. Fahd as-Simārī, "Die Saudi-Deutschen Beziehungen in einem Zeitabschnitt von König Abdulaziz (1926–1939)," in *Die Beziehungen zwischen der Bundesrepublik Deutschland und dem Königreich Saudi Arabien* [Würzburg Geographische Manuskripte, Berling/Irbid: 2001], 44–50; Uwe Pfullmann, "Die deutsch-saudischen Beziehungen am Vorabend des Zweiten Weltkrieges – der Waffenhandel und die Etablierung diplomatischer Missionen im Kontext der regionalen und europäischen Politik," *Asien, Afrika, Lateinamerika* (Berlin) 23, no. 4 (1995): 355–77.
87. Compare Michael Wolffsohn, "The German-Saudi Arabian Arms Deal 1936–1939," in *The Great Powers in the Middle East 1919–1939*, ed. Uriel Dann (New York/London, 1988), 283.
88. Helmut Mejcher, *Saudi-Arabiens Beziehungen zu Deutschland*, 110; C. Leatherdale, *Britain and Saudi Arabia 1925–1939: The Imperial Oasis* (London, 1983), 300–306.
89. BArch Berlin, R 49.02 (German Institute of Foreign Affairs), no. 3496, bl. 10.
90. On May 28, 1939, a lengthy conversation took place between Khālid Āl Hūd al-Qarqānī and, presumably, Dr. Schlobies, in the course of which the Saudi envoy expressed personal matters as well as his political views. Ibid., no. R 104 795 (no pagination), May 28, 1939. For the spelling of the Saudi envoy's name, ibid., Bl. 385 557.

91. Ibid., Bl. 385 604 (copy pol. VII 1058), notes of Werner von Hentigs about the reception of the special envoy of King Ibn Saʿūd, the royal counsel Khālid Āl Hūd al-Qarqānī, Berlin, June 20, 1939.
92. Ibid., Bl. 385 640; Wolffsohn, *The German-Saudi Arabian Arms Deals*, 295.
93. Ibid., Bl. 385 695.
94. Ibid., German Information Service no. 169, London, June 20, 1939.
95. Ibid., Bl. 385 602 Fritz Grobba to Foreign Office, Baghdad, June 20, 1939.
96. Heinz Tillmann, *Deutschlands Araberpolitik im zweiten Weltkrieg* (Berlin, 1965), 72.
97. Compare Josef Schröder, "Die Beziehungen der Achsenmächte zur Arabischen Welt," in *Hitler, Deutschland, und die Mächte*, ed. M. Funke (Düsseldorf, 1976), 373.

Figure 9. Reza Shah and the crown prince before the Apadana relief excavated by Eric Schmidt

German Research on the Ancient Near East and Its Relation to Political and Economic Interests from Kaiserreich to World War II

STEFAN R. HAUSER

The importance of ancient history and archaeology for the construction of national identities has repeatedly been stressed in recent years. This essay addresses the question of the importance of Ancient Near Eastern studies in Germany from 1870 to 1945. It is argued that this seemingly apolitical research developed hand in hand with the economic and political as well as cultural interests prevalent in Wilhelmian Germany. After World War I, this concern, for various ideological and political reasons, gave way to a reorientation toward ancient Greece. During the Nazi regime, the auspices for the study of the Ancient Near East changed again. Here it was put to use for the devaluation of the Semitic people and glorification of Aryan history. But whatever ideological stance was taken toward the Ancient Near East, its research remained a very important vehicle in international relations and a factor for German influence in the region.

Introduction

Research in history in general reacts to questions asked in the present. Often the influence of current ideologies and the importance attached to certain areas of research become clear only in retrospect. A prime example for the interrelation of political and economic interests, the search for cultural agendas suitable under specific circumstances, and interest in antiquity, is the study of the Ancient Near East in Germany. This essay addresses the question of the interrelationship between political agendas and historical research from the Kaiserreich to the Third Reich. The general objectives of historical research, and even the areas of historical and/or archaeological interest in ancient civilizations, changed in relation to political and economic developments.

Imperial Germany and the Rise of Ancient Near Eastern Studies

The founding of the German Empire in 1871 can be seen as a logical step in the economic development and Prussian politics of hegemony. Industrialization and urbanization, with large increases in population and social imbalances, characterized the period of the Kaiserreich. During the reign of Kaiser Wilhelm II (1888–1918), Germany became one of the world's leading industrial nations. The expansion of German industrial exports, especially at the beginning of the twentieth century, was accompanied by discussions of Germany's new position in international affairs. It was commonly believed that Germany's role as a continental power could last only if she exercised power on a world level, beyond the confines of Europe, as well (*Weltmachtpolitik*).[1] Being late in the race for colonies, particularly in comparison with Britain and France,[2] Germany developed a strong interest in the Near Eastern region after Bismarck's abdication in 1890.

For various reasons Germany concentrated on the weakened Ottoman Empire.[3] Important factors were its relative independence and its geopolitical strategic position between Russia, British-dominated Egypt, and Persia. The Ottoman Empire was not only rich in all kinds of raw materials, especially metals and oil, but also seemed a promising market for industrial products. Some experts saw an opportunity to retrieve agricultural products, cotton, tobacco and grains from Mesopotamia,[4] after a restructuring of the mode of production.

At the heart of these German calculations was the construction of a network of railways in the Ottoman Empire, in particular the Baghdad railroad, which was to connect Constantinople with the Persian Gulf via Baghdad. Its construction was to ensure the rapid transport of goods on the shortest route from Europe to the Persian Gulf and as far as India. Thus, the Baghdad railroad would become an immediate competitor to the British-controlled Suez Canal. Already in 1888, against Chancellor Bismarck's advice, but strongly urged by Kaiser Wilhelm II, the Deutsche Bank had granted a loan of 30 million marks to the Ottoman government for a concession to construct the first 1,000 kilometers of the Anatolian railway. "This was the beginning of Germany's paramount position in Turkey's economic and financial affairs."[5]

Germany's growing influence was accompanied by a unique expansion of German archaeological activity in the Ottoman Empire. In the latter half of the nineteenth century, in connection with European colonization of other parts of the world, explorers were to be found in the remotest parts of the globe. They spearheaded a new interest in foreign regions and cultures. Important in this connection is that in the later nineteenth century artifacts became accepted as additional or alternative sources to texts in the description of cultures.[6] This elevation of objects (and in its wake archaeology in general) enabled the exploration of cultures unaccounted for in Biblical or Greek and Latin texts, opening new avenues into the past.[7] This was not only true for prehistory, which in Germany became very popular as the archaeological adjunct to the study of local history, but was also broadly applied to the study of ethnology and archaeology around the world, as it coincided with a fascination for the exotic and with economic interests. As result, several museums for non-classical cultures were established around 1900 in Berlin, Bremen, Hamburg and Munich. In particular, the Royal Prussian Museums in Berlin created, within a few years, departments for African and Oceanic, Indian and Far Eastern art, as well as for Ancient Near Eastern, Islamic and Byzantine art.

This cultural re-orientation did not mean a complete departure from Germany's Philhellenism, which had been a defining part of German cultural identity since the late eighteenth century. Nevertheless, it showed a certain deviation from it, the break of a complete hegemony.[8] While the earlier nineteenth century had idealized and romanticized Greece and a presumed inner bond between ancient Greeks and modern

Germans, this neohumanist ideal had come under severe criticism in the Kaiserreich. The more professionalized the study of Antiquity became, the more pragmatic became the scholarly examinations. At the same time, with the support of Kaiser Wilhelm II, a general reform of the educational system elevated Realschulen and Technische Hochschulen to parity with the Humanistisches Gymnasium and University. Classical learning and especially the romantic notion of a close relation between ancient Greece and Germany were increasingly considered irrelevant to the demands of the day. Still, Greek superiority in aesthetic questions was widely accepted. And despite the Kaiser's interest in modernization, archaeologists [i.e., classical archaeologists] held a prominent position at court as well as in German society at large.[9] Classical study continued to hold sway in the cultural life of the educated elite, but its supremacy was no longer unchallenged. New emphasis on patriotism fostered a new German nationalism independent of classical Greece, and a strong fascination with the exotic diverted interests toward foreign cultures. Within this context, the Ancient Near East gained special importance.

The Discovery of the Ancient Near East

Until the middle of the nineteenth century, knowledge of Ancient Near Eastern history and cultures in Europe was basically derived from references in classical writings and the Bible. But in the 1840s, first the French consul at Mosul, Paul Emile Botta, and then the Englishman Henry Austin Layard started to unearth miles of reliefs that had adorned the palaces of Assyrian kings in the first half of the first millennium B.C.E. The excavations, which first started as clandestine operations, aroused enormous interest, especially after some of the reliefs were brought to Paris and London, where they were displayed to tremendous public acclaim.[10] In addition to the reliefs, tens of thousands of clay tablets with texts in the recently deciphered Akkadian cuneiform writing were found.[11]

A fierce French-British rivalry over sites to excavate developed. In 1895 the French even succeeded in obtaining a monopoly on archaeological exploration for the entire area of Persia.[12] Even though limited in scale, archaeological and philological research provided a constant flow of newly discovered cultures. This, and the Mesopotamian art that poured into the Louvre and the British Museum starting in the mid-nineteenth century, stirred the interest of the German and especially the Prussian public. This interest was further fostered by the commonly held opinion that the Mesopotamian texts and artifacts provided the background for the Bible, which together with the Greek intellectual world was regarded as the cornerstone for Western culture. Indeed, it was general interest in the Bible and the peculiar find of a cuneiform tablet telling the story of the great flood in a Mesopotamian version that helped to establish the first professorship for Cuneiform Assyrian in Germany as early as 1875.[13] In addition to the purely historical and theological interest, it was commonly accepted and desired that Germany's new political and economic status should be seen to rival that of France and Britain through its museum collections. Germany's widely recognized pre-eminence in scholarly analysis of the ancient world should be manifested as well in the public display of material artifacts.

In 1878 the Berlin museums started their first project in the Ottoman Empire, the excavations of the Pergamon Altar. It was not without significance that the excavator, Carl Humann, had become acquainted with the ruins during his tenure as railway engineer in western Turkey in 1871. Between 1895 and 1899 long-term excavations in western Turkey, at Priene, Miletos, and Didyma, were started and became renowned for their scale, approach, and advanced techniques of excavation, documentation, and analysis. But this research still concerned Greek antiquity and was carried out by official state institutions, the Berlin museums and the German Archaeological Institute (henceforth: DAI).

Research in Mesopotamia took a different route. Instead of the state, it was the private Orient-Committee, founded in 1887, which supported the first smaller campaigns in northern and southern Mesopotamia. These small-scale campaigns, however, led to interest by the government. In February 1897 a commission of the Prussian Academy of Science, prompted by an inquiry of the minister of culture, officially declared research in Mesopotamia to be "one of the most important tasks in the present time. It would correspond to the cultural importance of the German Reich"... if Germany were to participate in "resurrecting a world lost in the memory of humankind, in recovering millennia of human history from art and inscriptions." Especially since French and British excavations had revolutionized "our knowledge on the genesis of our culture."[14]

Only three months later, the Prussian Academy of Science constituted a formal commission for the exploration of the Tigris and Euphrates area (Kommission zur Erforschung der Euphrat- und Tigrisländer), which dispatched scholars to look for sites to excavate. After much debate, they settled for ancient Babylon, but the excavation itself became the enterprise of the Deutsche Orient-Gesellschaft (henceforth: DOG). This society was founded in 1898 and incorporated the older Orient-Committee. That this society was not established purely on philanthropic grounds can be surmised from the list of founding members and executive board. Among them we find the entire upper echelons of German bankers with interests in the Ottoman Empire, starting with von Siemens, Rothschild, and Delbrück, as well as industrialists like Krupp, Rathenau, and Borsig. In addition, we find leading politicians and scholars of the Orient. The society enjoyed the kaiser's enthusiastic support. He proclaimed his protective friendship of the Islamic countries on his second visit to Jerusalem and Damascus in 1900.[15] The following year he became the patron of the DOG and according to his memoirs never missed any of its public lectures. Thus, when the DOG launched major excavations at several Mesopotamian sites, such as Babylon or Asrur, in 1899 and 1903, they were hailed and generously supported by the kaiser. These excavations revolutionized archaeological methods in the area and greatly broadened general knowledge about ancient Mesopotamia.[16] From the outset, however, these undertakings served nationalist ambitions by providing objects for the Berlin museum, conceived of as a national museum, comparable to the British Museum and the Louvre. Together with the excavations in western Turkey, they made Germany's importance for archaeology in the Ottoman Empire paramount.

The wider German public took readily to Near Eastern studies, attracted by the steady stream of new discoveries that directly touched on their fascination for adventure and exotic foreign cultures as well as their interest in the origins of the Bible. Several plans for the Museum-island in Berlin included growing space for the Ancient Near East.[17] Although Mesopotamia was also popular in other countries, as exemplified by the 1896 plans for the University Museum in Philadelphia,[18] the intensity of political and public support of Ancient Near Eastern Studies was unique to Germany. Supported by high popularity, spurred by political and economic interests and patronized by Kaiser Wilhelm II, studies in the Ancient Near East "became the perfect field for non-classical, in the sense of open-minded, modern investment in culture, by the state as by private philanthropists."[19]

Germany's Return to the Near East after World War I

World War I destroyed Germany's ambitions to play a leading part in the concert of imperialist powers. Germany lost its colonies, and her influence in the Near East came to a halt. It is no surprise that Near Eastern archaeology, one of the ideological flagships of German cultural imperialism, suffered deeply. Hyperinflation and Germany's role as pariah on the international scene thwarted for years any hope of renewing excavations in the Near East. In addition to the political restrictions imposed on Germany internationally, German scholars found themselves barred from international forums because of their role during the war.[20]

Three essential political prerequisites would have to be met for Germans to regain their place in archaeological research: First was the settling of Germany's economic crisis; second was the re-establishment of political contacts with the new governments in the countries of research; and third was the softening of international tensions. Here the treaties of Rapallo in 1922 and Locarno in 1925, and Germany's admission into the League of Nations and its permanent council in 1926, paved the way to German research in Persia, Turkey, and Iraq.

Persia

The first German scholar to return to the Near East was Ernst Herzfeld, who started to work in Persia in 1923. Herzfeld played a special role in Near Eastern Studies in many respects.[21] One of his most important contributions was to have raised interest in the archaeology of Persia and to help the Persian government to eliminate the monopoly France had held on archaeological explorations since 1895.[22] Moreover, the political situation in Persia played an important part in Herzfeld's developing role as the premier archaeologist in that area. Although nominally independent, Persia had come under even stronger British influence after World War I than before.[23] This led to a low point in German-Persian economic relations. Nevertheless, the desire of the Persians, and also Russians, to lessen British influence favored German activities in the country. In January 1923, the first post-war German ambassador to Persia, Werner von der Schulenburg, arrived in Tehran via Moscow.[24] Thus, Herzfeld's arrival in Iran appears to have been related to the new German-Iranian rapprochement. But his stay, which lasted, with brief interruptions, until 1934, was not officially backed by the German government. During his early years in Persia, the only support Herzfeld received was full pay for a leave of absence from the professorship he had held in Berlin since 1919.

In 1926 Herzfeld became chief advisor for the preparation of a new antiquities law that ended the French monopoly. His ambition to become the first director of antiquities in Persia, however, was thwarted by limited official interest and support in Germany for his research. Due to French diplomatic pressure, Herzfeld, the only non-Persian member of the Anjuman Athar-i Milli (National Monument Council),[25] was superseded by the French architect André Godard as first head of the Persian Department of Antiquities and the projected National Museum.

Herzfeld, nevertheless, stayed in Tehran and continued his pioneering work, for example, on the Achaemenid capitals Pasargadae and Persepolis. But throughout the 1920s, the German Ministry of Foreign Affairs generally lacked any interest in furthering German political influence in Persia.[26] In addition, despite Persia's expressed interest in closer economic ties with Germany, trade relations between the two countries remained insignificant.[27] This coincided with Herzfeld's failure to gain German financial support for excavations and the establishment of a DAI branch in Tehran. Exhausted by years of fruitless pleading with the German government and German research foundations, Herzfeld finally started excavations at Persepolis with the financial support, and on behalf, of the Oriental Institute of Chicago.[28]

The limited support for Herzfeld in the Persian venture cannot be explained by financial shortages alone. Even more important was the fact that the resources available were largely tied to long-established projects in Turkey and Mesopotamia, which had been revived after 1926.

Turkey

As described above, Germany and the Ottoman Empire had strong political, economic and archaeological ties before World War I. But resumption of work after the war was not only obstructed by Germany's economic and political situation. Conditions had also changed within the territory of the now-dissolved Ottoman Empire. New states had emerged, most importantly Turkey and Iraq, and new diplomatic, political, and economic ties had to be established. Only after Mustafa Kemal (Atatürk) had abolished the Caliphate and replaced it with a presidial system were diplomatic relations between Turkey and Germany resumed, in 1924.[29] This step was soon followed by the opening of a branch of the Deutsche Bank in Constantinople and contracts between Turkey and Junkers, the German airplane manufacturer, for the establishment of an arms factory.

Given the political situation in Turkey, it is no surprise that German archaeological research there was halted until 1927. However, considering the state of the economy of Weimar Germany, the revitalization of German excavations in Turkey indicates the high priority archaeology still enjoyed in Germany and the importance attached to it in Germany's foreign policy. Soon after the German embassy in Constantinople opened, the DAI inquired about and lobbied for the opening of a DAI in Turkey. Although difficult negotiations delayed the institute's opening until 1929,[30] once most of Germany's prewar archaeological activities in the field were resumed, they concentrated into the 1930s on Greek classical heritage. Entirely independent from these negotiations, Eckhard Unger, who had published his habilitation thesis in Near Eastern archaeology in Berlin in 1924, was appointed director of the Archaeological Museum in Istanbul for one year in 1924/25 and again in 1932 until 1935.[31] The resumption of German archaeological research followed intensified trade relations between the two countries. However, Germany never regained the considerable influence on Turkish foreign policy she had once had.

Iraq

While Persia never commanded much archaeological and historical interest, and German archaeology in Turkey concentrated on classical periods, the heart of Near Eastern Studies and the scene of extensive and highly popular excavations before World War I had been Mesopotamia. After the war this area now formed the British Mandate of Iraq. For German archaeologists the situation looked discouraging. Germany had neither official ties to the new government nor economic interests. The kaiser and his cabinet were gone and so was their erstwhile support. The number of DOG members had dropped considerably. Financial problems at home and the new political situation thwarted any hope of reviving research in Mesopotamia. In addition, except for earlier shipments, which included the glazed bricks of the famous Ishtar gate from Babylon, archaeological finds from the pre-war excavations in Babylon and Assur had not yet arrived in Berlin. In this situation the newly founded Notgemeinschaft der Deutschen Wissenschaft (Emergency Union of German Scholarship) saved the field from falling into oblivion. In its inner circle we find several strong supporters of Near Eastern Studies, especially the historian Eduard Meyer and Theodor Wiegand, as well as its president Friedrich Schmidt-Ott, who had been an active board member of the DOG from the beginning. A large number of archaeologists received grants for the publication of DOG excavations and work on objects for the projected new Near Eastern Museum in Berlin.[32]

Support was even increased for re-launching excavations after 1926. The Study of Antiquity in general and Orientalistik in particular became two of the best-funded fields of research, above, for example, biology, agronomy, and the remaining humanities, social sciences, and engineering.[33] Although the lion's share went to Classics, Mesopotamian studies were heavily subsidized.

In 1926, when Germany became a member of the League of Nations, the finds from Assur, which had been held up at Porto during the war, were released by Portugal and shipped to Berlin.[34] Soon afterwards, Walter Andrae, now curator at the museum, received permission in Baghdad to export (more than) half of the finds from Babylon to Berlin.[35] While in Baghdad, he was also encouraged to renew field research, which resulted in the relaunching of activity in 1928 at two highly prestigious sites: Uruk/Warka and the former Parthian and Sasanian capital Ctesiphon. Both excavations were officially organized by Eduard Meyer, who had become the foremost figure in the fields of Ancient History and Near Eastern Studies as well as influential in German research institutions, especially the Notgemeinschaft.[36]

It is important to note that throughout the Weimar era, there was virtually no German economic interest in Iraq. The first German envoy to Iraq, Fritz Grobba, was sent as late as 1932.[37] This circumstance certainly did not help German archaeological undertakings in Mesopotamia. Nevertheless, friendly personal ties with international colleagues and enormous support from the Notgemeinschaft enabled German archaeologists to regain their place in the field.

The Notgemeinschaft's backing of Near Eastern Studies shows how much the intellectual climate had changed: these studies were now accepted as an academic discipline and supported by public money, not only by private foundations. And while there was almost no official political, and very limited economic, German interest in Iraq, archaeology became once more a vehicle of German influence.

Responses to the Ancient Near East in Weimar Germany

Growing public funding of Near Eastern Studies during the Weimar years contrasted with reduced public attention and dwindling interest by scholars of other academic disciplines. As early as 1908, Eduard Meyer had scolded most of his fellow scholars for their lack of "intellectual elasticity" to come to grips with the changes in historical understanding necessitated by the discovery of Assyrian texts.[38] But the mushrooming knowledge about these cultures and the variety of languages an expert needed to learn posed a serious problem. As more research was carried out and more was learned about the Ancient Near East, scholars developed specific areas of in-depth knowledge. This trend toward specialization paralleled developments in the industrial sector. For non-specialists it became increasingly difficult to follow the debates. This became particularly problematic for historians in the field. Therefore, most made a more or less conscious decision to concentrate on Greek and Roman history again. The Ancient Near East was neglected by non-specialists. During the entire decades of the 1920s and 1930s, only Josef Vogt among German historians repeatedly taught a course in the cultural history of the Ancient Near East.[39] By and large, Near Eastern history and archaeology was non-existent at universities. Herzfeld, the only professor expected to teach Near Eastern archaeology, was on permanent leave since 1923. Assyriologists, for their part, were slow to advance their position as historians. Akkadian and Sumerian were still solely taught as languages and within departments of Oriental languages.

The Near East suffered from comparable difficulties in the public mind. While fieldwork and Bible-Babel controversies were greeted enthusiastically before World War I, the novelty of Ancient Near Eastern cultures had worn off. And without new excavations no spectacular new finds were brought to light. In competition with other fields for funding and public attention, scholars specializing in the Ancient Near East were now fighting a losing battle against local German Prehistory and especially the Classics.

At first this seems at odds with the modernization of many areas of society, but among the many different strands of intellectual life in the Weimar Republic, Classics increasingly filled the vacuum of meaning for an audience frustrated by Germany's loss of status and resources in the World War. The orientalist Carl H. Becker, a modernizer who had become Prussian minister of culture in 1921, may serve as an example. He was a staunch supporter of reforms to modernize the school and university systems. But in programmatic writings, he sought a reconciliation of spirit and body, art, religion, and engineering, something he called "real Humanism." As models for his concept of the "neue deutsche Vollmenschen" (new well-rounded Germans), he invoked the ancient Greeks.[40] Like Becker, many others, of various political backgrounds and disillusioned by modernity, found a model in the idealized, glorious past of ancient Greece. Most influential became the classical philologist Werner Jaeger. A former student of Ulrich von Wilamowitz-Moellendorff, whose historicism had promoted a purely academic, lifeless picture of the ancient world, Jaeger attempted to bring the Greeks' "timeless values of humankind" back to life as paradigmatic ideals for contemporary culture and character.[41] A growing number of influential classicists and educated laypersons followed his lead. The movement, called "Third Humanism," propounded the notion that classical ideals should have relevance for and substance in contemporary life.[42] With the re-invention of classical Greece as the ideal and model for a new humanism, the fascination with older cultures came full circle. And in connection with the return to the ideal, the Near East once again became the negative Other, the antagonist of the Western classical tradition.

The Nazi Regime: Aryans in the Ancient Near East

The ground was thus laid for the historian Helmut Berve's attack in 1935 on Ancient Near Eastern Studies as useless, because they were "dealing with alien, and therefore not comprehensible races." A "new demand for values," which according to Berve forfeited these studies' right to exist,[43] meant the new basis for writing history had to be "völkisch" and "rassisch" (ethnic and racial). History had to be written from the perspective of the present and had to contribute to the illumination of German and Aryan history. In this highly ideologized approach, archaeology and ancient history became prime targets for political influence on scholarly work. In turn, they gained considerable importance in Nazi ideology, which purports the superiority of Aryan Germans throughout history. Prehistory, in particular, enjoyed the immediate support of several state institutions (which started fighting each other for influence), especially the Amt Rosenberg with the Reichsbund für Deutsche Vorgeschichte (Reich Association for German Prehistory), and the SS-Ahnenerbe (SS-ancestor heritage).[44]

On another level, the generally high esteem in which classical antiquity, especially Greek culture, was held survived.[45] The classical world, nevertheless, suffered from the use it was put to by a number of scholars. While the older generation of historians had been political conservatives, many of the younger generation were active Nazi supporters even in the early years. Their interpretation of ancient history and the topics chosen for research changed under the impact of Nazi ideology. For example, Sparta as military might and the Roman Emperor Augustus as "Führer" received unprecedented acclaim.[46]

The Orient, by contrast, was relegated to inferior status on two basic lines of argument. One was the earlier, rather traditional approach to belittle accomplishments of the East and to elevate Western cultural superiority, now often called "Orientalism."[47] But while the supposed backwardness of the Orient was formerly attributed to political organization, climate, and culture, differences were now increasingly ascribed to racial inferiority.

Several Ancient Near East scholars had left Germany in the 1920s for positions in the United States. Now others followed.[48] Among them were Benno Landsberger, one of the most influential Assyriologists of the twentieth century, who became professor in Ankara and later in Chicago,[49] and Ernst Herzfeld, the important Near Eastern archaeologist. They were forced out of their academic posts and Germany because they were Jews.[50]

Herzfeld's departure cleared the path for Eckhard Unger's appointment to the first full professorship for Near Eastern archaeology in Berlin. Already in 1934 Friedrich Wachtsmuth had been appointed professor for Near Eastern Art at Marburg. At first glance, the creation, or in the case of Berlin the re-naming, of two chairs for Near Eastern archaeology seems to indicate growing interest in the Ancient Orient, but a closer look reveals that both new appointees were strong supporters of the regime. In addition, their lines of inquiry had changed according to the new dogma to search for "Indo-Germanic," that is, Aryan, contributions to Near Eastern civilization.[51] Hittites and Hurrians gained new popularity and research into their Indo-European languages and their material artifacts, which had started in the later 1920s and early 1930s, was encouraged.[52] Parenthetically it should be noted that due to the Nazis' misuse of the term, "Rasse" (race) is no longer used in Germany, except in the classification of animals. For most Germans of the post-war generations, it is associated with Nazi ideology. In recent years this has led to indiscriminate allegations against scholars writing in the 1920s and 1930s as fascists. In fact, this stance is ahistorical. The use of "Rasse" during this period is comparable to the use of "race" in current American English. Although these early writings may have racist or fascist connotations, this is not necessarily so.[53] The new trend also became clear in the aforementioned lecture course of Josef Vogt, a member of the NSdAP since 1937. He changed the title of his course on Near Eastern cultural history to "The Empires of the Ancient Near East and the Indo-Germans."

Indo-Europeans, Aryans, these were research topics that kept Ancient Near Eastern Studies alive. Even the SS Ahnenerbe created a Near Eastern department whose aim it was to establish the Aryan-Indogermanic influences on the progress of Near Eastern civilizations.[54] The new agenda finally shifted the focus from Mesopotamia to Iran. While Herzfeld had found it impossible to acquire funding from official sources more intrigued by excavations in Mesopotamia, the "cradle of civilization," now Persian history, regarded as Aryan, received unprecedented press. And as historians stressed the Aryan roots of the ancient Persians,[55] modern Iranians were explicitly exempted from the Nuremberg laws as "reinrassig" (of pure race).[56]

German interest in Aryan history dovetailed with the shah's interest in an ideology that would support his regime (picture 9). In 1934 the shah started a program for the Iranization of Persia. The "vahdat-i melli" (National Unity Campaign) involved "purification" of the Persian language, the creation of national consciousness through mass publications, and the deliberate use of Iran's glorified past.[57] Supposedly at the suggestion of diplomats posted in Berlin, Reza Shah ordered the country to be called Iran instead of Persia. The ideological closeness between Iran and Germany in many respects paved the way for the signing of several far-reaching trade and other treaties by the two governments.[58] In the late 1930s, Iran increasingly depended on Germany for machinery as well as trade in general. In 1940/41, 47.2 percent of all imports into Iran originated from Germany, while 42.9 percent of all Iranian exports were sent to Germany.[59] In an atmosphere of growing exchange and trust, Wilhelm Eilers was sent to Isfahan in 1938 to establish a German institute that would include archaeological research among its pursuits. But "activities were limited to philological and linguistic studies after 1939; in 1941 the institute was closed and Eilers was deported to Australia."[60]

Despite German economic influence and strong sympathies for Germany in Iran, the country managed to remain neutral in the first years of World War II. In August 1941, in a pre-emptive strike against German plans to use Iran as a base for action against India, an Anglo-Soviet invasion forced the shah to expel all German citizens, before he himself was compelled to resign.[61] This move by Britain and the Soviet Union eliminated Germany's only stronghold in the Near East.

It might have been this loss that finally encouraged the German government to turn its attention toward Near Eastern Studies. In the fall of 1942, the Nazi government sent out invitations for a conference of German Near East scholars and Near East archeologists, as part of a series devised by Paul Ritterbusch.[62] It was organized by Walther Wüst, the "curator" at Ahnenerbe and president of the University of Munich.[63] In this position he played an important role in the prosecution and execution of members of the anti-Nazi student group "Weiße Rose" in 1943.

If it was the government's aim to enlist the invited Orientalists for their ideological or political support, the conference was a complete failure. According to Hausmann, Ritterbusch was in general heavily criticized by the Nazi association of university professors, because he invited scholars to his conferences without regard for their sympathies for Nazi ideology.[64] These Orientalists may not have been particularly nonconformist, but surprisingly the published speeches of most contain no, or at most superficial, allusions to the current *zeitgeist*.[65] Many scholars simply enumerated earlier accomplishments in their respective fields and tried to advance their field's position for future increase of support for their activities, or, in the case of archaeologists, for re-initiation of their work. Thus even in 1942, Oriental Studies was deemed unimportant to either the war effort or Nazi propaganda.

Only the lofty tone of Walther Wüst's closing words hints at some of the more successful ancient historians under the Nazi regime, above all Berve. In the introduction to *Das neue Bild der Antike*, a two-volume work he edited in 1942, Berve describes the new affinity between Nazi Germany and the ancient Greeks and Romans. And while his words of the reconciliation between body and spirit are at times reminiscent of Jaeger's goal of a Third Humanism or even Becker's *Vollmenschen*, for Berve, the ideal had become reality in Nazi Germany. The *Wesensverwandtschaft* (congeniality) with the ancient Greeks and Romans, he considered deeply felt because of revived racial instincts that would lead modern Germans to recognize instantly the link with their glorious past.[66] While Berve was celebrating his success of having restored order to the ancient world, Ritterbusch was courting Berve's victims. But as we know, the Nazi government's endeavors to enlist the remaining Near East scholars were not decisive for the war's outcome.

Conclusion

The importance attached to Antiquity in general and the Ancient Near East in particular was a specifically German phenomenon. The close connection between politics, culture, and antiquity, as demonstrated above, had its origins in Germany in the early nineteenth century. In the Kaiserreich, research into the Ancient Near East was allied with German economic and political imperialist designs in the Ottoman Empire. In the Weimar Republic, Ancient Near Eastern Studies, which had been thriving on this connection and enjoyed great general popularity, was again excluded from the canon of general knowledge. The field survived only because of the financial support provided by older, influential supporters within the Notgemeinschaft der Deutschen Wissenschaft. Still, archaeologists working in the Near East largely helped to improve bilateral relations. The focus of research and the importance given to Near Eastern Studies changed again during the Nazi period. Now Ancient Near Eastern Studies was put to use in support of claims to Aryan, "Indo-European" pre-eminence throughout history. The importance of, and arguments drawn from, these studies by the Nazis were the last flickering of the intense ideological role of these studies. The abuse of Antiquity and the various disciplines of Classical Studies certainly contributed to their decline in public opinion after World War II.

Today, professors of Ancient Near Eastern Studies, Assyriology, and/ or archaeology are found at thirteen German universities. Approaches have changed; many scholars consider their field as either cultural-historical or social science, and their work as reconstructing ancient settlement systems and their ecological settings or the workings of relations between nomadic and settled communities. The cultural-imperialist approach, the *Sendungsbewußtsein* (sense of mission) of the Kaiserreich, is gone. Also the direct connection with economic or political interests, which was so intense in the formative period of these studies before World War I, are less obvious, if not altogether peripheral. Nor do we see ideological constraints like the obligatory *Arierforschung* (Aryan research) under the Nazis. Ancient Near Eastern Studies, Assyriology, and archaeology have found their place in the academic world as small but respected fields.

Yet, neither the art nor the history of the Ancient Near East are subjects taught in art history or history departments. And in German school textbooks the Ancient Near East is almost totally absent. Based on handbooks by Berve and Bengtson, written or drafted in the Nazi period, Ancient Near Eastern powers are still mostly reduced to the position of Oriental enemy of Greek freedom, which is presumed to be at the root of European civilization.[67] Nevertheless, in an atmosphere of generally friendly relations with all modern states in the area, generalizations of "Oriental" behavior from ancient sources are rare. On the contrary, recent political events clearly indicate that only a small segment of the German public seems unsensitized by the Nazi abuse of history and still susceptible to such simplifications as a clash of civilizations or the division of the world into good and evil. But as is the case currently in the United States, active involvement in discussions about the multiplicity of approaches to the world, whether ancient or modern, remains a must for scholars of the Ancient Near East.

Notes

The present article is the extended and annotated version of a paper presented at the German Studies Association meeting in Washington, D.C., on October 2, 2001. I would like to thank Dr. Hans-Ulrich Seidt for his invitation to participate in the panel on Germany and the Middle East. I am very grateful to Prof. Dr. Elspeth Dusinberre, who went through the paper with great care to correct my non–native speaker's English. All opinions and mistakes remain my responsibility.

The following abbreviations are used:

Bast 2001 = Oliver Bast, "Germany I: German-Persian diplomatic relations," in *Encyclopedia Iranica* X, 2001, 506–19.
Gunter and Hauser (in press) = Ann C. Gunter, and Stefan R. Hauser, eds., *Ernst Herzfeld and the Development of Near Eastern Studies, 1900–1950* (Leiden, in press).
Hauser 2001 = Stefan R. Hauser, "Not out of Babylon? The Development of Ancient Near Eastern Studies and Its Current Significance," in *Historiography in the Cuneiform World*, Part I, Proceedings of the XLVe Rencontre Assyriologique International, ed. Zvi Abush et al (Bethesda, Maryland, 2001), 211–37.
Hauser (in press) = Stefan R. Hauser, "Ernst Herzfeld and Eduard Meyer: Near Easter Studies, Orientalism and Universal History," in Gunter and Hauser (in press).
Hirschfeld 1980 = Yair Hirschfeld, *Deutschland und Iran im Spielfeld der Mächte: internationale Beziehungen unter Reza Schah 1921–1941* (Düsseldorf, 1980).
Marchand 1996 = Suzanne L. Marchand, *Down from Olympus: Archaeology and Philhellenism in Germany, 1750–1970* (Princeton, N.J., 1996).
Mousavi (in press) = Ali Mousavi, "Ernst Herzfeld, Politics, and Antiquities Legislation in Iran," in Gunter and Hauser (in press).
Renger 1979 = Johannes Renger, "Die Geschichte der Altorientalistik und der vorderasiatischen Archäologie in Berlin von 1875 bis 1945," in *Berlin und die Antike*, ed. Willmuth Arenhövel and Christa Schreiber (Berlin, 1979), 151–92.
Rezun 1982 = Miron Rezun, *The Iranian Crisis of 1941: The Actors Britain, Germany and the Soviet Union* (Cologne, 1982).

1. Cf. "Deutsche Politik im Zeitalter des Imperialismus: Ein Teufelskreis?," in *Flucht in den Krieg? Die Außenpolitik des kaiserlichen Deutschland*, ed. Gregor Schöllgen (Darmstadt, 1991), 170–86; Immanuel Geiss, "'Weltpolitik': Die deutsche Version des Imperialismus," in ibid., 148–69.
2. It is often forgotten that besides the most successful powers, France and Britain, Russia, Spain, Portugal, Belgium, and the Netherlands were also active as colonial powers. At least in Germany, the scale and success of imperial activities by Japan and the United States at the turn of the century are usually forgotten.
3. Repeatedly the Persian government tried to gain German support, or even to win Germany over as a third power in the political struggle for influence in Persia between Russia and Britain. Nevertheless, Bismarck and later Wilhelm II did every-

thing possible to demonstrate their lack of interest in Persia, as part of their policy to conciliate Britain and Russia, cf. Bast 2001.
4. Gregor Schöllgen, *Imperialismus und Gleichgewicht: Deutschland, England und die orientalische Frage 1871–1914* (Munich, 1984), 433.
5. Kurt Grunwald, "Pénétration Pacifique—the Financial Vehicles of Germany's 'Drang nach Osten,'" in "Germany and the Middle East 1835–1939," ed. Yehuda L. Wallach, *Jahrbuch des Instituts für Deutsche Geschichte*, supplement 1 (Tel Aviv, 1975), 85–101, here p. 87.
6. This also changed the archaeological practice in field research. While archaeology in earlier times generally meant the hunt for treasures illustrating what was known from written sources, archaeologists, in their attempt to break the narrow scope of textual evidence, developed precise methods modeled on hard science (Adolf H. Borbein, "Klassische Archäologie in Berlin vom 18. bis zum 20. Jahrhundert," in *Berlin und die Antike*, ed. Willmuth Arenhövel and Christa Schreiber (Berlin, 1979), 99–150, here p. 138). For a short history of archaeological methods and theories see Stefan R. Hauser, "Archäologische Methoden," in *Der Neue Pauly: Rezeptions- und Wissenschaftsgeschichte*, vol. 13 (Stuttgart and Weimar, 1999), 201–16. For a detailed account of the history of archaeology see Bruce G. Trigger, *A History of Archaeological Thought* (Cambridge, U.K., 1989).
7. Suzanne L. Marchand. "The Rhetoric of Artifacts and the Decline of Classical Humanism: the Case of Josef Strzygowski," *History and Theory* 33 (1994): 106–30, here p. 112.
8. The literature on German Philhellenism, especially on specific aspects and periods, is vast. For a summary see above all Marchand 1996.
9. Marchand 1996, 243.
10. Cf. Frederick N. Bohrer, "Inventing Assyria: Exoticism and Reception in Nineteenth-Century England and France," *Art Bulletin* 70 (1998): 336–56; Frederick N. Bohrer, "Layard and Botta: Archaeology, Imperialism, and Aesthetics," in *Historiography in the Cuneiform World*, Part I, Proceedings of the XLVe Rencontre Assyriologique International, ed. Zvi Abush et al. (Bethesda, Maryland, 2001), 55–64.
11. The first cuneiform signs were deciphered by Georg Grotefend in 1802. A much broader understanding of signs and language was independently gained by Henry C. Rawlinson in the 1830s. His work was based on Darius's trilingual inscription from Bisotun, which he published in full in 1846. In 1857 the British Academy officially declared cuneiform as deciphered. For the most detailed account see Mogens Trolle Larsen, *The Conquest of Assyria: Excavations in an Antique Land, 1840–1860* (New York, 1996).
12. Cf. Francine Tissot, "La délégation archéologique française en Iran," *Encyclopaedia Iranica* vol. 7 (1996), 238–40; Rémy Boucharlat, "Ernst Herzfeld and French Approaches to Iranian Archaeology," in Gunter and Hauser (in press); Mousavi (in press).
13. Cf. Renger 1979, 153. Six years earlier, the first chair for Assyriology was created for Jules Oppert at the Collège de France.
14. Quoted after Matthes Olaf and Johannes Althoff, "Die 'Königliche Kommission zur Erforschung der Euphrat- und Tigrisländer,'" *Mitteilungen der Deutschen Orient-Gesellschaft* 130 (1998), 241–54, p. 243. Interestingly Mesopotamia was

chosen over Egypt, as the minister had asked for advice on inaugurating research into Egypt or Mesopotamia (Matthes and Althoff, ibid., 242). Nevertheless, in 1899 a "Generalkonsulat" for archaeology was established in Cairo, which in 1907 was transformed into the "Institut für ägyptische Altertumskunde." In 1928 this institute became part of the Deutsches Archäologisches Institut [DAI] (Marchand 1996, 195).

15. cf. Jan Stefan Richter, *Die Orientreise Kaiser Wilhelms II. 1898: Eine Studie zur deutschen Außenpolitik an der Wende zum 20. Jahrhundert* (Hamburg, 1997).
16. cf. among others Seton Lloyd, *The Archaeology of Mesopotamia* (London, 1978), who in his foreword praises the excavators Robert Koldewey (Babylon) and Walter Andrae (Assur) for their techniques laying the ground to all later discoveries.
17. Nicola Crüsemann, *Vom Zweistromland zum Kupfergraben: Vorgeschichte und Entstehungsjahre (1899–1918) der Vorderasiatischen Abteilung der Berliner Museen vor fach- und kulturpolitischen Hintergründen*, Jahrbuch der Berliner Museen N.F., Beihefte Bd. 42. (Berlin, 2001).
18. The 1896 master plan for the museum, not completed as planned, envisaged "Three central rotundas ... devoted to the ancient civilizations of Greece & Rome, Egypt, and Mesopotamia, flanked by courtyard buildings dedicated to the traditional cultures of America, Asia, Africa, and Oceania." Douglas M. Haller, "Architectural Archaeology: A Centennial View of the Museum Buildings," *Expedition* 41, (2000). <http://www.upenn.edu/museum/Overview/buildinghistory.html>.
19. Hauser 2001, 218.
20. Bernhard vom Brocke, "'Wissenschaft und Militarismus': Der Aufruf der 93 >An die Kulturwelt!< und der Zusammenbruch der internationalen Gelehrtenrepublik im Ersten Weltkrieg," in *Wilamowitz nach 50 Jahren*, ed. William M. Calder III, Hellmut Flashar, and Theodor Lindken, (Darmstadt, 1985), 649–719.
21. See Gunter and Hauser (in press).
22. Mousavi (in press).
23. Hirschfeld 1980, 17.
24. Hirschfeld 1980, 32.
25. The Anjuman Athar-i Milli was a private society founded in 1922 to support care of Persian cultural heritage. On the developing interest in and the changing role of archaeology in Persia/Iran see Kamyar Abdi, "Nationalism, politics, and the development of archaeology in Iran," *American Journal of Archaeology* 105 (2000): 51–76.
26. Bast 2001, 511.
27. According to Hirschfeld (Hirschfeld 1980, 331) during the Weimar years imports by Persia accounted for 0.1 to 0.2 percent of Germany's overall exports, and imports from Persia, including oil, amounted to 0.2 to 0.6 percent.
28. Hauser (in press).
29. On behalf of Germany, the Swedish ambassador inquired about entering into relations in November 1923. In April 1924, the first German ambassador, Nadolny, was delegated. See *Akten zur deutschen Auswärtigen Politik 1918–1945 aus dem Archiv des Auswärtigen Amtes* (Göttingen ,1991), Serie A vol. IX, nos. 18, 88, and 241. This appointment coincided with the passing of the new constitution in Turkey.
30. Marchand 1996, 283–84.

31. Ernst Weidner, "Nachruf Eckhard Unger (April 11, 1885 to July 24, 1966)," *Archiv für Orientforschung* 22 (1968/69): 210–11.
32. The foundation stone for the museum was laid in 1910. After protracted quarrels the museum finally opened in October 1930. On these quarrels cf. Nicola Crüsemann, *Vom Zweistromland zum Kupfergraben*, passim. The Near Eastern exhibition was completed in 1936 and closed with the outbreak of World War II in 1939. The exhibition was designed by Walter Andrae, the former excavator of Assur, who assumed the directorship of the museum in 1928. The museum was heavily damaged in bombing raids during the war; most of the artifacts were removed by Soviet troops in 1945 and returned in 1957. In the German Democratic Republic, the displays were redesigned following Andrae's original concept, except for the missing pieces, particularly those in gold. On the difficulties of concept and design see Reinhard Bernbeck, "The Exhibition of Architecture and the Architecture of an Exhibition: The Changing Face of the Pergamon Museum," *Archaeological Dialogues* 7 (2000): 98–145.
33. Marchand 1996, 295.
34. Walter Andrae, "Der Rückerwerb der Assur-Funde aus Portugal," *Mitteilungen der Deutschen Orient-Gesellschaft* 65 (1927): 1–6.
35. Walter Andrae, "Reise nach Babylon zur Teilung der Babylon-Funde," *Mitteilungen der Deutschen Orient-Gesellschaft* 65 (1927): 7–27.
36. Wolfhart Unte, "Eduard Meyer und die Notgemeinschaft der Deutschen Wissenschaft," in *Eduard Meyer*, ed. William M. Calder III. and Alexander Demandt (Leiden, 1990), 505–37; Hauser (in press).
37. See the contribution by Schwanitz in this volume.
38. Renger 1979, 155.
39. Diemuth Königs, *Joseph Vogt: Ein Althistoriker in der Weimarer Republik und im Dritten Reich* (Basle, 1995), 307–308.
40. Carl Heinrich Becker, *Die pädagogische Akademie im Aufbau unseres nationalen Bildungswesens* (Leipzig, 1926), 52–56.
41. Werner Jäger, "Einführung," *Die Antike* 1 (1925): 1–4. It is no coincidence that among Jaeger's many publications the most important and still reprinted one is his *Paideia: Die Formung des griechischen Menschen* (Engl.: *Paideia: The Ideals of Greek Culture*). The first volume was published in Germany in 1934 and translated into English in 1939. At that time Jaeger had already accepted a chair at Harvard University. Calder emphasizes that Jaeger was entirely apolitical (William M. Calder, "Werner Jaeger," in *Classical Scholarship: A Biographical Encyclopedia*, ed. Ward M. Briggs and William M. Calder (New York and London, 1990), 211–26, here pp. 217–18). His ideas found a very positive response in the Third Reich. Nevertheless, the offer from Harvard was very fortunate as his wife was Jewish. Volumes 2 and 3 of his *Paideia* appeared first in English and shortly afterwards in German. The books went through several editions in both languages and are still available as reprints.
42. Albert Henrichs, "Philologie und Wissenschaftsgeschichte: Zur Krise eines Selbstverständnisses," in *Altertumswissenschaft in den 20er Jahren: Neue Fragen und Impulse*, ed. Hellmut Flashar (Stuttgart, 1995), 423–57, here pp. 454–55.
43. "Die Wissenschaft vom Alten Orient. soweit sie fremdrassige, uns wesensfremde und darum in ihrer tiefen Eigenart nicht zu begreifende Völker betrifft, ist in dem

Augenblick, da die Problemsetzung über das rational Feststellbare hinausgeht, zur Resignation verdammt. Sie versagt damit vor der neuen Wertforderung und verliert infolgedessen ihr Lebensrecht." (The study of the ancient Orient, inasmuch as its focus is an alien race, alien to us in nature, and therefore concerns peoples that are incomprehensible in their deeper character, is, at the moment when the problem exceeds anything that is rationally determinable, condemned to resignation. It thus fails the test of the new value demand and consequently loses its right to exist.) Helmut Berve, "Zur Kulturgeschichte des Alten Orients," *Archiv für Kulturgeschichte* 25 (1935): 216–30, here pp. 229–30.

44. See Henning Haßmann, "Archaeology in the Third Reich," in *Archaeology, Ideology and Society: The German Experience*, ed. Heinrich Härke (Frankfurt am Main, 2000), 65–139.
45. Among Nazi racist historians even the Greeks came under general doubt concerning their Aryan blood. Their special role in history was no longer sufficiently explained by their being Aryan, but by their "nordic" blood, see Hans F. R. Günther, "Der Einschlag nordischer Rasse im hellenischen Volke," *Vergangenheit und Gegenwart* 25 (1935): 529ff. But in general ancient Greece and Rome were highly valued. According to *Kürschners Deutscher Gelehrtenkalender*, the number of classical archaeologists, especially at universities, remained far higher than the number of prehistorians.
46. Volker Losemann, *Nationalsozialismus und Antike: Studien zur Entwicklung des Faches Alte Geschichte 1933–1945* (Hamburg, 1977). Franz Georg Maier, "Review of Volker Losemann, *Nationalsozialismus und Antike* (1977)," *Gnomon* 53 (1981): 215–16. Beat Näf, *Von Perikles zu Hitler? Die athenische Demokratie und die deutsche Althistorie bis 1945* (Berne and New York, 1986). Beat Näf, "Deutungen und Interpretationen der griechischen Geschichte in den zwanziger Jahren," in *Altertumswissenschaft in den 20er Jahren. Neue Fragen und Impulse*, ed. Hellmut Flashar (Stuttgart, 1995), 275–302; Ines Stahlmann, *Imperator Caesar Augustus: Studien zur Geschichte des Principatsverständnisses in der deutschen Altertumswissenschaft bis 1945* (Darmstadt, 1988).
47. Edward W. Said, *Orientalism* (New York, 1995). For a discussion of Orientalism and its importance for the interpretation of the Ancient Orient and its history see Stefan R. Hauser, "Orientalismus," in *Der Neue Pauly: Rezeptions- und Wissenschaftsgeschichte* 15/1 (Stuttgart and Weimar, 2001), 1233–43. Examples of prejudiced interpretations are shown in: Stefan R. Hauser, "'Greek in subject and style, but a little distorted.' Zum Verhältnis von Orient und Okzident in der Altertumswissenschaft," in *Posthumanistische Klassische Archäologie*, ed. Stefan Altekamp, Matthias Hofter, and Michael Krumme (Munich, 2001), 83–104.
48. See Renger 1979; Johannes Renger, "Altorientalistik und jüdische Gelehrte in Deutschland—Deutsche und österreichische Altorientalisten im Exil," in *Jüdische Intellektuelle und die Philologien in Deutschland: 1871–1933*, ed. Wilfried Barner and Christoph König (Göttingen, 2001), 247–61.
49. Renger 2001.
50. Like many German scholars, Landsberger was courted by the Turkish government and started to teach in Ankara. Herzfeld went first to London and in 1936 joined Albert Einstein and John von Neumann at the Institute for Advanced Study in Princeton, New Jersey. Although Herzfeld's parents had converted to Protestant-

ism before he was born, the Nuremberg Laws of 1935 defined him as Jewish. Both had been highly decorated in World War I.

51. Eckhard Unger, *Das antike Hakenkreuz als Wirbelsturm, Welt und Mensch im Alten Orient*, vol. 1 (Berlin, 1937); Friedrich Wachtsmuth, *Die Widerspiegelung völkischer Eigentümlichkeiten in der alt-morgenländischen Baugestaltung* (Leipzig, 1938).

52. See Julius Jordan, "Leistungen und Aufgaben der Deutschen Ausgrabungen im Vorderen Orient," in *Der Orient in deutscher Forschung: Vorträge der Berliner Orientalistentagung, Herbst 1942*, ed. Hans H. Schaeder (Leipzig, 1944), 228–38. Jordan emphasizes the importance of the excavation at Boghazköy, because of its former "Indo-European" inhabitants. It is important to note that not all scholars were able or willing to collaborate in the efforts of redefining Ancient Near Eastern Studies. For example, Bittel, the excavator of Boghazköy, seems to have sacrificed his scholarly standing in that respect. He started to excavate the capital of the Hittite Empire in central Anatolia in 1931. In the 1960s he became president of the DAI. Most notable is Walter Andrae, head of the Vorderasiatische Museum in Berlin, who in addition became chairman of the Deutsche Orient-Gesellschaft. His writings are free from all allusions to anti-Semitism and the cult of Aryans. In his contribution to the *Propyläen Kunstgeschichte*, for example, he insists on a linear development of Mesopotamian art despite ethnic/racial changes. We should expect that his obvious refusal to define "race" in the then-prevailing zeitgeist would have caused raised eyebrows in 1942 (Walter Andrae, "Vorderer Orient," in Heinrich Schäfer and Walter Andrae, *Die Kunst des Alten Orients, Propyläen Kunstgeschichte* 2 (3rd ed.) (Berlin, 1942), 131–68, 704–46, here pp. 136–37).

53. See the discussion in Stefan Altekamp et al., *Posthumanistische Klassische Archäologie* (Munich, 2001), 249.

54. Michael H. Kater, *Das "Ahnenerbe" der SS: 1935–1945, ein Beitrag zur Kulturpolitik des Dritten Reiches* (Heidelberg, 1974), 111.

55. The most prominent historic figures of Persian history, such as Zoroaster or the Achaemenid kings Cyrus and Darius, were even described as "nordic;" see Hans F. R. Günther, *Die nordische Rasse bei den Indogermanen Asiens: Zugleich ein Beitrag zur Frage der Urheimat und Rassenherkunft der Indogermanen* (Munich, 1934); Fritz Schachermeyr, *Indogermanen und Orient* (Stuttgart, 1944). For some scholars the Aryan race of the ancient Persians soon became a problem in the context of their fights with the Greek heirs of European (and German) heritage. The explanation found for the Persian defeat was their intimate contact with their non-Aryan subjects in Mesopotamia, which resulted in loss of strength through mingling of races (see Schachermeyr, 171). On the general problem of how the Achaemenid (Persian) Empire was interpreted in Nazi Germany, see Josef Wiesehöfer, "Das Bild der Achaimeniden in der Zeit des Nationalsozialismus," in *Achaemenid History III: Method and Theory*, ed. Heleen Sancisi-Weerdenburg and Amélie Kuhrt (Leiden, 1998), 1–14. Shockingly enough Schachermeyr's view is generally repeated in Bengtson's handbook on Greek history (Hermann Bengtson. *Griechische Geschichte von den Anfängen bis in die römische Kaiserzeit, Handbuch der Altertumswissenschaft III.4*, 5th ed. (1st ed. 1950), [Munich, 1977], 180), which, until recently, served as the basis for German schoolbook texts. See Stefan R. Hauser, "Der hellenisierte Orient: Bemerkungen zum Verhältnis von

Alter Geschichte, Klassischer und Vorderasiatischer Archäologie," in *Fluchtpunkt Uruk, Archäologische Einheit aus methodischer Vielfalt: Schriften für Hans Jörg Nissen*, ed. Hartmut Kühne, Reinhard Bernbeck, Karin Bartl (Rahden, 1999), 316–41, here p. 330.
56. Rezun 1982, 29.
57. M. Reza Ghods, *Iran in the Twentieth Century: A Political History* (Boulder, Colo., 1989), 106–108. My due thanks go to Dr. Kamyar Abdi who was so kind to provide me with the picture that shows Reza Shah and the crown prince in front of the Apadana reliefs (picture 1).
58. Yair Hirschfeld, "German Policy Towards Iran: Continuity and Change from Weimar to Hitler, 1919–1939," in "Germany and the Middle East 1835–1939," ed. Yehuda L. Wallach *Jahrbuch des Instituts für Deutsche Geschichte*, supplement 1 (Tel Aviv, 1975), 117–41, here pp.127–28.
59. Hirschfeld 1980, 330.
60. Dietrich Huff, "Germany ii. Archaeological Explorations and Excavations," *Encyclopaedia Iranica* vol. 10 (2001), 519–30, here p. 525. The DAI's former director, Wolfram Kleiss, seems blissfully ignorant about its history in Iran. His article "Deutsches Archäologisches Institut" for the *Encyclopaedia Iranica* vol. 7 (1996), 331–33, turns the development upside down in stating that Herzfeld's publications were sponsored by the Isfahan station, which was founded after the publications had appeared. For his publications in Germany after 1935, Herzfeld paid himself using his pension, which due to the laws on money transfer had to remain in Germany. Kleiss also claims that there had been German excavations in Persepolis before 1938. This must be a reference to Herzfeld's and later Erich Schmidt's work at this important site. But although both of them were German, they worked for the Oriental Institute of Chicago (on Schmidt see Jack M. Balcer, "Erich Friedrich Schmidt, 13 September 1897–30 October 1964," in *Achaemenid History VII: Through Travellers' Eyes*, ed. Heleen Sancisi-Weerdenburg and Jan W. Drijvers (Leiden, 1991), 147–72).
61. Bast 2001, 506–19; Rezun 1982.
62. Frank-Rutger Hausmann, "Deutsche Geisteswissenschaft im Zweiten Weltkrieg: Die 'Aktion Ritterbusch' (1940–1945)," *Schriften zur Wissenschafts- und Universitätsgeschichte* 1 (Dresden, 1998).
63. Wüst, who was born in 1901, had been appointed professor for "Indo-Germanische Studien" in 1932. According to Kater (*Ahnenerbe*, 295), Wüst never worked in Iran. Although Wüst was curator, that is CEO, of Ahnenerbe, the Notgemeinschaft refused him a grant for a new documentation of the famous Bisotun inscriptions during the war (Ibid., 97). Nevertheless, from 1938 to 1943, the same institution granted him money for research in Iran relevant to the war. (I would like to thank Willi Oberkrome, Freiburg, for this information.) The exact use of these grants is uncertain. They might have helped him to publish his *Indogermanisches Bekenntnis: Sechs Reden* (Berlin-Dahlem, 1942). In his lecture on the Reich, idea and reality among the ancient Aryans, he describes what he called *Entartung* (loss of ethnic character) and *Entnordung* (loss of Nordic character) of Aryans in contact with their Near Eastern neighbors (among others: "the subversive influence of the highly developed money economy in Mesopotamia"), and expresses his hope of a new dawn with Reza Shah Pahlevi (Wüst, 29–30).

64. Hausmann, 43. Hausmann describes these conferences as "Leistungsschauen" (scholarly fairs).
65. The contributions were published in two volumes: Hans H. Schaeder, *Der Orient in deutscher Forschung: Vorträge der Berliner Orientalistentagung, Herbst 1942* (Leipzig, 1944); and Richard Hartmann, ed., *Beiträge zur Arabistik, Semitistik, und Islamwissenschaft* (Leipzig, 1944). Some of the articles are still useful summaries of German research in certain areas until 1942.
66. Berve, 7.
67. In an atmosphere where many, if not most, historians of Greek and Roman history were either conservative or outright fascist, Berve later became the war-time representative of the German study of Antiquity. His articles and leaflets, about the battle at Thermopylae, for example, where the Spartans fought against the Near East invaders to the last man, were distributed to German soldiers at the front as means to boost morale and lift their spirit. After the war, he was at first banned from teaching, but was re-appointed to a full professorship in 1949. He later became head of the Commission for Ancient History and Epigraphy of the DAI and as such was a spokesperson for Germany's Greek and Roman historians. A collection of his articles was published anew in 1966. Except for the deletion of a few sentences, the articles were published in their original form. On Berve cf. Karl Christ, *Neue Profile der Alten Geschichte* (Darmstadt, 1990), 125–87.

Figure 10. Prophecy: "Hitler is great, and Papen is his prophet," after Papen's Vienna mission 1938

Berlin – Ankara – Baghdad

Franz von Papen and German Near East Policy during the Second World War

KARL HEINZ ROTH

Franz von Papen as German Special Envoy to Ankara

Hitler named his former vice chancellor, Franz von Papen, ambassador to Turkey and assured him of his "special protection" for this very perilous assignment (figures 10–11) on April 20, 1939.[1] Papen remained in this post until the Turkish government severed diplomatic relations with Germany on August 2, 1944. Most researchers, except Papen's biographers,[2] place little importance on this phase of his political life. They tend to regard his Turkey mission as the final stage in a gradual fall from political power and, therefore, not warranting closer analysis.[3] Many studies about the German-Turkish relations in the thirties and forties regard Papen merely as a typical representative of Nazi Germany's foreign policy. He is seen as executing the Turkey policy of the Third Reich without any initiatives of his own.[4]

Even a quick glance at the archival sources contradicts this assessment. Due to his variegated political past, neither was Papen in Ankara tied completely to a routine and the instructions from the hierarchy of the foreign office, nor were his activities limited to Turkey. As a former staff officer of the German Orient Corps, who had fought in 1917/18 on several fronts of the Ottoman Empire, he had excellent knowledge of the Arab East and had close connections to the military-political elite of the host country. He stood for a specific alternative to German expansionist policy, one that was to grant the satellite and subject nations under the umbrella of German world hegemony certain autonomous rights, including in trade. Berlin was quite tolerant of this approach as long as it helped keep collaborators, especially the authoritarian regimes in southeastern Europe, under control, leaving Papen to make conscious use of this fact for his own initiatives. He had a much freer hand than has been presumed up to now, and he enriched German foreign policy during the Second World War by suggesting remarkably imaginative alternatives to German foreign policy. A closer analysis of his activities during the war is therefore absolutely warranted.

In the years 1934 to 1938, when he served as special envoy to Vienna reporting directly to Hitler, Papen had earned the reputation of troubleshooter, who, with remarkable negotiating skill and clever political intrigues, knew to bend even seemingly hopeless situations in favor of the interests of the Reich.[5] It was this image, more than anything, to which Papen owed his new mission to Ankara. In late July 1934, all attempts by the Austrian Nazis to topple the government and unite Austria with Nazi Germany had ended in hopeless failure. Papen, who was promptly dispatched to Vienna, nevertheless succeeded, within a few years, in bringing the Austrian state under dominant German influence and thereby preparing for the *Anschluß*. In the spring of 1939, the German position in Turkey also declined dramatically. Alarmed by the German-Italian incursion into the Balkans,[6] the Turkish government began to waver in its traditional course of neutrality and sought a rapprochement with the Western Powers. Here, too, it was Papen who was charged with attempting to halt this development and to repair German-Turkish relations. For this purpose, the envoy was given direct access to Hitler. Reich foreign minister Joachim von Ribbentrop was not always present during discussions concerning the trump cards of German war and expansionist policy between the *"Führer"* and his "old jockey" at the time of critical events in May and August 1939, in the summer and November 1940, the spring of 1941, and March 1942.[7]

Adding to the prestige of the ambassadorship to Turkey was the geostrategic position of that country as a land bridge between southeastern Europe, the Near East, the Caucasus, and Central Asia. Since the Balkan Pact of 1934, Turkey was seen as an important guarantor of stability of the postwar political order established in the southeast region of Europe in 1918.[8] Two years later, Turkey regained sovereignty over the Straits through the Treaty of Montreux and shared control over the Black Sea region with the Soviet Union.[9] Within the framework of the Pact of Saadabad, Turkey was also considered as an important stabilizing factor in the Middle East, especially with regard to Iran and Afghanistan.[10] By the same token, the importance of Turkey's concealed influence in the Arab world could not be underestimated. Although these regions had exchanged the Ottoman yoke for the authority of the British-French Mandate as a result of the First World War, they nevertheless were casting a jealous eye on Atatürk's military dictatorship, which had risen from the ruins of the Sublime Porte.

Turkey as a German Sphere of Action during the Second World War

In the 1930s and during the Second World War, Turkey was thus the only regional power on the cutting edge between the Balkans, the Near and Middle East as well as the Caucasus which the enemy powers had to give serious consideration, especially since she pursued an ambitious industrialization and armaments program. When the Axis powers shattered one by one the Turkish regional alliances by virtue of their expansionist policies in the Balkan,[11] the top politicians in Ankara sought, starting in the spring of 1939, to cover their back with a friendship treaty with Great Britain and France, which was signed on October 19, 1939, following mutual assurances of guarantees in May/June.[12] However, when France collapsed under the Nazi invasion in June 1940, Turkey, rather than fulfilling its treaty obligations, took refuge in a seesaw position, which she continued in April 1941 when the Germans, by attacking Yugoslavia and Greece, made short shrift of the Balkan Pact as well. On June 18, 1941, five days before the German invasion of the Soviet Union, Turkey finally concluded a friendship treaty with Nazi Germany (figure 12).[13] Now, she was allied with Great Britain and, at the same time, on friendly terms with Germany. Turkey thus acknowl-

Jn Namen des Deutfchen Volkes

ernenne ich
unter Berufung in das Beamtenverhältnis
auf Lebenszeit
den Botfchafter
Franz von Papen
zum Botfchafter in Ankara.
Ich vollziehe diefe Urkunde in der Erwartung,
daß der Ernannte getreu feinem Dienfteide
feine Amtspflichten gewiffenhaft erfüllt und
das Vertrauen rechtfertigt, das ihm durch
diefe Ernennung bewiefen wird. Zugleich
fichere ich ihm meinen befonderen Schutz zu.

Berlin, den 20. April 1939
Der führer und Reichskanzler

Figure 11. Papen's appointment by Hitler. It was missing and recently discovered in the State Military Archives of Moscow (see English translation opposite)

> In the Name
> of
> the German People
> I appoint
> under admission into civil servant status
> for life
> Ambassador
> Franz von Papen
> Ambassador to Ankara.
> I execute this document in the expectation
> that the candidate will fulfill the duties of his office faithfully
> in accordance with his oath of service and
> that he will justify the trust in him to which this appointment
> testifies. By the same token, I assure him of my special protection.
>
> Berlin,   April 20,   1939
>
> The Führer and Reich Chancellor
>
> [Signed:] Adolf Hitler

Translation of document shown in Figure 11

Figure 12. After the signing of the German-Turkish Friendship Treaty June, 18 1941: Franz von Papen (right) and Foreign Minister Shükrü Sarachoğlu shaking hands

edged the fact that since the German deployment in Bulgaria against Greece in February/March 1941, several Wehrmacht units were massed on the northern border of European Turkey, which reinforced the previously existing threat from Italian sea and air bases on the Dodecanese. Several months later, British and Soviet military expeditions appeared in neighboring Iraq, Syria, and lastly also Iran. In the course of the summer of 1941, Turkey became a neutral buffer state encircled by the Near and Middle East secondary theater of war, which kept the opposing armed forces apart. Ankara remained the most important diplomatic outpost of the enemy blocs during the war as long as the Axis powers were engaged in their strategic offensive in the Mediterranean and the Middle East. The Turkish center of trade and commerce, Istanbul, advanced to the status of espionage capital of the world.[15]

These were the overall conditions Franz von Papen was confronted with in the last phase of his political career. Papen subjected the characteristics and changes to a careful, thorough study in order to determine the possibilities for German trade. In his voluminous correspondence with Foreign Minister Joachim von Ribbentrop, State Secretary Ernst von Weizsäcker, and other top foreign office officials, he presented a constant stream of new proposals whereby he always alluded to his direct contact with Hitler. The archival sources reveal a surprisingly multi-layered panorama of German foreign policy initiatives that spread from Ankara and Istanbul to the neighboring subcontinents. These show Papen as a diplomat who resembles a passionate gambler. He loved surprise moves. He skillfully used the opponent's psychology, exploited instinctively any suddenly emerging opportunities, and abstained as long as possible from bellicose blackmail maneuvers in spite of instructions to the contrary from the Foreign Office.

Papen also gambled with unconventional methods in pursuit of his diplomatic chess moves. These derived, in large part, from his aristocratic background as landowner and real estate speculator.[16] Since his accreditation in Ankara, Papen had kept a secret "mobilization fund" which he used to finance extensive propaganda operations and bribery schemes. In the course of 1941, he engaged in arbitrage transactions in the free Turkish gold market seeking to revive the collapsed German-Turkish trade by setting up bogus shipping firms. In December 1942, the secret coffers of the German embassy in Ankara were stocked with stolen gold from the so-called Ribbentrop Fund in a value of five million Reichsmark. This enabled Papen to keep afloat the pro-German clientele in the Turkish press and in Turkish government circles who had fallen on hard times due to mandatory confiscation of their property. Finally, Papen, and the majority of the Axis diplomatic corps and their allies, engaged, beginning in the spring of 1943, in gold transactions of their own, which yielded such high profits that he was able to transfer certificates of deposit for his children to Swiss bank accounts.[17]

Papen's general repudiation of blackmail methods was certainly not a typical characteristic of Nazi foreign policy; systematic bribery and support for collaborators and informants was a common practice among other German envoys. But since the Nazi leadership agreed repeatedly to Papen's initiatives, it gained, despite a tendency for ruthless power politics, in the case of Turkey and the Near and Middle East a measure of flexibility and unpredictability. The placement of its flamboyant special envoy on the Anatolian merry-go-round introduced an element of agility and daring that was absent from other European outposts under German domination. It was, therefore, no coincidence that Papen was the only prominent German diplomat who became the target of an assassination plot during the Second World War, behind which was at least one of the Allies, namely the Soviet Union.[18]

Figure 13. Adolf Hitler and Franz von Papen at the Obersalzberg, July 1940

Even if Papen's many proposals were not followed in the end, they are significant inasmuch as they enable us to trace in detail the planning and decision-making processes of the Near East, Balkan, and Middle East politics during the Second World War. In addition, they also led to a remarkable practical result which was not totally without consequences for the war: Papen managed to detach Turkey, in several stages, from the Triple Alliance with the Western powers and to lead her on a course of a surprisingly far-reaching "evolutionary" rapprochement with the Axis powers. Thus was laid the basis in 1941/42 for a Turkish policy of neutrality, which lasted until the final days of Nazi Germany.

In the following, I shall reconstruct in a basic outline Franz von Papen's Middle East policy. According to my thesis, Papen attempted to transform Turkey into a satellite power under German control. Turkey, in return for regaining the status of a world power, was to serve the vital interests of Germany in the Near and Middle East. Papen's first order of action was to win Turkey over to the Axis as an alliance partner to enable the Fascist powers to strike a decisive blow against the British Empire in the Near East. Second, she was to guarantee the German takeover of the oil resources in Iraq and secure the strategically important ports on the Persian Gulf. She would thus take on the function of policing the entire Near East, which would entail putting a considerable crimp into Italian ambitions in the eastern Mediterranean. Third, after the German assault on the Soviet Union, Turkey would be charged with securing a broad stretch of the southern flank of the "continental European economic realm" in association with the expansion of her cultural and political hegemony over the Caucasus and Central Asia, two areas overwhelmingly populated by Muslims and people of Turkic stock.

My thesis is supported by voluminous quantities of source material I had at my disposal. While most research until now has been limited to either the Archives of the Foreign Office in Bonn (now in Berlin) or the Central State Archives in Potsdam (now Bundesarchiv Berlin), I was able to use both reserves and close crucial gaps in the sources.[19] I also made use of the resources in the National Archives in Washington,[20] the Public Record Office in London,[21] the Swiss Bundesarchiv in Bern, the State Military Archives (formerly Special Archives) in Moscow,[22] and various German special collections (the Historical Archives of the Deutsche Bundesbank, the Historical Institute of the Deutsche Bank, the Archives of the Institute for Contemporary History and several Papen collections in Bundesarchiv Koblenz), which were indispensable for my analysis of various important questions. However, the archives of the Turkish Republic and the Vatican remained closed despite my intensive efforts to gain access.

Papen as Primary Contact for Arab Collaborators

As far back as 1917/18 when he was chief of staff of the Fourth Ottoman Army, Papen had recognized the significance for the conduct of war of the "Arab problem": the alliance of the Bedouin tribes and the Pan-Arabic movement with Great Britain was based on promises of political independence after the war. Since they represented a threat to the strategic supply lines and the right flank of the Palestine front, the Ottoman Empire was able to neutralize this danger only by issuing respective declarations of guarantees for the Arabic national movement. Papen had then been unable to get a hearing for his proposals concerning this situation.[23] About twenty years later, he was again confronted with these questions, though under drastically altered conditions. He was no longer a military adviser to the Young Turks, but a prominent representative of the Greater German Reich, which had eliminated one of the two Near East Mandate powers when it defeated France in June 1940 and, at the same time, had constantly broadened the war against England, the latest archenemy of the Arab national movement. However, Germany's policy of bowing to its Italian Axis partner, which had few friends in the region, in matters of the Near and Middle East made it difficult for Arab nationalists to make contact with the German representatives.

Their choice finally fell on Franz von Papen, who, since his arrival in Ankara, had maintained secret contacts with the Egyptian royal court and who, due to his political past, was in good standing with the notables of the Arab national movement. On July 5, he had a visit from Najī Shaukat, the Iraqi minister of justice. He spoke in the name of all those tendencies within his government opposed to England, but also in the name of the Mufti of Jerusalem, Muhammad Amīn al-Husainī, from whom he carried a letter dated June 21.[24]

Shaukat informed Papen of efforts to retract Iraq's breaking of diplomatic relations with Germany that had taken effect the previous September, to topple the present minister president Nūrī as-Saʿīd, to restore the Syrian government which had been ousted by the French in March 1939, and to renew the struggle against the British Mandate in Palestine. Papen's first answer was that Italy was the relevant authority for any discussions of this matter. For this reason, he himself "could only be regarded as an intermediary of suggestions and requests via the German government." Papen pricked his ears, when Shaukat replied that the Arab national movement opposed Italian imperialist expansion in the Near East as much as the British or French, and that it was imperative for Germany to act in the interest of the Axis powers and to get Italy to agree to a solution that was acceptable to the Arab movement. He emphasized, "All nations who fight for independence naturally have to make a contribution themselves." "Now that the final battle against England is imminent," Germany should "expect the Iraqi popular government to do everything possible militarily in support of this fight." Accordingly, Shaukat held out the possibility of the Iraqi army's support against England, and Papen promised to inform his government in a confidential report.

Thus the contact between one of the most influential conservative elite groups of the Arabic national movement and Nazi Germany was established. Papen's proposed course, to accept the offer of collaboration in the interest of Germany's military and economic needs, was confirmed as early as July 1940, notwithstanding "Italy's priority."[25] In the months that followed, the German ambassador in Ankara advanced to become the top contact address for Arab nationalists. As early as July 22, 1940, the Mufti of Jerusalem announced a visit of his secretary ʿUthmān Kamāl Haddād who would continue the exchange started by Shaukat, whereby al-Husainī pressed for immediate cooperation of the Axis powers with the Arab countries.[26] Haddād paid a visit to Papen on August 6 at the latter's summer residence on the Bosporus and informed him of a guarantee for independence issued meanwhile by the Italian government to all Arab areas under the Mandate. In addition, he requested Germany's help in preparations of a renewed uprising in Palestine and pointed to the growing conflict between England and the Iraqi government, which had just refused to grant British Commonwealth troops marching rights through its territory. Plans for a new political order were also discussed for the first time and the secretary requested permission to travel to Berlin and Rome to negotiate the terms.[27] Papen was now absolutely certain that interesting new opportunities for intervention were emerging here. He was impressed and urged Berlin to act with dispatch. On August 15, 1940, he finally received a telegram from Ernst Woermann, head of the political division of the Foreign Office, informing him that the Mufti's secretary had been granted a visa and would be received by Fritz Grobba, the former German envoy to Baghdad and Jidda.[28]

From then on, the contacts went on uninterrupted. The German embassy in Ankara functioned as protective mailbox for Haddād's correspondence with the Mufti and the "Committee for Cooperation among Arabic Countries" which had meanwhile been formed in Baghdad and to which belonged prominent notables and government representatives from the countries of the Arab East as well as the Arabian Peninsula. Again and again we find in the letter exchanges and news reports discussions between Papen and Shaukat as well as other emissaries of the committee. The German ambassador became the most important German negotiating partner for Arab nationalists. He engaged with them in detailed discussions and increasingly developed in the context of his reports his own ideas that he frequently interjected into the negotiations taking place in Berlin. For example, after a meeting with Shaukat in late September 1940 in Istanbul, he emphasized in his report to Berlin the Arab leaders' reservations toward Italy and requested authorization for an oral assurance of support for the Arabs' push for independence.[29]

Following Papen's advice, in Berlin on October 18, 1940, Weizsäcker handed the Mufti's secretary a declaration of solidarity from the Reich government, which created a huge sensation when it was made public a few days later.

Papen Coordinates the German Intelligence Service in Ankara and Istanbul

The role of intermediary led to the creation of a tightly woven net of communications, which made Papen not only one of the best-informed experts on developments in the Near East, but also a key figure of the various support actions for the increasingly stressed Arab national movement. In the spring of 1941, the intelligence service of the Wehrmacht expanded its "war organization" to the Near East and installed at the embassy in Ankara and the general consulate in Istanbul a branch office for this purpose.[31] Apart from purely military reports, all politically relevant information was to be cleared with Papen, who decided on its use and whether to forward it to Berlin. In the course of this activity, Papen developed a joint effort with Paul Leverkuehn, the man in charge of the Wehrmacht intelligence office in Istanbul.[32] This collaboration became a precondition for the manifold actions of assistance for Arab nationalist refugees in Turkey which became necessary in the summer of 1941 with the British occupation of Iraq, Syria, and Iran. In addition, an Orient department was set up at the German embassy to coordinate the activities of the German diplomatic missions expelled from these countries.

Papen soon had a good system of information with wide-ranging contacts at his disposal in close collaboration with the Orient division of the Foreign Office in Berlin and the Wehrmacht Intelligence Service, even though Papen's system sometimes acted independently. Papen's success in gaining the trust of Ludwig Moyzisch, head of the Security Service of the SS in Turkey,[33] made him the best-informed source for German espionage activities in the Near and Middle East. Until the debacle of the Wehrmacht Intelligence Service in Turkey in February/March 1944,[34] Papen held all threads of the various divisions of the German Information Service undisputedly in his hands.

For the time being, however, the most pressing problem was how to deal with acute needs. When 350 Arab mercenaries, who had fought on the side of the French Levant army during the British attack on Syria in 1941,[35] crossed the border into Turkey, it was Paul Leverkuehn who took them under his protection. The financial resources for this were channeled from the legations budget of the Foreign Office through the embassy budget in Tehran.[36] After the German embassy in Tehran was closed, secret transfer deposits in the Japanese and Spanish embassies were activated, which Papen had previously set up for just such a eventuality.[37] In November 1941, Papen and Leverkuehn assisted the ousted Iraqi Prime Minister, enabling him, in the course of an adventuresome special action, to flee to Germany.[38] Such engagements gained Papen the reputation of a friendly intermediary, who was open to Arab nationalist aspirations and did not shy away from taking risks to further their cause.

Papen's Arab Policy

But what significance did the Arab world really have for Papen? An analysis of his diplomatic correspondence and his political notes shows that he had a very clear conception from the very beginning of his Turkey mission. Although he adjusted that vision, in the course of the years that followed, to the development of the military-political conditions, in principle he held it to be unalterable. A few weeks after assuming his post in Ankara, he wrote in a memorandum during his first visit to Berlin that in the coming war, England "had to be struck in its most vital spot in India" and "the Axis powers must, therefore, be in possession of the land bridge to India (the Syria-Palestine pathway to Mosul)."[39] The Arab world was for Papen mostly of importance because the ultimate victory of the Axis powers presupposed the expulsion of Great Britain from the Suez Canal, the Palestine-Transjordanian land bridge, from the Persian Gulf, and finally from India. In addition, Papen was, from the beginning, an inveterate opponent of the frequently proclaimed priority of Italian power in the Mediterranean region and in Asia Minor. However, since he could not simply make this strategic basic decision of the Nazi leadership disappear, he wrote about a year and half later in an essay about Germany and the Arab Question in the Near East: "Italy's hegemony in the Mediterranean, that is, her absolute control of the passage (through the Suez Canal) to our former Central African possessions, which we seek to regain, and to the oil reserves in the

Near East seems to make it imperative for the Reich to secure at least one of the maritime routes independent of the land connection to the Persian Gulf."[40] In accordance with this concept, the areas of Iraq and the Persian Gulf were of vital German interest and the entire Arab East assumed the role of a strategic staging area and the "treatment of the problems of Asia Minor" thus became for Papen "a question which we cannot evade."

He bolstered this military-strategic option with concrete examples of economic interests. To Papen's mind, control over the Iraqi oil resources was one of the main goals of German expansionist policy. In this his thinking dovetailed with that of Fritz Grobba, the Arabia specialist in the Foreign Office. Like Grobba, Papen became indirectly involved in the Deutsche Bank's pursuit of oil interests.[41] In the summer of 1940, the experts of the Berlin branch of the Deutsche Bank started to unearth their collapsed Iraq concession dated to the golden era of the Baghdad railroad and the Turkish Petroleum Company, in order to assure themselves preferential treatment in case of a German advance on Mosul and Basra. The foundation for it stood, however, on a tottering footing and did not meet with the complete agreement of Grobba and state secretary Wilhelm Keppler. This was probably the reason why the Deutsche Bank resorted to engaging its veteran lobbyist Franz von Papen. In November 1940, the director of the Deutsche Bank, Kurt Weigelt, asked Papen to initiate negotiations with the Iraqi government for the return of crude oil concessions.[42] In this context he recommended two tactical approaches, either to revive past claims or to request new concessions within the framework of a future peace treaty. Papen agreed and announced that he would keep the Deutsche Bank in Ankara informed.

By the same token, the Dresdner Bank was to be compensated as well. In the spring of 1941, Papen named the director of the Deutsche Orientbank, an affiliate of Dresdner Bank, Curt Lebrecht, an economic advisor at his embassy. In Ankara, Lebrecht was primarily responsible for economic and financial planning of the Orient department at the embassy. A few months later, he was assigned to the staff of Arabia experts of the Foreign Office and, together with the director of the Deutsche Reichsbank, was designated currency and financial advisor for a "liberated" Iraq. Until the summer of 1941, the plans for the economic integration of Iraq had matured to a considerable extent. On August 23, a concluding department meeting voted and passed the stipulations for the economic foundation of the treaty with the future collaborationist government of al-Kailānī. These stipulations projected the introduction of a currency based on German gold credit, the deployment of economic and financial advisors as well as an agreement on the delivery of crude oil in exchange for German war equipment.[43]

Meanwhile, Papen was by no means content with mere memoranda, agreements, and declarations of intent. In addition, he geared all his diplomatic and political activities in Ankara toward drawing the Asia Minor land bridge to the Persian Gulf into the German domain. From the summer of 1940 on, he swamped the Foreign Office and the Reich Chancellery with memoranda and other submissions in which he proposed that the Axis powers join with the Soviet Union, at that time still allied with Germany, to advance on the Near and Middle East in order to strike a blow against the central life line of the British Empire.[44] On September 30, a few days after the signing the Three Power Pact between German, Italy, and Japan, he sent a telegram to Berlin, urging an attempt at last to "secure by treaty Russia's participation in a final settlement of her already existing interest in the Danube region, the question of the Straits, and Near Eastern oil resources."[45] Papen's exhortations then became the basis of the famous/infamous secret Berlin talks of Ribbentrop and Hitler with the Soviet foreign minister, Vyacheslav Molotov, on November 12 and 13, 1940. The Soviet Union was to join the Three Power Pact, whereby her attention would be diverted from the Balkans toward India, which would force Turkey to agree to a new statute concerning the Straits, and expel England from the Near and Middle East.[46] However, Stalin and Molotov were not about to abandon either their Balkan strategy nor their demands for sea and air bases on the Dardanelles and the Bosporus. Giving in to these demands would have placed considerable restrictions on Turkish sovereignty, which was not in the German interest.[47] The Nazi leadership's decision, on December 18, 1940, to initiate "Operation Barbarossa," that is, the complete military destruction of the Soviet Union,[48] was in large part due to the failed attempt to curb the Soviet sphere of influence in the Balkans and the uncertainty concerning her control over the strategic route to Ankara, Baghdad, and Basra. The German military and political elites projected an eight-week blitzkrieg and declared the subsequent intensification of operations in the Mediterranean region as the most important, strategic step in the continuation of the battle against the British Empire.[49]

Papen, however, remained undeterred in his strategic ideas by this dramatic reversal of his proposed plan of action, though he did regard the war against the Soviet Union as a dangerous detour that made the realization of his most important strategic goal, namely the defeat of England in the Near and Middle East, for the time being unattainable. For him, the most decisive war aim remained securing the German land bridge to Mosul and Basra. It constituted the anchor of his world power concept whereby he detached himself from the ambitious treaty partner Italy, to whom he was at best willing to grant junior partner status. As he saw it, Turkey would no longer be blackmailed by the power phalanx of the German-Italian-Japanese-Russian Four Power Pact, but would have to be won over to join the side of the Axis in its "crusade" against the Soviet Union. The overtures that then began were made easier in the spring of 1942 by the German military's assessment that a march on Mosul and Basra could be launched from the Caucasus and Turkey and the treacherous terrain in the Taurus Mountains could be circumvented. All that was necessary was a gesture of "benign neutrality" on the part of Turkey by holding her fifty divisions in abeyance. Papen held to this point of view until the late fall of 1942, when the German conquest of Trans-Caucasia had ended in failure. Under pressure of the new situation and a change to strategic defense, he had to resign himself to the fact that a neutral Turkey would not only protect the southern flank of the German-Soviet front, but also prevent the formation of an Allied front in the Balkans. The dream of placing the oil-rich areas under German patronage and of taking possession of the Iraq Petroleum Company's refineries and pipelines as well as of the transfer ports on the Persian Gulf had come to an end.

These political-strategic considerations were still very much on Papen's mind as he obtained entrance visas to Berlin and Rome for the Arab nationalists. His outwardly friendly façade toward them, as was befitting for future collaborators, concealed his cold calculations. He was willing to serve al-Husainī's, Haddād's, and al-Kailānī's moves for independence only inasmuch as they furthered the step-by-step realization of his strategic goal. In this context, it seemed useful and plausible to Papen to hold out promises of autonomy to the representatives of the various Arab states if such promises secured a frictionless economic, military, and political German takeover of Iraq. It also relieved the Near Eastern states, recently liberated from Ottoman rule, of the sense of being encircled on all sides by the dominant Mediterranean power Italy,[50] and would thus further a lasting rapprochement with Germany. Unlike Fritz Grobba and several other Foreign Office Orient experts, Papen viewed a federation above and beyond a rapprochement with great skepticism. For Turkey could live with politically independent neighbors like Syria, Iraq, Palestine, and Transjordan, but not with an Arab federation that would sooner or later challenge her unofficial position of hegemony in the Near East.

A Greater Turkish Regime as Southern Cornerstone of German World Power

Papen clearly regarded Turkey as a pillar of a future German hegemony in the Near East. In this scheme, the interests of Arab nationalists had to take second place within the German-Turkish alliance. However, the Turkish satellite regime he wanted to create did not yet have the necessary insignia of a solid medium-size power. Militarily this could be easily helped through arms supplies. To further this goal, Papen became the tireless mentor of the famous armaments credit negotiations that gave birth to the Chromerz Cannon Consortium steered by the Krupp company and initially with a credit of 100 million.[51] Turkey was especially vulnerable on its borders. For example, the Baghdad railroad crossed the northern border of Syria at several points and could therefore easily be paralyzed in the middle of its run. Equally unstable was the only Turkish railway connection to Europe where it passed through the area bordering Thrace. The former Ottoman fortress Edirne/Adrianople in that area had lost its protective function when the Bulgarian-Turkish border was redrawn in 1918. And above all, there was the island group of the Dodecanese, situated just offshore of the Anatolian mainland, which Italy had annexed back in 1912, as well as the economically disadvantageous redrawing of the borders with Iraq and the Caucasian Soviet Republics, which could not but challenge nationalist politicians to demand their revisions.

Papen was closely familiar with the unfavorable situation at the Turkish borders. He saw them as bargaining chips in a power play for German hegemony in the future, which would guarantee the rounding out of the borders in return for negotiating far-reaching concessions to German interests in the Near and Middle East. Papen's familiarity with the mentality of Turkish military and political leaders, who were about to detach themselves from Atatürk's policy of renouncing all imperialist claims, permitted him again and again to make subtle use of this particular weakness of Turkish nationalism.

Within a few months of presenting his credentials to President Ismet Inönü, Papen recommended to the foreign ministers of the Axis powers to return two of the Dodecanese islands, situated within the Turkish three-mile zone, as a token of good will toward Turkey and a guarantee of her European positions, in return for a policy of neutrality and leaving exposed the flank of the English land bridge to India.[52] In July 1940, he went one step further and suggested offering the Turkish government the entire island group as security if she was willing to support the German-Italian-Soviet pincer operations, then being debated, against key British positions in the Near and Middle East.[53] During the Berlin-Moscow Four Power Pact discussions, Papen felt empowered to offer leading Turkish politicians comprehensive territorial assurances in order to tie them to the dawning European and Near Eastern "new order."[54] This, however, came to naught, for Inönü and Foreign Minister Shükrü Saraçoğlu were cautiously awaiting the consolidation of this generally forgotten alternative to the German war aims of November 1940.

Nevertheless, a strategic arrangement between the two regimes came closer to fulfillment after the Nazi leadership had decided, in part because of rivaling interests in the Balkans and the Near East, to embark on a war of total destruction against the Soviet Union, prior to which Germany attacked Yugoslavia and Greece in April 1941. Even now, Papen opened the new round of the gambit with tempting offers of border corrections. In May 1941, he offered his Turkish negotiating partners parts of North Syria and a strip near Edirne/Adrianople to gain their agreement for the transfer of war materiel and supplies from Syria to Iraq in support of an uprising there. These discussions soon produced a draft treaty negotiated between Papen and the Turkish state secretary for foreign affairs, Numan Menemencioğlu, which in return for permission to transfer extensive arms shipments—a de facto abandonment of Turkish neutrality—anticipated, in case of an early end to the war, extensive territorial concessions in Thrace and in the Eastern Mediterranean archipelago and, in case of an expansion of war, "guarantee of Turkish wishes in southern and eastern neighboring zones."[55] This enterprise too came to naught because the Turkish government retreated at the last moment in face of massive British pressure to prevent the annulment of the last remnant of the alliance treaty of October 1939; because the Nazi leadership was too preoccupied with "Barbarossa" priorities that it failed to take advantage of the opportunities for intervention in the fighting in Iraq and Syria in May/June 1941; and because, after British successes in the conflict, Germany no longer regarded the transfer of arms through Turkish territory as important. Once again, the casual, ad-hoc decision making on the part of the German political-military leadership left Papen's vision of Turkey as a German satellite power in the Near and Middle East unfulfilled in the end.

Papen and the "Pan-Turanian Movement"

This renewed setback in the summer of 1941 was followed by a third rapprochement phase, which gave German-Turkish diplomatic relations its peculiar stamp until the fall of 1942. This was preceded by the German invasion of the Soviet Union on June 22, 1941, which set off in Turkish military and government circles a veritable outburst of enthusiasm while it aroused among broader segments of the population the hope for a revival of specific pan-Turkic dreams of expansion as formulated during the First World War.[56]

These developments enabled Papen to lead his agitation on two tracks simultaneously. On the one hand, he was able to grab hold of the Turkish center of power and intensify the push for his imperialist interests, and on the other, he could spin unofficial threads, placing Ankara under more pressure by exploiting the newly awakened nationalist expansionist movement. Papen reported in a dispatch to Berlin of July 18, 1941, for the first time about the Pan-Turanian Movement.[57] He invoked the name of his friend the commander of the Turkish military academy, Ali Fuad Erden, who let it be known that Turkey would welcome a discussion with Germany concerning "a federation in the Caucasus of the more or less Turkic tribes in that region while for the region east of the Caspian Sea, an autonomous Turanian state was regarded as the best solution." These remarks outlined the basic points. Ribbentrop immediately requested a detailed report and a week later Papen presented a first scenario.[58] He pointed to the "more than 40 million Turkic Muslims" populating the southern provinces of the Soviet Union and with whom the Turkish Pan-Turanian movement was increasingly identifying. Encouraged by the German military successes in the region, this movement was experiencing almost automatic growth spurts: "Even the lowliest Turk has a pronounced race and ethnic consciousness and understands that his desires in this regards can only be fulfilled with the [help of the] German Reich and never with England." This opportunity must now be given "concrete form."

In the months that followed, Papen clarified the steps that had to be taken toward this concretization. If handled skillfully, it would be possible to kill two birds with one stone: With the help of Turkey, Germany would at last be able to draw the pan-Turkic movement to her side and, at the same time, exploit Turkish expansionist interests in achieving a political and cultural consolidation of the southern border of the future German sphere of power on the European Continent all the more so, since Germany's interest in this region was limited to the economic exploitation of strategic raw materials.[59]

Here, too, Papen bolstered his argument with a comprehensive catalogue of practical suggestions for step-by-step action. As his vision of a Pan-Turanian bloc on the southern flank of Continental Europe under German control created a stir among the planning staff of the Foreign Office, the Wehrmacht, and among leading industrialists, Papen continued to present his plans in greater and increasingly concrete detail.[60] He recommended launching a propaganda campaign to give the Pan-Turanian followers the impression of being recognized as an important element in the "new order" to be established. He was the first to suggest isolating Muslim and Turkic prisoners-of-war in special camps, where they would be "re-educated" with the help of suitable representatives of the pan-Turkish-Muslim ideology, and then deployimg them behind the front lines as agents of a Pan-Turanian uprising. Papen obtained for the representatives of the Pan-Turanian movement as well their first entrance visas to Berlin, whereby he placed, in this case, his entire personal prestige on the line so that they would be well received. The cast of characters ranged from Nuri Killigil, named Pasha, the brother of the legendary Enver Pasha, to the influential ex-general Hüsnü Emir Erkilet and the Pan-Turanian ideologist Zeki Velidî Togan, to a dozen or more nameless trans-Caucasian, Caucasian, and Turkmen irredentists, who had wintered for decades in Turkey and Western Europe in isolated emigré circles, and who now felt their time had come.[61] Above and beyond these efforts, Papen hinted as early as August 1941 at the formation of a secret Turkish government committee, dedicated to the Pan-Turanian cause. Two months later, at his initiative, two prominent Pan-Turanian military leaders, generals Ali Fuad Erden and Hüsnü Emir Erkilet, visited selected areas along the German-Soviet front, following which they were received at the Führer's headquarters.[62] Papen's idea of turning Turkey into an imperial satellite state within the German sphere of hegemony with the help of the "Pan-Turanian idea" had gained him a following that, at times, reached into the higher Nazi leadership and his practical proposals found, in many cases, a quick transformation.

However, even then, Papen and the power group behind him were unable to reap a lasting success. This was due in large part to the course the war was taking in Europe, in contrast to the Near East options, which remained relatively open until the fall of 1942. The German attack ground to a halt in the southern part of the Soviet Union, the Crimea and the Northern Caucasus, as early as late fall 1941. The Wehrmacht's summer offensive during the following year likewise failed to take the strategic Caucasus passes. The Soviet barrier in the trans-Caucasian region and the eastern border of Turkey was just as unbreachable as the Don-Kuban front, which sealed all access to Azerbaijan and Central Asia.

Only then did those factions in Alfred Rosenberg's Reich ministry for occupied territories and in various SS administrative centers, which favored a policy of pillaging and Germanizing, gain the upper hand. Up till then, they had had to accommodate themselves to the experts in the Foreign Office who favored collaboration with national movements. When Hitler subordinated the Foreign Office to the eastern schemes of the Rosenberg ministry in late July 1942 and, two months later, ordered the cessation of the Pan-Turanian campaign,[63] it had become clear that the Pan-Turanian committee, established on Papen's initiative and directed by Werner Otto von Hentig of the Foreign Office, had as little influence on political-military decisions in Nazi Germany as Fritz Grobba's coordination efforts in the Near East.

In the end, the Pan-Turanists Nuri Pasha, Ali Fuad Erden, and Hüsnü Emir Erkilet were as frustrated as the Arab nationalists around the clans of Rashīd ʿAlī al-Kailānī and Muhammad Amīn al-Husainī. Both groups of collaborators had for the time being put their trust in Papen since he had advocated a contractually agreed upon division of labor between the German hegemonial power and their satellite regimes whereby the satellites of this utopian imperium were to have certain autonomy rights. But Papen was not a decisive actor in the Berlin center of power and the functionary elites of Near East and greater Turkish collaborators were put off with vague assurances while being kept away from their followers. Nuri Pasha, Erkilet, al-Kailānī, and al-Husainī recognized, after a long learning process, that they had put their trust in a streak of German imperialism that represented only a tactical sideline of the genocidal expansion politics of German fascism.

Exploitation of the Pan-Arab and Pan-Turanian Movements during the Transition to a Strategic Defensive

Regardless of these circumstances, beginning in late 1942 and early 1943, the actors responsible for military and occupation policy went through a new process of learning that steered the further course of the war and prompted them to regard the options presented by previously silenced rival groups with different eyes. In November/December 1942, the Wehrmacht was placed for the first time since the start of the Second World War on the strategic defensive in North Africa and at Stalingrad. While the Reich was able to accommodate fairly quickly to the new situation of a "total" defense of "Fortress Europe," it became increasingly difficult to make up for the tremendous losses in manpower. The leadership of the Wehrmacht and the main office of the Waffen-SS, therefore, saw themselves increasingly forced into recruiting non-German mercenaries and collaborators. Most of these "volunteers" had been placed in the special prisoner-of-war camps as Papen had intuitively suggested back in July 1941. These could now be mobilized relatively quickly. In addition, the German recruiters resorted to campaigns among political groups leaning toward collaboration and national minorities in the occupied territories. In this context, the time had finally come for ethnic-nationalist collaboration, even if in pocket size, for without the participation of politicians, propagandists, and clerics of the Arab, Caucasian, and Turkmen organizations, it would be impossible to accomplish the difficult "re-education" and training programs. It now became clear that the administrators of the Foreign Office responsible for occupation and the Wehrmacht intelligence division had not turned an entirely deaf ear toward Papen's autonomy proposals.

Since the Wehrmacht had tendered limited autonomy offers during its invasion of the Soviet Union and had started recruiting for legionary units in the fall of 1941, it was relatively easy now to renew the initiatives first launched by Papen of exploiting the national movements among Arabs, Crimea-Tartars, Caucasian-Muslims, and Turkmen. An example is the Arab combat unit, with which Rudolf Rahn landed in Turkey in July 1941 after the defeat of the French Levant army. It was transformed into a "German-Arabic training division" under the command of the special staff of air force general Hellmuth Felmy (Special Commando Unit F).[64] This unit was transferred in the summer of 1942 from its training center on Cape Sunion in Greece to behind the German-Soviet front near Stalino. In case of a conquest of the Caucasus passes, the unit would be prepared to advance on Baghdad and Basra as the Arab part of a motorized German Orient Corps, equipped with the most sophisticated, modern weaponry.[5] After the collapse of the summer offensive on the southern German-Soviet front, the unit was transferred, together with an Arab combat unit set up by Italy, to North Africa where it participated in the fighting in 1942/43, under the moral-religious care of emissaries from the Mufti al-Husainī, against Allied troops, who had meanwhile landed in Morocco and Algeria.[66]

However, the Wehrmacht also made considerable progress in sorting out and recruiting Muslim-Turkmen mercenaries from among one and a half million Red Army prisoners-of-war who were condemned to starvation.[67] The religio-ideological care of these units by intellectual collaborators, primarily in service of the Foreign Office, functioned quite smoothly after some initial disputes. In the course of 1942, increasing numbers of East Turkic volunteers, among them units from Turkestan, Azerbaijan, Armenia, Georgia, the North Caucasus, and of Volga Tartars, were deployed in the fight against Bolshevism.[68] Their native caretakers and representatives were then gathered in "control offices" through which they managed to improve their at first very limited status in proportion to the increasing deterioration of the German war prospects. In the end, they even obtained basically useless promises of independence after the "final victory, for the ethnic-nationalist states they represented." Since these units were gradually scattered over the German army's entire field of operation in Europe, the army high command finally named a "general for volunteer units" who, in September 1944, commanded 160,000 soldiers who were deployed in fiercely disputed combat areas of the French and Italian invasion front. The last unit that was set up was an East Muslim regiment.[69]

Beginning in the summer of 1943, the SS leadership too followed in Papen's footsteps. However, it is still not clear that the SS's discovery of the Muslim Arab and Turanian fount of manpower is directly traceable to contacts with the special envoy to Turkey, who had until then received little recognition.[70] At any rate, Heinrich Himmler, the Reichsführer SS, and the Mufti al-Husainī met in Berlin in July 1943 for a long, detailed exchange that ended with mutual assurances of covert cooperation. In late July there followed concrete negotiations between the Mufti and the chief of the SS main office, Gottlob Berger.[71] Thanks to the Waffen SS's positive experiences with Muslim volunteer units on the Crimea and the Bosnian part of occupied Yugoslavia in 1942, it managed to catch up with the Wehrmacht which had so far held the advantage in this field of activity. In addition, it was clear that Himmler and Berger had a more receptive ear for the particular mentalities of these groups of collaborators and also were willing to respect the Mufti's wishes in broad outline.[72] The Bosnian volunteer units were expanded into the Bosnian division of the Waffen SS, which then served from 1943/44 as the model for other Muslim units of the Waffen SS. The units were soon faced with a lack of clerics since each battalion, like the Bosnian division, was to have an imam and the exercise of religious rituals was to be fully respected. On April 21, 1944, an imam training school opened in Guben and al-Husainī gave the opening address.[73] These battalion imams, under al-Husainī's close supervision during frequent visits, developed into the backbone of the Muslim units of the Waffen SS. Despite the increasingly deteriorating military situation, al-Husainī boosted the morale of the Bosnian and Turkestani divisions in carefully formulated missives to his religious emissaries.[74] The SS leadership was finally so impressed with the combat spirit of these units that they revived the "Pan-Turanian idea," fully two years after Hitler's rejection of Papen's proposals. Only through the mobilization of "a common political idea" would it be possible to strengthen the Turkic and Caucasian people's "sense of unity" and to organize their "fight against Bolshevism and for the German language," lectured a colleague of the official in the SS main office responsible for the Turkmen question in the Rosenberg ministry in September 1944.[75]

Broad Views

Franz von Papen was a politician who, in the course of his life, opened a Pandora's box on numerous occasions. Even during the Second World War, as special envoy to Turkey, he faithfully played this role. How would the victorious Allied Powers judge him? As the end of the war drew nearer, it is likely that Papen, who met Hitler from time to time (figure 13) and who had returned to Germany from Turkey in August 1944 and was decorated with highest honors by Hitler, could not but mull over this question again and again.

On April 10, 1945, Papen was arrested by American troops in a hunting lodge in Westphalia. Then began a series of endless interrogations. Of particular significance was a Special Investigation Mission of the U. S. State Department, which subjected Papen, on November 1, 1945, to intensive questioning about his Austria and Turkey policies.[76] From Westphalia he was transferred to the court prison in Nuremberg and was indicted in the war crimes trial together with leading Nazis. However, the prosecution was mostly interested in Papen as Hitler's stirrups holder in 1932/33. In addition, the prosecution sought to show that Papen had played a significant role in the annexation of Austria and had covered himself with guilt when he participated in the Nazi conspiracy against peace.[77] His activities in Turkey remained expressly unmentioned, giving Papen's defense attorney the opportunity to fill this gap by calling dozens of witnesses, who swore to Papen's dedicated service toward preserving Turkish neutrality and the cause of peace during the war.[78] The result was a not-guilty verdict against which the Soviet representative of the International Military Court entered a strangely unemphatic objection.[79] Even though they were by no means of the same mind, the members of the International Military Court deemed it advisable to leave Papen's activities in Turkey out of the protocol.

The not-guilty verdict proved at first a pyrrhic victory. Upon his release, Papen was placed under police surveillance and in the spring of 1947, he was cited by a Bavarian court to answer for his devastating role in the establishment of the Nazi dictatorship. The sentence was eight years' work camp and confiscation of much of his personal property. Here again, his years as envoy in Turkey were left out of the discussion. Two years later, the sentence was reduced. Receiving credit for time served since April 1945, he was released from incarceration.

After he had recovered his health, he devoted much energy in the following years toward seeking his rehabilitation. But despite the escalating Cold War and conciliatory tendencies in West Germany, he did not succeed. Even the conservative political currents in the Bonn republic never forgave Papen for his role in 1932/33. In contrast, nobody took any interest in Papen's service to the Nazi regime during the Second World War in spite of the fact that the balance sheet of those years is no less damning.

After being named special envoy in April 1939, Franz von Papen tried his best to draw Turkey to the side of the Berlin-Rome Axis and to transform her into a German satellite power. In doing so, he prepared the political groundwork for a broad-based pincer attack against British positions in the Arab West that would lead to the destruction of the most important territorial power centers in the British Empire. Papen approached this operational goal from two different angles. In the fall of 1940, he recommended including the Stalinist Soviet Union in the German-Italian-Japanese Three Power Pact as a means to blackmail Turkey, which was then allied with Great Britain, and to extend the European war to the Near and Middle East. When this option failed to get a hearing and Nazi Germany attacked the Soviet Union instead, Papen tried to force Turkey into the role of a German satellite with territorial offers, generous arms credits, and exploitation of newly revived imperial tendencies. In neither case was Papen concerned with maintaining Turkish neutrality; rather, his efforts were directed toward drawing Turkey into the fascist power bloc. It was only when Germany was forced into a strategic defensive position in 1942/43 that Papen was content with a benign neutral orientation of his diplomatic negotiating partner.

For the newly won over and stabilized satellite of German hegemony in the Near and Middle East, Papen had in mind the role of a political and cultural police. The nationalist aspirations of East-Arab nations would be satisfied under Turkish supervision, however, without formation of an Arab federation. Furthermore, once the Soviet Union had been defeated, the Turkish sphere of influence would be extended over the Caucasus and Central Asia. In both cases, according to Papen's vision, Germany, rising to a position of world domination, was to assume the role of a superimperialist power operating in the background of these events in achieving her vital strategic interest in the Near and Middle East. Part of this plan was the seizure of the crude oil resources in the Caucasus and Iraq as well as the strategically important ports on the Persian Gulf. However, the addition of a Berlin–Ankara–Baghdad–Basra axis, paralleling the Berlin–Rome Axis, would necessitate a revision of the Italian spheres of influence. The up-to-now dominant Italian partner would lose control of the land bridge bordering on the eastern Mediterranean. It was a matter of adapting to current conditions the model for expansion that had dominated German imperialist aspirations at the time of the Wilhelmian era and the First World War.

What would have happened had Papen's visions been adopted? This is by no means a moot question. On three occasions—in the fall of 1940, in May/June 1941, and in late summer 1942—the Near and Middle East were close to becoming the primary battlefield of the Second World War. On all three occasions, the alternatives of German war policy examined above almost became history. If Nazi Germany and the Soviet Union had agreed on an expanded renewal of the Ribbentrop-Molotov Pact, as Papen desired, then the British troops could have been expelled from the Near and Middle East and the power constellation led by Hitler, Mussolini, Tenno, and Stalin would in all likelihood have quickly won the war.

This opportunity appeared again on the horizon in May/June 1941 when Iraq and the French Levant army fought against the British expedition corps. The strategic constellation too was a favorable one. The United States had not yet entered the war, the British units in the Near and Middle East were relatively weak, and the Wehrmacht had just gained control over the central Mediterranean region. And yet, the Nazi leadership permitted this window of opportunity to close because they had meanwhile geared almost their entire military potential toward an attack on the Soviet Union. By contrast, in late summer 1942, a German victory was no longer seemed certain, despite the panic among the Anglo-American staff in Cairo.

Even if the Soviet Union had capitulated at this point and the German Orient Corps had crossed the Caucasus, it would immediately have come up against the massively strengthened Anglo-American armed forces. It is questionable whether a German breakthrough in the transCaucasus region and into northern Iran would have sufficed to take the pressure off the German Africa Corps and enabled General Erwin Rommel to conquer the Suez Canal. At any rate, the entire Near East and Middle East would have become a battlefield and would have sustained severe devastation. The outcome of the struggle was meanwhile open because of the full mobilization and the practically inexhaustible armaments potential of the United States.

Fortunately, the Near and Middle East was spared such a fate. The fascist axis was unable to exploit to its advantage the windows of opportunity that opened in this region as nowhere else during the Second World War. A thorough contemplation of these events makes clear how diabolical was the role Franz von Papen played in Turkey. At play were many incidentals and only a few absolutes that prevented the powder keg, to which he had attached the fuse, from blowing up.

Notes

1. The certificate of appointment was missing for decades. It was finally located a short while ago in "Fond Papen" of the State Military Archives in Moscow, 703-1-49.
2. In 1952, Papen published his autobiography, which is, despite a basically apologetic tone and omission of important, incriminating circumstances, in many details quite surprising. If used critically, this much-maligned work can, in many respects, be very useful for a study based on primary sources. See Franz von Papen, *Der Wahrheit eine Gasse* (Munich, 1952).
3. Compare Joachim Petzold, *Franz von Papen. Ein deutsches Verhängnis* (Berlin, 1955), 259–62, in which the Turkey mission is discussed in barely four pages.
4. Compare especially Lothar Krecker, *Deutschland und die Türkei im zweiten Weltkrieg* (Frankfurt am Main, 1964); Selim Deringil, *Turkish Foreign Policy during the Second World War: An "Active" Neutrality* (Cambridge, 1989). Frank G. Weber, by contrast, was first to point out Papen's special role. See his *The Evasive Neutral: Germany, Britain, and the Quest for a Turkish Alliance in the Second World War* (New York and London, 1979).
5. The most important study so far about this aspect of Papen's activities is Franz Müller, *Ein "Rechtskatholik" zwischen Kreuz und Hakenkreuz: Franz von Papen als Sonderbevollmächtigter Hitlers in Wien 1934–1938*, Europäische Hochschulschriften, series 3, vol. 446 (Frankfurt am Main, 1990).
6. The key events that caused Turkey's change were the German-Rumanian economic treaty of March 23, 1939, and the subsequent Italian invasion of Albania on April 7, 1939.
7. That Hitler described Papen as an "old jockey" was recorded by Hasso von Etzdorf, the Foreign Office representative with the Army High Command, on July 17, 1941, in a meeting at "Führer" headquarters where strategies for administering the conquered Soviet territories were discussed. In the course of this meeting, Hitler ridiculed Papen's memorandum that pleaded for the reintroduction of Christian religions in the occupied Soviet territories. Compare *Akten zur Deutschen*

Auswärtigen Politik 1918–1945 (hereafter *ADAP*), series D, vol. XIII.1 and 2, f. 6 to document no. 114, pp. 127–31; also Otto Bräutigam's diary entry about the meeting of July 16, 1941, mentioning "abusive criticism" of Papen, in Archiv des Instituts für Zeitgeschichte, Munich (hereafter IfZ Archive) MA–257.
8. The Balkan Pact was concluded on February 9, 1934, between Greece, Yugoslavia, Rumania, and Turkey.
9. The Montreux Agreement was signed on July 20, 1936, by the signatories of the Lausanne Treaty of 1923. It dissolved the International Straits Commission and returned sovereignty over the Straits to the Turkish Republic, including the right to fortify the Dardanelles. By stipulation of the Treaty of Versailles, Germany was not a signatory of the Treaty of Lausanne and was, therefore, not a participant at Montreux. Compare Ernst Woermann, Notiz zum Meerengen Abkommen von Montreux, July 20, 1936, in *ADAP*, series C, vol. V.1 and 2, document no. 462, 734–37.
10. The consultative pact of Saadabad was concluded on July 8, 1937, near Tehran between Afghanistan, Iraq, Iran, and Turkey.
11. The decisive turning point came with the dismantling of Czechoslovakia on March 15, 1939, and the subsequent Italian invasion of Albania on April 7, 1939.
12. Krecker, *Deutschland und die Türkei*, 51–66.
13. The German-Turkish friendship treaty was signed in Ankara on June 18, 1941; in *ADAP*, series D, vol. XII.1 and 2, document no. 548, 866–67.
14. The British-Iraqi conflict began on May 2, 1941, leading to British military occupation of the country by the end of the month. On June 8, 1941, British troops led an attack against the French Levant army stationed in Lebanon and Syria, which ended four weeks later in French capitulation. The British-Soviet occupation of Iran followed on August 25, 1941, giving Great Britain control over the land bridge from the Suez Canal, the Persian Gulf, to India. At the same time, she secured a direct access route for military support to her new war ally, the Soviet Union.
15. Compare Barry Rubin, *Istanbul Intrigues* (New York, 1989).
16. Compare in the following the detailed description in Karl-Heinz Roth, *Papens Raubgold. Franz von Papen als deutscher Sonderbotschafter in der Türkei 1939 bis 1944* (Hamburg, 2003). See also Wolfgang G. Schwanitz, *Gold, Bankiers und Diplomaten. Zur Geschichte der Deutschen Orientbank 1906–1946* (Berlin, 2002). Schwanitz was first to use U.S. sources documenting the German practice of laundering stolen gold in the Near East.
17. Compare the extensive records in National Archives and Record Administration, Maryland (hereafter NA II), Record Group 165, Boxes 3051, 3052; Record Group 226, Box 183; Entry 126 (Regional Series), Boxes 762, 768, 918, 1035; in addition, Schwanitz, *Gold, Bankiers und Diplomaten*, 398.
18. On February 24, 1942, Papen and his wife Martha survived an assassination attempt in Ankara by Yugoslav communists almost unscathed. The assassins' trail led to the Soviet General Consulate in Istanbul. A sensational trial followed against the perpetrators, who were sentenced to severe prison terms, but were released immediately after the breaking of Turkish-German relations. As far back as 1941, the Turkish security police had discovered assassination plots against Papen linked to the British Intelligence Service. The assumption by contemporary observers,

frequently reported in the source literature, that Papen might have arranged the assassination attempt to position himself for a leading role in a German transition government after the war is not supported by either Allied or Axis sources. However, the Turkish archives are still under seal.

19. Here mention should first be made of *Akten zur Deutschen Auswärtigen Politik* (*ADAP*), published up to series D by an international commission of historians and containing a representative sample of the most important documents. Since the publication of the source material under West German direction began (series E, documents since fall 1941), the previous approach is, unfortunately, no longer followed. As far as the documents used in this essay have been reproduced, the citations are from this easily accessible source.
20. I thank Wolfgang G. Schwanitz and Katharina Hering for their help in locating the source material.
21. For locating these sources I thank Heinrich Senfft of the London branch of the Institute for Twentieth Century Social History.
22. My thanks to Valerij Brun for his help.
23. Compare Donald M. McKale, *War by Revolution. Germany and Great Britain in the Middle East in the Era of World War I* (Kent, Ohio, and London, 1998), 123, 125–26, 222ff.
24. Papen to Foreign Office, political report, content: Conversation with the Iraqi Minister of Justice, July 6, 1940, with attachment of Memorandum from the Superior Arab Committee for Palestine of June 21, 1940. PA AA, embassy Ankara, no. 555. Printed as document no. 125 in *ADAP*, series D, vol. X, 117–19; the following citations from the same. Another copy of the attachment by the Mufti of Jerusalem to Papen's report can now be found in Gerhard Höpp, ed., *Mufti-Papiere. Briefe, Memoranden, Reden und Aufrufe Amin al Husainis aus dem Exil, 1940–1945* (Berlin, 2001), 15 f.
25. Notes of Ernst Woermann, head of the political division of the Foreign Office, dated July 21, 1940; printed as document no. 200 in *ADAP*, series D, vol. X, pp. 215–16.
26. Le Grand Moufti de Palestine, Mohamed Amin El Husseini, Baghdad, to Papen, July 22, 1940. PA AA, embassy Ankara, no. 555. Printed as document no. 209 in *ADAP*, series D, vol. X, p. 227, as well as in Höpp, *Mufti-Papiere*, 16.
27. Papen, telegram no. 602 to Foreign Office, August 6, 1940. Printed as document no. 289 in *ADAP*, series D, vol. X, 341.
28. Note 5 to document 289 in ibid.
29. Papen, political report no. A 4828 to Foreign Office, content: Germany and the Near Eastern Question, October 3, 1940. Printed as document no. 146 in *ADAP*, series D, vol. XI.1 and 2, 206–207.
30. Fritz Grobba, notes of a conversation of Weizsäcker with the private secretary of the Mufti of Palestine, October 18, 1940. Printed as document no. 190 in ibid., 272–74.
31. Compare political archive of the Foreign Office (in the following PA AA), R 101832, 101881, 101883.
32. Paul Leverkuehn, "Orient 1940–1944," Hamburg, October 1945, in Bundesarchiv Koblenz (in the following BArchK), N 1146/13.

33. This is attested to by the fact that Moyzisch's analysis of the situation, in a report to the Reich security main office, was in complete agreement with Papen's assessment and political options. Compare, for example, Moyzisch, Bericht zur Lage. Attachment to a letter by Schellenberg to Himmler of January 20, 1943, in BArchB, NS 19 / 2236, f. 2–16. Papen and Moyzisch provided the basis for one of the most spectacular successes of the German Secret Service (Cicero Affair) when the SS Foreign Intelligence Service recruited, in the fall of 1943, the Albanian manservant of the British ambassador in Ankara, Hughe Knatchbull-Hugessen.
34. In the first months of the year 1944, several Turkish agents of the Wehrmacht Intelligence Service switched over to the British Secret Service. As a result, German intelligence gathering in Ankara and Istanbul was largely paralyzed and Papen lost his dominant influence on German Near and Middle East espionage. Compare the documentation of the affair and its ramifications in: PA AA, R 101881, 101882; Public Record Office (hereafter PRO), FO 371 / 39132, KU 2 / 168; in addition, Roth, *Papens Raubgold*.
35. Rudolf Rahn, presenting legation counselor, Report about the German Mission in Syria from May 9 to July 11, 1941. Printed as document no. 165 in *ADAP*, series D, vol. XIII.1 and 2, 198–220.
36. The documentation can be found in BArchB, R 901 / 61125.
37. Compare relevant documentation in BArchB, R 901 / 61138.
38. After the collapse of the Iraqi resistance against the British expedition corps, al-Kailānī fled, in the company of the Mufti, from Jerusalem to Tehran. While the Mufti was able, in September 1941 after the British-Soviet invasion, to escape incognito with Italian diplomatic personnel to Rome, al-Kailānī fled to Istanbul via Anatolia in the summer of 1941. He was granted political asylum, but was prohibited from leaving Turkey and was placed under strict surveillance from the Turkish and Allied secret service. With the help of Papen and Leverkuehn, he evaded his pursuers and fled by plane to Berlin, disguised as a seriously ill German citizen. Compare Paul Leverkuehn, "Orient 1940–1944," 1, 28, 38 (see note 32).
39. Franz von Papen, Memorandum. Die militärpolitische Lage der Türkei und die Achsenmächte, May 20, 1939; printed as document no. 413 in *ADAP*, series D, vol. VI, 452–54 (citation on p. 452). Papen intended this memorandum to serve as a basis for the exchange between Ribbentrop and the Italian foreign minister, Count Galeazzo Ciano, on the occasion of the signing of the German-Italian alliance treaty. He dispatched it on the same day to state secretary Weizsäcker.
40. Papen, Political Report, no. A 4828 to the Foreign Office, content: Germany and the Near East Question, October 3, 1940. Printed as document no. 146 in *ADAP*, series D, vol. XI.1 and 2, 206–207 (citation on p. 207).
41. Compare the following with the comprehensive documentation in: BArchB, R 8119 F / P 3369.
42. Weigelt to Papen, November 11, 1940, in ibid.
43. Notes of the presenting legation counselor Davidsen from the economic political division of the Foreign Office concerning department discussion of August 23 about Iraq, August 25, 1941. Printed as document no. 253 in *ADAP*, series D, vol. XIII.1 and 2, 297–98.

44. Compare documentation in: PA AA, R 29776; in addition *ADAP*, series D, vol. X, document no. 96, 88–89; no. 196, 212–13; no. 272, 321–22.
45. Papen, telegram no. 792 of September 30, 1940, to Foreign Office, in IfZ-Archiv, collection Fd 42.
46. The minutes of the discussions and the drafts of the pertinent secret agreements are printed in *ADAP*, series D, vol. XI.1 and 2, documents no. 309, 428–30; no. 325, 448–55; no. 326, 455–61; no. 328, 462–72; no. 329, 472–78.
47. The German ambassador to Moscow, Friedrich Werner Count von der Schulenburg, telegraphed Molotov's reply, which he presented during a discussion on November 25, 1940, on the same day to Berlin. Compare *ADAP*, series D, vol. XI.1 and 2, document no. 404, 597–98.
48. Compare Hitler's instruction no. 21, Operation Barbarossa, December 18, 1940. Printed as document no. 532 in *ADAP*, series D, vol. XI.1 and 2, 750–53. The Army General Staff began planning the attack on the Soviet Union as far back as the summer of 1940. The final political decision, however, was made following Hitler's and Ribbentrop's discussions with Molotov on November 12 and 13 in Berlin.
49. Compare to Hitler's instruction no. 32: preparations for the time after Barbarossa, draft version of June 11, 1941, as well the subsequent instruction of the Army High Command, preparations for the time after Barbarossa of June 30, 1941. Printed as document no. 617 in *ADAP*, series D, vol. XII.1 and 2, 842–46.
50. Papen, Germany and the Near Eastern Question, 207 (see note 29).
51. Compare the comprehensive documentation in: BArchB, R 901 / 68460–68463 (dossiers of the economic political division of the Foreign Office concerning war equipment transactions with Turkey from 1939 to 1943); in addition *ADAP*, series D, vol. XIII.1 and 2, documents no. 390, 511–13; no. 402, 527–29; series E, vol. IV, document no. 331, 605–609.
52. Papen memorandum, content, the military political situation in Turkey and the Axis powers, prepared as basis for Ribbentrop's discussions with the Italian foreign minister, Count Ciano, May 20, 1939 (see note 39).
53. Papen memorandum, content, Turkey and the war against England, political report to the Foreign Office, July 20, 1940; printed as document no. 196 in *ADAP*, series D, vol. X, 212–13.
54. Papen, telegrams no. 971 and 977 to the Foreign Office, November 29, 1940. Printed in *ADAP*, series D, vol. XI.1 and 2, 619–21, 638–39.
55. Papen to Ribbentrop, telegram no. 598, May 23, 1941. Printed as document no. 545 in *ADAP*, series D, vol. XII.1 and 2, 721–22 (citation on p. 721).
56. Detailed historical documentation about this phenomenon was presented to the German planning staff in a small monographic study by the Orient expert Gotthard Jäschke. See Gotthard Jäschke, *Der Panturanismus der Jungtürken. Zur osmanischen Außenpolitik im Weltkriege* (Leipzig, 1941).
57. Papen, The development of Turkey foreign policy. Political report no. 1335, July 18, 1941. Printed as document no. 125 in *ADAP*, series D, vol. XIII.1 and 2, 147–49; the following citation is on p. 148.
58. Papen to Ribbentrop, Turkish influence on Soviet Russia, July 25, 1941, in BArchB, R 901/61174, f. 58–59; the following citations are on f. 58.

59. Papen, telegram no. 74 to the Foreign Office, August 26, 1942. Printed as document no. 233 in *ADAP*, series E, vol. III, 399–402; also political report to the Foreign Office, August 27, 1942, The new Turkish Prime Minister and the question of Turkish minorities and the future of Russia. Printed as document no. 238, in same, 411–14.
60. Compare to the following in BArchB, R 901/61174, 61175; PA AA embassy in Ankara, no. 479.
61. Correspondence of the embassy in Ankara and the general consulate in Istanbul with the Foreign Office concerning initiation of contact with the leaders and activists of the greater Turkish-Turanian movement is primarily in BArchB, R 901/61173, 61174; PA AA embassy Ankara, no. 479.
62. Papen, The travels of General Ali Fuad Erden, political report to the Foreign Office, November 10, 1941, in BArchB, R 901/61172, notes 201–203; notes of envoy von Hentig concerning an interview with General Erkilet, November 7, 1941, in BArchB, R 901/61174.
63. The power struggle, which ended in favor of the Reich ministry for occupied eastern territories, over occupation policies of the Crimea and the Caucasus, as well as the regions of the occupied Soviet Union important for the German Turanistan option, is documented in BArchB, R 6/66; R 901/61175; in addition, *ADAP*, series E, vol. III, document no. 70, 120–21; no. 83, 138–39; no. 135, 230–32; no. 284, 486–87.
64. Compare this and the following to the comprehensive documentation in BArchB, R 901 / 61123, 61124.
65. Compare Karl Schnurre/Curt Prüfer, Notes concerning the German-Arab training division, November 20, 1942, in BArchB, R 901 / 61125, notes 16–19.
66. Al-Husainî exhorted the Bey of Tunis and the Arab-Muslim population of North Africa to support Axis troops, which landed in Tunisia behind the Allied invasion forces, against the Anglo-Americans, because the latter were "allied with the Jews." Compare PA AA, embassy Rome, no. 141; R 29866.
67. Compare with the following BArchB, R 6 / 143, 247; R 901 / 61174, 61175.
68. Letter from the Army High Command, organization division (II) to the Army High Command Group A, concerning members of Turkic tribes, October 5, 1942, in BArchB, R 6 / 143.
69. Von Mende, notes concerning discussion with Dr. Oltzsche of the SS main office on September 13, 1944, in Berlin, September 18, 1944, f. 69–71.
70. This is quite possible since Papen maintained excellent relations with the SD (German Security Service) affiliate in Turkey and improved his standing with the SS leadership considerably in the fall of 1943 in connection with the "Cicero Affair."
71. Compare in this regard the documents in BArchB, NS 19 / 2637.
72. The relevant correspondence between al-Husainî and Berger is located in BArchB, NS 31 / 43.
73. BArchB, NS 19 / 2637, f. 33, front and back cover. Printed in German translation in Höpp, ed., *Mufti-Papiere*, 212–13.
74. Compare al-Husainî's addresses to the imams of the Bosnia SS division of October 4, 1944, and to the Turkestani members of the Waffen-SS about February 1945, in PA AA, R 27317; BArchB, NS 31 / 44, f. 4.

75. Thus a certain Dr. Oltzsche from the SS main office in a discussion with Professor von Mende from the division leading staff: Politics of the Reich Ministry for Occupied Eastern Territories, September 13, 1944. Mendes's notes are in BArchB, R 6/ 143, f. 69–71, front and back cover.
76. U. S. State Department Special Investigation Commission, interrogation of Franz von Papen by Harry N. Howard in Wiesbaden, November 1, 1945, in NA II, RG 332, Box 104.
77. The war crimes trial of top Nazis before the International Military Tribunal, Nuremberg, November 14, 1945 to October 1, 1946 (hereafter IMT), vol. VI, Nuremberg 1947, summation of the prosecution against Papen on January 23, 1946, 87–115.
78. IMT, vol. XVI, Nuremberg 1948, protocol of defense counsel Dr. Kubuschock's cross-examination of Papen in State Archive Nuremberg, Collection KV Trials IMT, Papen Documents 94, 95, 105, 107.
79. IMT, vol. XXII, Nuremberg 1948, 651–54, 674; *Judgment of Nuremberg*, with a preface by Lothar Gruchmann (Munich, 1977).

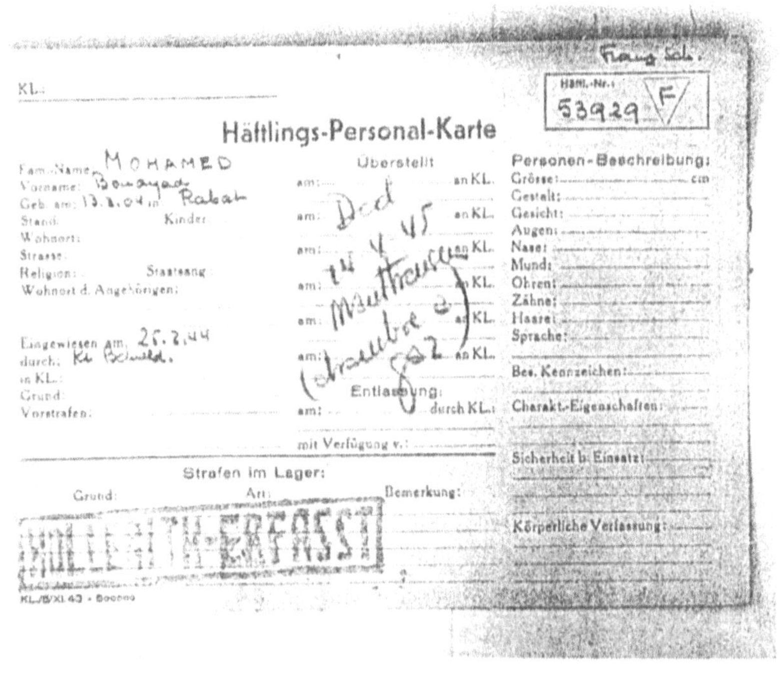

KL.:

Häftl.-Nr.: 53929 F

Frang Sch.

Häftlings-Personal-Karte

Fam.-Name: MOHAMED
Vorname: Bouayad
Geb. am: 13.3.04 in: Rabat
Stand: Kinder:
Wohnort:
Strasse:
Religion: Staatsang.:
Wohnort d. Angehörigen:

Eingewiesen am: 25.2.44
durch: KL Bchwld.
in KL.:
Grund:
Vorstrafen:

Überstellt

am: an KL.
am: Dead an KL.
am: 14 4 45 an KL.
am: Mauthausen an KL.
am: (chambre à an KL.
am: gaz) an KL.

Entlassung:
am: durch KL.:
mit Verfügung v.:

Personen-Beschreibung:
Grösse: cm
Gestalt:
Gesicht:
Augen:
Nase:
Mund:
Ohren:
Zähne:
Haare:
Sprache:

Bes. Kennzeichen:

Charakt.-Eigenschaften:

Sicherheit b. Einsatz:

Körperliche Verfassung:

Strafen im Lager:

Grund:	Art:	Bemerkung:

HOLLERITH-ERFASST

KL./8/XI.43 - 500000

Figure 14. The Moroccan Mohamed Bouazad was killed in the gas chamber of Mauthausen in April 1945, as the above register record indicates

In the Shadow of the Moon

Arab Inmates in Nazi Concentration Camps

GERHARD HÖPP[†]

This essay examines why, in contrast to intensive research about the collaboration of Arab politicians with Nazi Germany and Fascist Italy, Arab victims of National Socialism have received no attention. It presents the preliminary results of new research into Arab inmates of German concentration camps between 1939 and 1945. It makes clear that the number of inmates is comparable to those of other smaller nations and even though they were not incarcerated primarily for racist and/or religious reasons, their suffering was no less than that of millions of other non-Jewish inmates. At this time, Arabs did not belong by any means to the class of "privileged" inmates; today they belong to the "forgotten victims" of National Socialism. To recall their fate is a humane demand as well as a task of historians, who will, in many respects, have to rewrite the period of Arab-German history between 1933 and 1945.

In July 1942, three associates of the former Iraqi Prime Minister Rashīd ʿAlī al-Kailānī and an associate of the former Grand Mufti of Jerusalem, Amīn al-Husainī, visited the Sachsenhausen concentration camp near Oranienburg during a "training course" provided by the Se-

Gesandter Dr. F. Grobba   Geheim!   zu Pol VII 6447 g II

Obersturmführer Weise vom RSHA, dem ich die einer Teilnahme von Mitgliedern der Begleitung des Ministerpräsidenten Gailani und des Grossmufti an SD-Kursen und einer Besichtigung von Konzentrationslagern durch sie entgegenstehenden erheblichen Bedenken mitgeteilt habe, erklärte, dass die Besichtigung des Konzentrationslagers Oranienburg durch drei Begleiter des Ministerpräsidenten und einen Begleiter des Grossmufti bereits stattgefunden habe. Die Besichtigung habe etwa 2 Stunden gedauert und sei sehr befriedigend verlaufen. Der Kommandant des Lagers, ein Oberführer, habe die Araber empfangen und ihnen einen Vortrag über Einrichtung und den Zweck des Lagers und insbesondere seinen erzieherischen Wert gehalten. Dann habe die Besichtigung der angetretenen Lagerinsassen stattgefunden; insbesondere die Juden hätten das Interesse der Araber erregt. Anschliessend habe die Besichtigung der Baracken mit den von den Insassen selbst angefertigten, zum Teil künstlerisch hochwertigen Einrichtungsgegenständen, des Speiseraums, Waschräume, Küche und des Lazaretts stattgefunden. Alles habe auf die Araber einen vorzüglichen Eindruck gemacht. Es seien dann gerade eine Anzahl russischer Kriegsgefangener eingeliefert worden und andererseits seien 60 von uns neu eingekleidete russische Offiziere, die sich zum Kampf gegen die Bolschewisten gemeldet hätten, singend in frohester Stimmung aus dem Lager ausmarschiert.

Der Oberführer habe in seinem Vortrag darauf hingewiesen, dass eine ganze Anzahl früherer Lagerinsassen jetzt Soldaten an der Ostfront seien und zum Teil Kriegsauszeichnungen erhalten hätten. Infolge erzieherischer Beeinflussung im Lager und der Eindrücke im Konzentrationslager seien sie völlig bekehrt worden und hätten zum Teil dann Briefe an den Oberführer geschrieben.

Obersturmführer Weise erklärte, dass ohne Zweifel die Besichtigung bei den Arabern seinen sehr günstigen Eindruck hinterlassen habe. Für die Zukunft würde die Bedenken des

Auswärtigen

D 611974

Document 4. Three assistants of the Prime Minister al-Kailānī and of the Grand Mufti of Jerusalem Amīn al-Husainī visited a concentration camp near Berlin as Fritz Grobba reported in July 1942.

– 2 –

Auswärtigen Amts berücksichtigt werden und weitere Besichtigungen von Konzentrationslagern durch Araber würden nicht stattfinden.

    Hiermit über
       Pg. Pol.
      U.St.S.
      <u>bei D II</u>

vorgelegt.
    Berlin, den 17. Juli 1942

<u>Durchschlag an:</u>
Herrn LR Melchers

Stamped: Secret
Ambassador Dr. F. Grobba   to Pol VII 6447 g II

Obersturmführer Weise of RSHA, to whom I reported considerable concern about the participation of members of the entourage of Prime Minister Gailani and of the Grand Mufti in SD courses and site visits to concentration camps, declared that the visit by three assistants of the prime minister and one of the Grand Mufti at concentration camp Oranienburg had already taken place. The visit lasted about two hours with very satisfying results. The camp's commandant, an Oberführer, received the Arabs and made a presentation about the installation and the purpose of the camp, especially with regard to its educational value. Then took place the sighting of the line-up camp inmates; the Jews aroused particular interest among the Arabs. From there followed a visit to the barracks with their installation objects, which the inmates had made themselves, in part of high artistic quality, in the eating hall, the washrooms, the kitchen, and the dispensary. It all made a very favorable impression on the Arabs. As it happened, a number of Russian prisoners-of-war were brought in just then and, at the same time, sixty Russian officers, newly dressed by us, who had volunteered for the fight against Bolshevism, marched out of the camp singing and in the best of moods.

The Oberführer pointed out in his presentation that quite a few former camp inmates were now soldiers at the Eastern Front and some had been awarded war medals. Due to the educational indoctrination at the camp and the impressions in the concentration camp, they had been completely won over and some later wrote letters to the Oberführer.

Obersturmführer Weise declared the site visit no doubt left a very favorable impression on the Arabs. In the future, the concerns of the Foreign Office would be taken into consideration and future visits of concentration camps by Arabs would not take place.

Herewith submitted through Dg. Pol. U.St. S. Pol. at D II
Berlin, July 17, 1942
Grobba

cc: LR Melchers

Translation of Document 4

cret Service (SD) of the SS. A report of this visit (document 4), although expressly disapproved by the Foreign Office, stated that the almost two-hour tour "made a very positive impression on the Arab visitors" and "the Jews in particular" had aroused their interest; however, in the future they would take the Foreign Office's concerns into consideration, and "allow no further visits of concentration camps by Arabs."[1]

Whether this is true or not remains in dispute. Al-Husainī, in particular, who like al-Kailānī had been in Germany since late 1941 to work with civil and military agencies in Nazi Germany to gain the "independence" of Arab and Islamic countries from British and French rule, is said not only to have had knowledge of the concentration camps but also to have visited them. Various authors speak of the camps at Auschwitz,[2] Majdanek,[3] Treblinka,[4] and Mauthausen.[5] While the assumption that he visited the Auschwitz camp in the company of Adolf Eichmann is supported by an affidavit of Rudolf Kasztner, referring to a relevant note by the Eichmann collaborator Dieter Wisliceny,[6] the other allegations are entirely unfounded. Speculation on this and other misdeeds by the Mufti[7] appear unnecessary in view of his undisputed collaboration with the Nazis unless they are intended to demonize al-Husainī.[8]

However, the question of whether any of his countrymen or the Mufti's fellow-believers were incarcerated in the concentration camps he is said to have visited, never seems to have come to the eager researchers' minds. Quite the contrary is true. Hermann L. Gremliza went so far as to claim "that anti-Semitism has never brought any Arab into a German gas chamber."[9] Indeed, it was not anti-Semitism but quite "ordinary" racism and terrorism on the part of the Nazis, which brought Arabs and/or Muslims, in addition to millions of other people, to the concentration camps and the gas chambers.

Tracing the Victims

From mid-1944 there existed a list of "Inmates of Islamic belief" in German concentration camps (document 5) which would have given honest researchers a clue.[10] The list was compiled on order of Reichsführer SS Heinrich Himmler, who at that time intended to recruit Muslims from the concentration camps for the Muslim units of Waffen-SS, mostly Bosnian and Albanian volunteers and former Soviet prisoners of war. To this end the SS Wirtschafts-Verwaltungshauptamt (Main Eco-

Der Reichsführer-SS
SS-Hauptamt - Amt D II
D II/2 Az.9h10 Sie/Prz

Berlin-Grunewald, den
Douglasstr. 7-11

Betr.: Häftlinge islamitischen Glaubens - Gesamtzahl 1130.
Bezug: Diess.Schreiben D II/2 9h La/Ma vom 26.6.44

An das
Reichssicherheitshauptamt - Amt IV
z.Hd. SS-Hauptsturmführer B u r g
B e r l i n SW 11
Prinz-Albrecht-Str. 8

Das Amt D II erinnert nochmals an das unter dem 26.6.44 gegebene Schreiben, wonach darum gebeten wurde, zu prüfen, ob ein Teil dieser islamitischen Häftlinge für eine Verwendung in der Waffen-SS geeignet wären und herausgezogen werden könnten.
Des weiteren wurde darum gebeten, zwecks Unterrichtung des Reichsführers-SS eine schriftliche Mitteilung nach hier zu geben. Als Grundlage zu dieser Nachprüfung war den Schreiben eine Aufstellung über die in den Lagern befindlichen Häftlinge beigefügt. Um umgehende schriftliche Erledigung wird gebeten.

I.A.

SS-Obersturmführer

Document 5. 1,130 prisoners of Islamic faith in German concentration camps, June 1944

Reichsführer-SS   Berlin-Grunewald, (date illegible)
SS-Main Office - Bureau D II   Douglas Street 7 - 11
D I 2 Time 9:10 a.m. Sie/Prz

Re: Prisoners of Islamic Faith -- total number 1,130.
Reference: Letter D II/2 9a.m. Lu/Ma of June 26, 1944

To:
Reich Main Security Office -- Bureau IV
c/o SS-Hauptsturmführer Burg
B e r l i n SW 11
Prinz-Albrecht Strasse 8

This is a reminder from Bureau D II of the letter of June 26, 1944, wherein a request was made to examine whether some of the Islamic prisoners are suitable for use in those Waffen-SS and should be detached.

Furthermore, a request was made to inform the Reichsführer-SS in writing about this matter. As basis for this examination, a list of prisoners incarcerated in the camps was enclosed with the letter. An immediate written follow-up of this matter is requested.

           Sincerely,

           SS-Obersturmführer
           (name illegible)

Translation of Document 5

nomic Administrative Office) responsible for the concentration camps produced this list under Oswald Pohl's direction with inmate numbers, nationality, and place of detention. Based on these figures, 1,130 Muslim men and 19 Muslim women from Africa, Albania, Bulgaria, France, Greece, Italy, Yugoslavia, the Netherlands, Poland, the Soviet Union, and Turkey were inmates in the camps Auschwitz I and II, Bergen-

Belsen, Buchenwald, Dachau, Flossenbürg, Gross-Rosen, Mauthausen, Natzweiler, Neuengamme, Ravensbrück, Sachsenhausen, and Stutthof.

No Arabs are named in this list. However, there is no reason not to look for them. And indeed some have been found: Most were concealed under the origin "France"; they came from the French colonies and/or mandate territories in North Africa and the Middle East. Colonial coding had been applied for a long time in Europe and also for other Arab victims of the Nazi regime, among them forced laborers and prisoners of World War II. This kind of coding removed the national identity from many so-called colonial nationals, pushed them as subjects of the colonial strongholds into the shadow of the moon, so to speak, and thus, consigned them to oblivion.

Searching for them was like protracted detective work. The colonial code was cracked during a search of the databases and archives of the concentration camp memorial sites for people who by their name and birth might have been Arabs. So far I have found more than 350 Arab inmates, mostly Muslims but also Christians and Jews, in the Nazi concentration camps, which is much more than the 72 "French" on Pohl's list; considering the fact that no more than half of all inmates of concentration camps can be identified by name and only half of those are today listed in databases, it might well be that these camps saw about 1,500 Arab inmates.

Arab inmates—men and women—could be found not only in those camps mentioned in Pohl's list but in all Nazi concentration camps. There is evidence for their presence in Auschwitz (25 persons), Bergen-Belsen (21), Buchenwald (152), Dachau (78), Flossenbürg (39), Gross-Rosen (12), Hinzert (3), Mauthausen (57), Mittelbau-Dora (40), Natzweiler (34), Neuengamme (36), Ravensbrück (25), Riga (1), Sachsenhausen (38), Stutthof (2), Warsaw (1) and Wewelsburg (2), and even in the extermination camp Lublin-Majdanek (2).[11] At the time of al-Husainī's and al-Kailānī's collaborators' visit to the Sachsenhausen camp in July 1942 not less than seven Arabs were inmates of German concentration camps, and two of them were at Sachsenhausen.

Most of the inmates came from North Africa—Algeria (205), Morocco (23) and Tunisia (19)—but also from Egypt (5), Iraq (4), Lebanon (1), Palestine (4), and Syria (1).[12] Arab Jews came mostly from Libya and Yemen. The majority of inmates lived in France when they were arrested and imprisoned, some as working migrants, some in the second generation. Many of those taken to the camps were prisoners of war from the defeated French army.

Individual Fates

The existence of these groups of victims and their fate never found a place either in the collective nor in the institutionalized memory of the peoples, their own among them.[14] Arab inmates appear only accidentally, as strangers from a faraway place in the memory of former inmates from other nations[15] and in works of poetry and fiction,[16] even more rarely in the lists of nationalities of scientific literature,[17] or in memorial sites of some concentration camps.[18] There seem to be no first-person, written memoirs of their time in prison. The Arab inmates of concentration camps belong, no doubt, to the forgotten ones, the "other" victims of the Nazis.[19] The question arises whether the loss of their (national) identity due to the colonial coding of their origin is the only reason, or whether, as Jan Assmann notes, there are other "jeopardies to memory" and "social conditions of oblivion"[20] to which Arab inmates of concentration camps may have fallen a prey.

Some Consideration about Forgotten Inmates

The estimated number of 1,500 Arab concentration camp inmates was and is simply too small to secure a place in the peoples' collective memory. Although this argument has some merit, even smaller numbers of people from "smaller" nations, such as Albanians, Bulgarians, Estonians, Swiss, or Turks, are expressly mentioned as groups of victims in research literature and the institutionalized memory. Even the far greater number of hundreds of thousands of Arab prisoners of war and slave workers in Germany and the occupied territories could not keep their compatriots in the concentration camps from being forgotten.

Arabs in the society of concentration camp prisoners might have been less exposed to sufferings than other inmates. If such an argument can be made at all—there are no tales of Arab woes, and, as we have noted, other inmates do not mention them in their memoirs—it might be possible along with the following criteria.

Reasons for committal to concentration camp

Most Arab inmates were arrested in France starting in 1943 and brought by German security police (Sipo), mainly from the central assembly camp at Compiègne near Paris but also from Belfort, Bordeaux, Drancy, Grenoble, Lyon, Metz, Nancy, Perpignan, Toulon, and Toulouse, to the concentration camps; a smaller number was arrested in various cities of the Reich and Austria (among them, Danzig, Frankfurt am Main, Halle, Karlsruhe, Cologne, Leipzig, Troppau, and Vienna); there are also records of transports of Arabs from Brussels and Tunis.

The reasons for their imprisonment and deportation can only barely be gleaned from the few records (picture 14) that still exist. Dates and places of arrest and imprisonment, respectively, and categorization of inmates allow us to project at least three reasons for the arrests: First, identification of some Arabs as so-called NN inmates and their committal to the camps at Gross-Rosen, Hinzert, Mauthausen, and Natzweiler indicates that they fought for the French Résistance or were close to it. They were arrested under the *Nacht-und-Nebel* ("under cover of darkness") decree,[21] subjected to "special treatment," and kept isolated from the outside world in select camps. Some were arrested in spring 1944 under the Sperrle Decree[22] and primarily taken to the concentration camp Neuengamme.

Second, large number of Arabs sent to the concentration camps presumably had committed a "breach of contract" as slave workers or prisoners of war bound for work in occupied Europe and the Reich and were sentenced by courts on grounds of absence from work, leaving the place of work, crime against wartime economy, and other offenses. So far, most of the documenting on the fate of a number of Arab slave workers has been made in Central Germany and Austria where they were either sent to the work education camps of Gestapo[23] or directly sent by Sipo to concentration camps as "parasites," "shirkers" (*Arbeitsscheue* – ASR), and "dropouts" (*Asoziale* – Aso),[24] respectively, and as "police prisoners" (*Polizeihäftlinge* – PH).[25] A case in point is the Algerian Allaoua J., who was sent in 1942 by the police in Leipzig to the work education camp Maltheuern in Bohemia. In 1943, he was transferred for a year to Buchenwald. A worse fate befell his compatriot Mohamed Raachi, who was convicted in 1943 in Leipzig as a "parasite" and was sent to Bergen-Belsen, where he died on March 7, 1945. The

Iraqi student Sayd Daud Y. was luckier. He was convicted in 1944 in Würzburg for aiding a deserter and sentenced to three years imprisonment. He was transferred to Dachau where he was liberated by American troops.

Third, the overwhelming majority of Arab inmates (over 95 percent) fell under the SS category of "political" (*Politische* – Pol.) or "protective custody" (*Schutzhäftling* – Sch.) and was marked with a red triangle on jacket and trousers of the prison clothes. Among them, apart from the separately marked NN inmates, were apparently many former slave workers, unless they were wearing (although this was rare) the black triangle marking them as "shirkers" or "dropouts," or the green triangle of "criminals" (SV – *Sicherheitsverwahrte*), that is, protective detainees. Since most Arab inmates were registered as French, they received names like "Pol. Frz." (Political French) or "Sch. Frz." (protective custody French) and in addition the letter "F" (for "France") inside the red triangle.

Ranking among the inmates

The SS categories where national and colonial, political and racist codes were mixed, served to discriminate and dissociate inmates and finally determined whether they lived or died. The closer an inmate was to the SS guards, the more likely it was that he or she could survive. Especially the Arab prisoners marked "Pol. Frz." and "Sch. Frz." (including NN) were in a social position far distant from the SS. So, they belonged to that group of inmates that, as Wolfgang Sofsky writes, was exposed to a high "pressure of destruction."[26]

In some concentration camps, such as Buchenwald, Dachau, Mauthausen, and Natzweiler, categories with Arab national codes were allocated occasionally and only by chance (for example, "Arab. Sch." for Arab protective custody, "Pol. Egypt" for Political Egyptian and "Sch. Irak" for Protective custody Iraqi). But there is no evidence that this circumstance changed the ranking of the inmates in the taxonomy of the SS, nor that it resulted in different treatment or bettered their chance for survival. Even assurances by the Office for Racial Policy—which, in answer to al-Kailānī's questions concerning the German attitude toward the "Arab race" (document 6), said in 1942 that the National Socialist racial theory considers the Arabs as "members of a high-grade race"—

had no perceptible influence on the position of Arabs in the society of inmates. This assurance, as well as the statement that National Socialism "was exclusively directed against the Jews as undermining the nations, but not against people of Semitic tongue since they have held an anti-Jewish attitude since ancient times," was part of Nazi propaganda aimed at getting Arab support for the Axis war aims. It should be noted that the declaration was published as late as 1944.[27]

The fact should also be noted, as recognized by several authors, that the Nazi racial policy apparently had no uniform official position with regard to "non-Jewish non-Aryans" and "non-whites," among them Arabs and Africans, which made "special treatment" of these people conceivable.[28] There is also no evidence of special attention or treatment granted to the imprisoned Muslims. Just as little is known whether they developed any specific relationship of solidarity, as was the case with Jewish and Christian inmates.[29]

Accommodation and mobility of the inmates

Most Arab prisoners were accommodated in category I and II concentration camps. These were provided for "heavily incriminated but still educable and capable of being reformed" and "heavily incriminated" and "hardly educable" inmates.[30] Within the boundaries of these camp categories, they had relatively considerable mobility. About 37 percent spent time in two camps, about ten percent three camps, and at least five inmates saw no less than four camps. Except for the NN inmates, a relatively large number of Arabs was ordered to outer camps for work assignments. Whether this was a result of their professional eligibility, physical robustness, or a network of connections within the society of inmates remains unknown.[31]

Age distribution and mortality of prisoners

The majority of Arab inmates, about two-thirds, were between the ages of twenty and forty. About one quarter was over forty and few were under twenty. According to the incomplete information available, every fifth Arab inmate did not survive the concentration camp. Diseases (primarily tuberculosis) and general physical weakness were the most frequent indicated causes of death. At least one inmate (the

Moroccan Mohamed Bouayad—see his registration record at picture 14) was killed in a gas chamber (Mauthausen). The proportion of those deceased was similar for the individual age groups, that is, about twenty percent, except for inmates under twenty. Comparable figures for other nationals are not known; the generally valid assumption that about two-thirds of all camp inmates died[32] cannot be applied here for comparison because it includes the above-average mortality of Jews, Russians, and Poles.

Jeopardies of Memory

Arab inmates, according to preliminary findings of my not-yet-completed investigations, were not an exception but a common phenomenon of the Nazi terror. They were not preferred but ordinary victims. Their number can be compared to that of victims from other smaller nations. Their sufferings were probably no less than those of most other inmates in protective custody (leaving the Jews, Russians, and Poles out of consideration). Thus far no plausible reason can be seen for their sufferings being less regarded than those of other inmates and thus, not worth being told or taken down. Arab inmates belong, along with Africans, Sinti and Roma, "dropouts," victims of euthanasia, homosexuals, and prostitutes, to the "forgotten" victims of the Nazis. However, one thing has not yet happened. Whereas the latter were rescued from oblivion a long time ago, published their stories and were recognized as victim groups in the institutionalized memory,[33] Arab inmates are still in the "shadow of the moon." If their sufferings, a primary experience of the inmates, can be excluded as a reason for the fact that they were forgotten, then it must sought elsewhere in the ex-post experience.[34]

Remarks about Arab Inmates

First: Assuming that after their liberation from the concentration camps most of the surviving Arab inmates returned to and also stayed in France where they had lived before as migrant workers in most cases, some even having been born there, their stories should have been told, written down, or published there. So far I have not found a single such work about the Arab experience. The almost four hundred pages of the *Grand livre des témoins* issued by Fédération nationale des déportés et internés résistants et patriotes contains not a single witness of Nazi persecution who by name might be an Arab. This does not mean that the sufferings of Algerians, Moroccans, Syrians, and Tunisians were not documented. Based on the known classification system, they have been included as "French" in the collective memory of the French people. Evidence for this are the "Memorials," the commemorative books for the French victims of Nazi persecution, most of them painstakingly compiled in the 1990s at considerable expense. These important historical sources contain numerous names and essential details of life and imprisonment of Arabs from North Africa and Syria, and even of Vietnamese, but list them as French.

I am not quite sure how to assess this ambivalent circumstance, which combines remembrance and oblivion. Aleida Assmann once talked about a "nationalization of memory" with the inherent danger of bringing about or reviving "official memory with no individual and social memory."[36] Such a practice may be one of the "conditions of oblivion" discussed earlier. It also makes reference to the fact that forgetting is not simply a negation of remembering.

Second: Assuming former Arab inmates returned to France or their countries of origin, the question arises as to which psychological, social, cultural, and political circumstances in the family, religious community, and society may have caused, or at least contributed, to the fact that they did not talk about their sufferings, or if they did so, they did not make it public. Apart from the high barriers that also prevented former inmates from other countries and cultural backgrounds to talk or write about the "unspeakable,"[37] we have to consider here one possible reason for a man's reticence in discussing his experience: the need to support his family as a working migrant in France, or as a foreign worker in Germany, and then, due to various circumstances, being told of his deportation and "violation of contract," ending up in a concentration camp, and thus failing to fulfill his familial obligations. His story would have been understood as a story of failure rather than heroism and would hardly have been told by a man in a patriarchal Islamic society .

Third: Assuming that Algerian inmates immediately returned to their homeland after liberation, on May 8, 1945, the day of German surrender, their experiences may have been lost in the events that followed. A French wave of terrorism was then unleashed on Algeria, which cost the lives of about forty thousand compatriots. This massacre and the Alge-

Antisemitismus oder Antijudaismus?

Wir geben einen bereits einige Zeit zurückliegenden Briefwechsel wieder, der klarmacht, warum wir den Begriff „Antisemitismus" nicht mehr gebrauchen. Das Wort wird sich nicht immer durch „Antijudaismus" oder ähnliches (Judengegnerschaft, Judenfeindschaft) ersetzen lassen — dann nicht, wenn es geschichtlich festliegt. Das Gesagte betrifft die Ausdrucksweise unserer Zeit. Die Gegenwart kennt keine „Antisemiten" mehr, sondern Judengegner.

Der irakische Ministerpräsident Gailani hat an den Leiter des Rassenpolitischen Amtes der NSDAP., Prof. Dr. Groß, folgende Anfrage gerichtet:

Die Feinde der Achsenmächte stellen in ihrer Propaganda die Behauptung auf, daß Deutschland die Araber in gleicher Weise wie die Juden für rassisch minderwertig halte oder die arabische Rasse auf der Werttafel der menschlichen Rassen an ungünstiger Stelle einstufe.

Als Ministerpräsident des Irak kenne ich meine Landsleute wie überhaupt die Araber so gut, um nicht zu wissen, daß sie jener Behauptung keinen Glauben schenken, weil sie im Kampf um ihre Freiheit und ihre Rechte von den Deutschen so viel Anerkennung und Unterstützung erfahren haben, daß sie von ihrer Achtung und Freundschaft überzeugt sind. Da aber die feindliche Propaganda jene Lüge ständig wiederholt, halte ich es für zweckmäßig, daß ihr von amtlicher deutscher Seite die Wahrheit über die deutsche Haltung zu der arabischen Rasse entgegengestellt wird.

Ich wäre Ihnen deshalb zu besonderem Dank verbunden, wenn Sie als Leiter des Rassenpolitischen Amtes der NSDAP, und hervorragender Vertreter der deutschen Rassenforschung mir den Standpunkt der nationalsozialistischen Rassenlehre und der deutschen wissenschaftlichen Rassenkunde zu dieser Frage bekanntgeben wollten.

Mit dem Ausdruck meiner vorzüglichsten Hochachtung bin ich   gez. Raschid Ali el Gailani

Dr. Groß hat darauf unter dem 17. Oktober 1942 wie folgt geantwortet:

Der in Ihrem Brief ausgedrückten Bitte entsprechend, ergreife ich gern die Gelegenheit, Ihnen in folgendem den Standpunkt der nationalsozialistischen Rassenlehre und der deutschen wissenschaftlichen Rassenkunde zu den Fragen, welche die arabische Rasse betreffen, darzulegen:

1. Sinn und Ziel der nationalsozialistischen Rassenpolitik ist u. a. der Schutz des deutschen Volkes vor den zersetzenden Einflüssen des Judentums, bei dem es sich um ein unharmonisches Rassengemisch handelt, das rassenbiologisch wie charakterlich eine geschichtlich anormale Erscheinung darstellt und von den Völkern vorderasiatischer und orientalischer Rasse, also auch den semitisch sprechenden Völkern des Vorderen Orients, streng zu unterscheiden ist.

2. Dementsprechend ist der seit Jahrzehnten in Europa für die antijüdische Bewegung gebrauchte Ausdruck „Antisemitismus" falsch, da sich jene Bewegung ausschließlich gegen das alle Völker zersetzende Judentum, aber nicht gegen die — seit alter Zeit ebenfalls antijüdisch eingestellten — anderen Völker semitischer Sprache richtet. In gleicher Weise treffen die Abwehrmaßnahmen der deutschen Rassengesetzgebung den Juden nicht wegen seiner Herkunft aus dem Orient oder wegen der semitischen Eigenart seiner Sprache, sondern einzig und allein wegen seines asozialen und antisozialen Charakters als Weltfeind.

3. Während von uns das Judentum als rassenbiologische und geschichtliche Erscheinung schroff und unbedingt abgelehnt wird, sind die semitisch-arabischen Völker, Sprachen und Kulturen stets Gegenstand liebevollen Interesses der deutschen Wissenschaft gewesen.

An dieser Haltung hat die Rassenlehre in neuerer Zeit nichts geändert. Vielmehr entspricht diese Einstellung der großen Achtung, die gerade das deutsche Volk stets den wertvollen kulturellen Leistungen fremder Völker und Kulturen entgegenbringt.

Von keiner ernstgenommenen Seite in Deutschland ist jemals gesagt worden, daß die Araber rassisch minderwertig seien oder in der Werttafel der menschlichen Rassen an ungünstiger Stelle stehen. Die nationalsozialistische Rassenlehre erkennt vielmehr die Araber als Angehörige einer hochwertigen Rasse an, die auf eine ruhmvolle und heldenhafte Geschichte zurückblickt.

Deshalb ist auch der politische Freiheitskampf der Araber gegen die jüdische Usurpation Palästinas von deutscher Seite stets mit besonderer Anteilnahme verfolgt und unterstützt worden.

Mit dem Ausdruck meiner vorzüglichen Hochachtung bin ich

            Ihr sehr ergebener
            Prof. Dr. Groß,
            Hauptdienstleiter

Document 6. Anti-Semitism or anti-Judaism? An Arab question and the official German answer in 1942

Anti-Semitism or Anti-Judaism?

We are presenting a correspondence of some time ago which makes clear we are no longer using the concept "anti-Semitism." The word cannot always be replaced with "anti-Judaism" or something like that (opposition to Jews, enmity toward Jews)— not when it is historically fixed. The term is an expression of our time. The present no longer recognizes "anti-Semites," but opponents of the Jews.

The Iraqi Prime Minister Gailani directed the following question to the director of the Race Political Bureau of the NSDAP, Prof. Dr. Groß:

The propaganda of the enemies of the Axis Powers claims that Germany considers the Arabs on a par with the Jews as racially inferior or places the Arabic race in a very unfavorable place on the value scale of human races.

As prime minister of Iraq I am too well acquainted with my countrymen and the Arabs in general not to know that they give no credence to these allegations since they received much support and recognition from the Germans in their struggle for freedom and justice so that they are convinced of their friendship and respect. But since the enemy propaganda constantly repeats this lie, I think it would be useful if it were opposed by the truth of the German attitude toward the Arabic race on the part of the official German side.

I, therefore, would be particularly grateful if you, as director of the Race Political Bureau of the NSDAP, and outstanding representative of German race research, would explain to me the standpoint concerning this question of the national socialist racial ideology and of the German scientific race research.

I remain sincerely yours,

Rashid Ali el Gailani

Translation of Document 6. Anti-Semitism From *Weltkampf: Die Judenfrage in Geschichte und Gegenwart*, (Berlin) 3 (1944): 168.

Dr. Groß replied on October 17, 1942:

In response to your request, I am glad to take the opportunity to explain to you in the following the standpoint of the national socialist racial ideology and of German race research with regard to the questions concerning the Arabic race.

1. The purpose and goal of the national socialist racial policy is, among other things, the protection of the German people from the subversive influence of the Jews, who constitute an unharmonious mixture of races, which represents an abnormal historical entity from race biological and characterlogical viewpoint, and who are to be strictly distinguished from the peoples of the Near Eastern and Oriental races, that is, also from the semitic-language groups of the Near East.

2. For this reason, the expression "anti-Semitism," which has been used for decades in Europe by the anti-Jewish movement, is incorrect since this movement was exclusively directed against Jewry that subverts all nations, but not against other peoples who speak a Semitic language—and who have likewise for ages been opposed to the Jews. By the same token, the defensive measures of the German racial laws are not aimed at the Jew because of his oriental origin or the Semitic specificity of his language but solely because of his asocial and antisocial character as enemy of the world.

3. While we are rejecting Jewry sharply and absolutely as a race biological and historical entity, the Semitic-Arabic peoples, languages, and cultures have always been the object of loving interest of German science.

This has remained unchanged even in view of recent race research. If anything, this standpoint reflects the great respect which the Germans more than any people has always paid the valuable, cultural achievements of other nations and cultures.

Nobody in Germany, whose opinion is taken seriously, has ever stated that the Arabs are inferior or occupy on the value scale of human races an unfavorable position. Rather, the national socialist racial teaching recognizes the Arabs as members of a highly valued race, which can look back on a glorious, heroic history.

It is for this reason as well that the political struggle for freedom by the Arabs against the Jewish usurpation of Palestine has always been followed and supported from the German side with particular sympathy.

With the expression of foremost respect, I remain,

Yours truly,
Prof. Dr. Groß

Translation of Document 6, continued

rian war a few years later might have relativized the experience of the Algerian victims of Nazi persecution in view of the innumerable new victims and sufferings, and dismissed or even obliterated their memories about their imprisonment in concentration camps. Likewise, the independence struggles soon flaring up in other Arab countries brought out new groups of victims among the population, which then filled the collective memory of their peoples and determined the institutionalized memory.[38]

Fourth: The conflict that broke out in 1948 between Arabs and Israelis paradoxically played a part, too, in forgetting the Arab victims of Nazi persecution. In addition to other things, it separated the sufferings of Arab Jewish Nazi victims from that of their Arab Muslim and Christian fellow-inmates and fellow-countrymen; this went down into the sufferings of another group, the Jewish people, and is still today part of the Jewish memory of the Shoah.[39]

Fifth: All these conditions of oblivion are part of a process which Reinhart Koselleck called the "crossover" from the "primary experience" of the suffering generation, that is, Arab inmates, to the "institutionalized memory" which established the "ex post experience."[40] Aleida Assmann defines this process by saying: "Memory is to be replaced by history". Memory, she writes, is not a "static container where experiences can be preserved unchanged"; instead it is the society "always defining new reference frameworks and interpretation patterns for the past."[41] Authors like Peter Reichel, Peter Steinbach, and Michael Wolffsohn call this process a "memory and history policy" respectively.[42] The following is an example.

The memorial at the concentration camp Mittelbau-Dora in Thuringia includes an inscription, in steel letters, about inmates from Arab states. Some time after the German reunification, presumably in 1992, an Israeli diplomat visited the former camp and saw this inscription which is unfortunately overly general and requested its removal. The management dismissed this request and looked instead for evidence that might justify the "offensive" words. The archives were searched for names like ʿAlī, Ahmad, Muhammad, and Mustafa, and when they found some, the holders of which were born in Arab countries, they sent copies of these documents to the diplomat, who made no reply. Meanwhile, I have found in the Mittelbau-Dora concentration camp records twenty-two Algerians, three Moroccans, two Tunisians, and thirteen Arabs of unknown origin.

This story is an example of how memory and history policy, respectively, are practiced under the conditions of the Arab-Israeli conflict. Victim monopolization, observed by Tom Segev on both sides of the conflict, also seems to mean on the Israeli side to negate and ignore Arab victims of Nazi persecution. While this aspect of victim monopolization has not yet attracted public attention, the alleged and actual denial of the Holocaust by Arabs as an aspect of *their* victim monopolization undergoes widespread and heated debates. This type of history policy has at least two negative aspects. First, the conflict that contributed to the erasure of Arab sufferings under the Nazi regime has turned this loss of memory into a deficiency, that is, the absence of suffering and consequently of victims. Second, it also made it possible that the written memories of Arab perpetrators, that is, collaborators with Nazism, among them from the Grand Mufti of Jerusalem, draw a picture of this historical period where Arab victims seem nonexistent.

When Yāsir ʿArafāt in 1998 cancelled his visit to the Holocaust Memorial Museum in Washington, D.C., Eli Wohlgelernter wrote a comment in *Jerusalem Post* headlined "Learning to See 'the Enemy' as Victims." This article also dealt with Irit Abramski-Bligh's efforts at Yad Vashem, to teach the Holocaust to the Israeli Arabs.[45] These efforts are doubtless very laudable and must be appreciated. However, neither there, nor anywhere else, did I find anything about efforts to recall the Arab victims of Nazi genocide.

Research about Arab victims of the Nazis is still in its initial stages. However, it should not be restricted to concentration camp inmates, about which this essay presents the first research results, but should include other groups of victims like forced laborers and prisoners of war. Another area that needs to be investigated concerns Arabs who actively fought against the Nazi regime and Fascism, including those who fought on the Republican side in the Spanish Civil War, members of the French Résistance, and soldiers and officers in the Allied anti-Hitler coalition. This will cast a critical light on Arab-German history between 1933 and 1945 and might lead in many respects to its revision.

Notes

1. Politisches Archiv des Auswärtigen Amtes (Political Archives of the Foreign Office), Berlin (PArchAAB), R 100702. The visit is presumably mentioned for the first time by David Yisraeli, *Ha-Reich Ha-germani we-eres Yisra'el* (Ramat Gan, 1974), 278. See also Israel Gutman, ed., *Enzyklopädie des Holocaust*, vol. 2 (Berlin, 1993), 631; Elliott A. Green, "Arabs and Nazis — Can It Be True?" *Midstream* 40, no. 7 (1994): 11; Rafael Medoff, "The Mufti's Nazi Years Re-examined," *The Journal of Israeli History* 17, no. 3 (1996): 332. Medoff also mentions that an Arab delegation visited and inspected Laurahütte, a slave labor subcamp of Auschwitz, in 1944.
2. See Maurice Pearlman, *Mufti of Jerusalem: The Story of Haj Amin El Husseini* (London, 1947), 73. See also Joseph B. Schechtman, *The Mufti and the Fuehrer: The Rise and Fall of Haj Amin el-Husseini* (New York and London, 1965), 160; Derek Hopwood, "Amin al-Husayni," in *The Encyclopaedia of Islam*, new edition, supplement 1–2 (Leiden, 1980), 69, which, however, confuses the affidavits of Imre Steiner and Rudolf Kasztner.
3. See Simon Wiesenthal, *Großmufti — Großagent der Achse* (Salzburg and Vienna, 1947), 37–45. See also Quentin Reynolds, Ephraim Katz, and Zwy Aldouby, *Minister of Death: The Adolf Eichmann Story* (London, 1961), 174; Siegfried Einstein, *Eichmann: Chefbuchhalter des Todes* (Frankfurt am Main, 1962), 166; Klaus von Münchausen, "Der Traum vom großen Arabien," *Die Zeit* (September 7, 1990): 45.
4. See Reynolds et al., *Minister of Death*; see also Einstein, *Eichmann*.
5. See Hannes Stein, "Die DDR, das Dritte Reich, und Israel," *Die politische Meinung* 44, no. 357 (1999): 82.
6. For Kasztner's affidavit see Nicholas Bethell, *The Palestinian Triangle: The Struggle between the British, the Jews, and the Arabs 1935–1948* (London, 1979), 225.
7. This includes the absurd accusations that al-Husaynī represented the Muslim peoples at the Wannsee Conference in January 1942 and "influenced Hitler's gas chamber concept." See Marzio Pisani, "'Resistenza' e 'collaborazionismo' nella seconda guerra mondiale Islam," *L'Uomo libero* 4, no. 16 (1983): 68; Martin Ros, *Schakale des Dritten Reiches: Untergang der Kollaborateure 1944–1945* (Stuttgart, 1997), 329.
8. See Gerhard Höpp, "Der Gefangene im Dreieck. Zum Bild Amin al-Husseinis in Wissenschaft und Publizistik seit 1941. Ein bio-bibliographischer Abriß," in *Eine umstrittene Figur: Hadj Amin al-Husseini*, ed. Rainer Zimmer-Winkel (Trier, 1999), 523; Gerhard Höpp, ed., *Mufti-Papiere: Briefe, Memoranden, Reden und Aufrufe Amin al-Husainis aus dem Exil, 1940–1945* (Berlin, 2001).
9. Hermann L. Gremliza, "Ein skandalöser Text," in *Israel, die Palästinenser, und die deutsche Linke* (Wuppertal, 2002), 58.
10. Bundesarchiv (Federal Archives), Berlin (BArchB), Reichsführer SS, film no. 2922, frame 699524.
11. This and the following information is mostly based on sources accessible to me at the memorial sites of the concentration camps and the Federal Archives in Berlin.

My express thanks to the staff of these institutions and the former inmate of Natzweiler and Dachau camps, Ernest Gillen (Howald/Luxembourg), for their valuable help and support in my investigations.

12. The national origin of ninety-five additional Arab inmates could not yet be established. The difference between the absolute number of inmates and the total number of inmates in the individual concentration camps results from the fact that many inmates were in more than one camp.
13. See Rachel Simon, "It Could Have Happened There: The Jews of Libya during the Second World War," *Africana Journal* 16 (1994): 391–422. See also the files not used by the author in PArchAAB, R 41507, 41508, and 412583.
14. A very brief and superficial chapter on "Muslime im KZ" (Muslims in concentration camps) is in Bernd Bauknecht, *Muslime in Deutschland von 1920 bis 1945* (Cologne 2001), 136ff.; for African victims compare the studies by Robert W. Kesting, "Forgotten Victims: Blacks in the Holocaust," *The Journal of Negro History* 77 (1992): 30–36, and Maguéye Kassé, "Afrikaner im nationalsozialistischen Deutschland," *Utopie kreativ,* 115–116 (2000): 501–507, which also need to be supplemented.
15. See G.-L. Fréjafon, *Bergen-Belsen bagne sanatorium* (Paris, 1947), 73f.; Aimé Bonifas, *Häftling 20801* (Berlin, 1968), 40f.; Jean Degroote, *Prisons de la Gestapo et camps de concentration* (Steenvorde, 1995), 23; Jean-Louis Vigla, *Evadés d'Aurigny: Hiver 1942–1943* (Cherbourg, 1995), 187f.; *Un pas, encore un pas...pour survivre (Kommando Buchenwald)* (Amiens, 1996), 220. Inmates of Sachsenhausen camp remember some "black people, Arabs" as fellow-inmates. See Brandenburgisches Landeshauptarchiv (Brandenburg County Archives), Potsdam (BrLHArchP). Pr.Br.Rep.35 H KZ Sachsenhausen, no. 8/1, 426.
16. See Alois Hotschnig, *Ludwigs Zimmer* (Cologne, 2000), 138, which mentions Algerians in the Mauthausen camp.
17. Olga Wormser-Migot, *Le système concentrationnaire nazi 1933–1945* (Paris, 1968), 431, mentions Algerians; Hans Maršálek, *Die Geschichte des Konzentrationslagers Mauthausen* (Vienna, 1974), 119, mentions Arabs and Egyptians; Bärbel Schindler-Saefkow, "Ein Gedenkbuch für die Opfer von Ravensbrück," in *Tod oder Überleben? Neue Forschungen zur Geschichte des Konzentrationslagers Ravensbrück,* ed. Werner Röhr and Brigitte Berlekamp (Berlin, 2001), 186, inmates from Egypt and Morocco.
18. A commemorative plaque on the former roll call square of the Buchenwald camp tells of Algerians, Egyptians, and Moroccans among others. See *Gedenkstätten für die Opfer des Nationalsozialismus* (Bonn, 1999), 865 and 898. An inscription at the former roll call square of concentration camp Mittelbau-Dora refers to inmates from Arab countries. Ibid., 865.
19. Ina R. Friedman, *The Other Victims: First-Person Stories of Non-Jews Persecuted by the Nazis* (Boston, 1990), 1, wrote: "Fifty years after the Holocaust many people believe, that only Jews were the victims of the Nazis. That is not true. While six million Jews were killed in the Holocaust, five million Christians were also deliberately murdered by the Nazis." Muslims are not mentioned.
20. See Jan Assmann, "Die Katastrophe des Vergessens. Das Deuteronium als Paradigma kultureller Mnemotechnik," in *Mnemosyne: Formen und Funktionen der kulturellen Erinnerung,* ed. Aleida Assmann and Dietrich Harth (Frankfurt am Main, 1991), 344ff.

21. The decree of December 12, 1941, called "Nacht- und Nebel-Erlass," by the Supreme Commander of the German Army (Chef des Oberkommandos der Wehrmacht), Wilhelm Keitel, provided that any persons "who infringes on the law of German Reich or occupying power will be transferred under cover of darkness to the Reich as a measure of deterrence." Philippe Waxrenier, member of the Résistance, mentioned for instance a Tunisian who joined his resistance network. See Raymond de Lassus Saint Geniès, *Si l'echo de leurs voix faiblit...* (Paris, 1997), 147ff.
22. The decree issued on February 3, 1944, by the Supreme Commander West, Hugo Sperrle, for the fight against French guerillas, also sanctioned reprisals against civilians.
23. See Gabriele Lotfi, *KZ der Gestapo: Arbeitserziehungslager im Dritten Reich* (Stuttgart and Munich, 2000).
24. See Wolfgang Ayaß, *"Asoziale" im Nationalsozialismus* (Stuttgart, 1995).
25. My thanks to the Saxon and Thuringian State Archives and the Brandenburg County Archives for their valuable help and support while I was reviewing personal files of inmates of Brandenburg, Ichtershausen, Leipzig, and Untermassfeld jails.
26. See Wolfgang Sofsky, *Die Ordnung des Terrors: Das Konzentrationslager* (Frankfurt am Main, 1999), 138ff.
27. See "Antisemitismus oder Antijudaismus?" *Weltkampf* 3 (1944): 168 (document 6 above). As early as the summer of 1936, after the passing of the *Nürnberger Rassengesetze* (Nuremberg racial laws) stirred up anxiety in the Middle East as well. Nazi politicians from the Foreign Office (Pilger), the Ministries of Interior (Globke, Stuckart), Justice, and Propaganda, and the Office for Racial Policy (Gross) met and discussed the issue of "racial" classification of Egyptians, for example. The participants categorized them as a race of "alien blood" ("fremdblütig"), but in view of the upcoming Olympic Games in Berlin they agreed "the time for an official declaration [of this ranking—G.H.] vis-à-vis foreign countries was not yet ripe." See PArchAAB, R 99173 and R 99174.
28. See Susann Samples, "African Germans in the Third Reich," in *The African-German Experience: Critical Essays*, ed. Carol Aisha Blackshire-Belay (Westport, Conn., 1996), 53–69; Marianne Bechhaus-Gerst, "Afrikaner in Deutschland 1933–1945," *Zeitschrift für Sozialgeschichte des 20. und 21. Jahrhunderts* 12 (1997): 10–31.
29. See Thomas Rahe, "Die Bedeutung von Religion und Religiosität in den nationalsozialistischen Konzentrationslagern," in *Die nationalsozialistischen Konzentrationslager —Entwicklung und Struktur*, ed. Ulrich Herbert, Karin Orth, and Christoph Dieckmann, vol. 2 (Göttingen, 1998), 1006–1022.
30. See Maršálek, *Geschichte des Konzentrationslagers Mauthausen*, 21.
31. See Sofsky, *Ordnung des Terrors*, 147f.
32. Ibid., 57.
33. The historian Koselleck questioned the sense of putting up a memorial for each group of victims and argued not to remember the victims by "SS categories" but "based on the facts created by the perpetrators," that is, "that they were murdered." Reinhart Koselleck, "Die Diskontinuität der Erinnerung," *Deutsche Zeitschrift für Philosophie* 47 (1999): 222.

34. Ibid., 215.
35. See *Le grand livre de témoins* (Paris, 1994).
36. See Aleida Assmann, "Gedächtnis ohne Erinnerung? Die Probleme der Deutschen mit ihrer Geschichte," *Gedenkstätten Rundbrief* 10, no. 97 (2000): 12.
37. See Michael Pollak, *Die Grenzen des Sagbaren: Lebensgeschichten von KZ-Überlebenden als Augenzeugenberichte und als Identitätsarbeit* (Frankfurt am Main and New York, 1988), 163ff.; Ulrike Jureit and Karin Orth, *Überlebensgeschichten: Gespräche mit Überlebenden des KZ-Neuengamme mit einem Beitrag von Detlef Garbe* (Hamburg, 1994), 164ff.; Ulrike Jureit, *Erinnerungsmuster: Zur Methodik lebensgeschichtlicher Interviews mit Überlebenden der Konzentrations- und Vernichtungslager* (Hamburg, 1999), 116ff.
38. See Benjamin Stora, *Le dictionnaire des livres de la guerre d'Algérie* (Paris, 1996).
39. See Michael M. Laskier, *North African Jewry in the Twentieth Century: The Jews of Morocco, Tunisia, and Algeria* (New York and London, 1994), 55ff.
40. See Koselleck, "Die Diskontinuität der Erinnerung," 215.
41. See Assmann, "Gedächtnis ohne Erinnerung?" 11 and 7.
42. See Peter Reichel, *Politik mit der Erinnerung* (Munich, 1995). Peter Steinbach, "Die Vergegenwärtigung von Vergangenem. Zum Spannungsverhältnis zwischen individueller Erinnerung und öffentlichem Gedenken," in *Aus Politik und Zeitgeschichte* B 3–4 (1997), 7; Michael Wolffsohn, "Von der äußerlichen zur verinnerlichten 'Vergangenheitsbewältigung.' Gedanken und Fakten zu Erinnerungen," in ibid., 17.
43. See Tom Segev, "Der Holocaust gehört in seinen historischen Kontext," *Universitas* 51 (1996): 90.
44. A good survey on the discussion is given by Rainer Zimmer-Winkel, ed., *Die Araber und die Shoa: Über die Schwierigkeiten dieser Konjunktion* (Trier, 2000).
45. See Joseph Massad, "Palestinians and Jewish History: Recognition or Submission?" *Journal of Palestine Studies* 30 (2000): 61. See also <http://www.yadvashem.org.il//download/education/conf/Abramski.pdf>

About the Authors

WOLFGANG G. SCHWANITZ, born in 1955, researches Middle Eastern history and foreign relations. Born in Germany, he spent his childhood in Egypt and now lives near Princeton. For twelve years he taught Middle Eastern history and policy at universities in Berlin and Potsdam. Educated at Leipzig University as an Arabist and economist, he received his Ph.D. there on Egypt's *infitāh* in 1985. He has been a researcher at the German Academy of Science and the Center of Modern Orient Berlin, and a visiting fellow in Cairo, Princeton, and Washington. He has edited eight books on the Middle East and authored *Deutsche in Nahost 1946–1965* (*Germans in the Near East, 1946–65*) and *Gold, Bankiers und Diplomaten: Zur Geschichte der Deutschen Orientbank 1906–1946* (Gold, Bankers, and Diplomats: A History of the German Orient Bank 1906–46) in a series of comparative history "America–Middle East–Europe" (www.trafoberlin.de), as well as the forthcoming *Middle Eastern Policy of German Empires and Republics*.

THOMAS L. HUGHES is a senior visiting research scholar at the German Historical Institute in Washington, D.C. His article expands a lecture delivered there on January 29, 2002. A Washingtonian since 1955, he has had a many-sided career as a lawyer, author, diplomat, and foundation executive. He was the former U.S. Assistant Secretary of State for Intelligence and Research in the Kennedy and Johnson Administrations (1963–69), Minister and Deputy Chief of Mission at the U.S. Embassy in London under the Nixon Administration (1969–70), and president of the Carnegie Endowment for International Peace (1971–91). He holds degrees from Carleton College, Oxford University, and Yale Law School, and is a trustee of several German-American organizations.

HANS-ULRICH SEIDT, born in 1952, joined the German Foreign Service in 1982. He has held assignments in Moscow, at NATO Headquarters in Brussels, and in Washington, D.C. He earned his Ph.D. on French Middle Eastern policy and was Lecturer for International Security Policy of the Robert Bosch Foundation (1994–97). He served as vice-chairman of the Bosnia Special Task Force (Sobos: Sonderstab Bosnien). He has written, translated, and edited numerous books and articles, among them the classical Russian biography on Carl Philipp Gottfried von Clausewitz by Alexander Swetschin and recently *Berlin, Kabul, Moskau: Oskar Ritter von Niedermayer und Deutschlands Geopolitik* (www.herbig.net). Seidt.Berlin@t-online.de

UWE PFULLMANN, born in 1956, pursues historical research about the Middle East with concentration on West Asia and the Arabian Peninsula. Educated at Leipzig University as an Arabist and historian, he earned there a Ph.D. about North African history with special regard to Morocco. In the 1990s he was a researcher at the Berlin Center of Modern Orient and taught at Hamburg University. He has traveled extensively in Arab lands and edited numerous books, among them historical reports and diaries of Julius Euting, Johann Ludwig Burckhardt, Richard Francis Burton, Georg Augustus Wallin, and Adolph von Wrede. He has authored *Throhnfolge in Saudi-Arabien. Wahhabitische Familienpolitik von 1744 bis 1953* (Succession to the Throne in Saudi Arabia: Wahhabi Family Policy, 1744–1953), the biography *Ibn Saud. König zwischen Tradition und Fortschritt* (Ibn Saud: King between Tradition and Progress), and the *Endeckerlexikon arabische Halbinsel* (Encyclopedia of Discoverers of the Arabian Peninsula). (www.pfullmann.de).

STEFAN R. HAUSER, born in 1962, specializes in the history of the Ancient Orient at the Institut für Vorderasiatische Altertumskunde of the Free University in Berlin. Current research topics include "Burial, Status and Ritual: The Social Structure of Neo-Assyrian Assur," "History and Archeology of the Arsacid Empire," and "The Living Presence: On the Power of Images in Ancient Mesopotamia." Among his articles is "Archäologische Methoden und Theorien" (*Der Neue Pauly Wissenschafts- und Rezeptionsgeschichte*, vol. 13) (Archaeological Methods and Theories [The New Paul History of Research and Reception]); his books include *Assur: Ausgrabungen der Freien Universität Berlin I:*

About the Authors

Die nachassyrischen Schichten (Assur: Excavations by the Free University of Berlin I: The Post-Assyrian Stratas). Together with Ann C. Gunter he edited "Ernst Herzfeld and the Development of Near Eastern Studies, 1900–1950" (hauser@orientarch.uni-Halle.de).

KARL HEINZ ROTH, born in 1942, is the co-founder and head of the German Foundation of Social History of the 20th Century in Bremen. He holds an M.D. and a Ph.D. He has authored many articles and books about the social and economic history of the world crisis in the 1920s, about Nazi Germany, the Cold War, and current history, among them *Facetten des Terrors. Der Geheimdienst der "Deutschen Arbeitsfront" und die Zerstörung der Arbeiterbewegung 1933–1938* (Facets of Terror: the Secret Service of the German Arbeitsfront and the Destruction of the Labor Movement 1933–48), and *Der Krieg vor dem Krieg. Ökonomik und Politik der "friedlichen" Aggression Deutschlands 1938/1939* (The War before the War: Politics and Economics of the German "Peaceful" Aggression 1938–39). He is the co-editor of *Sozial.Geschichte* (formerly *1999*), the German journal for the history of the 20th and 21st century. Currently he is completing a biography on *Franz von Papen and the German Policy towards Turkey during World War II* (www.stiftung-sozialgeschichte.de).

GERHARD HÖPP, 1942–2003, professor, worked at the Center for Modern Oriental Studies in Berlin. Educated as an Arabist and Islam scholar at Leipzig University, he did his Ph.D. there about the intellectual conflicts in Arab countries, and his habilitation thesis on the history of the Arab Nationalist Movement, 1948–75. He researched the history of the Muslim immigration to Germany, Muslim biographies between the cultures, and Arab personal experiences with Nazi Germany. He was the editor and author of many articles and books, among them *Fremdeinsätze: Afrikaner und Asiaten in europäischen Kriegen, 1914–1945* (Among Strangers: African and Asian Soldiers in European Wars), *Texte aus der Fremde: Arabische politische Publizistik in Deutschland, 1896–1945. Eine Bibliographie* (Literature on Foreign Soil: Political Publicatioins by Arabs in Germany, 1896–1945. A Bibliography), and *Mufti-Papiere: Briefe, Memoranden, Reden und Aufrufe Amîn al-Husainîs aus dem Exil, 1940–1945* (Mufti-Papers: Letters, Memoranda, Speeches and Appeals by Amīn al-Husainī from his Exile, 1940–45) (www.zmo.de).

www.ingramcontent.com/pod-product-compliance
Lightning Source LLC
Chambersburg PA
CBHW020945230426

43666CB00005B/174